An **INTRODUCTION** to

R

for **SPATIAL ANALYSIS**
& MAPPING

WITHDRAWN

For my cousin John Poile (1963–2013) – Missed by many people in many ways. CB
To Mandy – we didn't break each other. AJC

An **INTRODUCTION** to

R

for **SPATIAL ANALYSIS**
& MAPPING

⑤SAGE

Los Angeles | London | New Delhi
Singapore | Washington DC

CHRIS
BRUNSDON
and
LEX
COMBER

Los Angeles | London | New Delhi
Singapore | Washington DC

SAGE Publications Ltd
1 Oliver's Yard
55 City Road
London EC1Y 1SP

SAGE Publications Inc.
2455 Teller Road
Thousand Oaks, California 91320

SAGE Publications India Pvt Ltd
B 1/I 1 Mohan Cooperative Industrial Area
Mathura Road
New Delhi 110 044

SAGE Publications Asia-Pacific Pte Ltd
3 Church Street
#10-04 Samsung Hub
Singapore 049483

Editor: Robert Rojek
Assistant editor: Keri Dickens
Production editor: Katherine Haw
Copyeditor: Richard Leigh
Proofreader: Neil Dowden
Marketing manager: Michael Ainsley
Cover design: Francis Kenney
Typeset by: C&M Digitals (P) Ltd, Chennai, India
Printed and bound in Great Britain
by Bell and Bain Ltd, Glasgow

© Chris Brunsdon and Lex Comber 2015

First published 2015

Library of Congress Control Number: 2014939813

British Library Cataloguing in Publication data

A catalogue record for this book is available from the British Library

ISBN 978-1-4462-7294-7
ISBN 978-1-4462-7295-4 (pbk)

At SAGE we take sustainability seriously. Most of our products are printed in the UK using FSC papers and boards. When we print overseas we ensure sustainable papers are used as measured by the Egmont grading system. We undertake an annual audit to monitor our sustainability.

CONTENTS

ABOUT THE AUTHORS

Chris Brunsdon is Professor of Geocomputation at the National University of Ireland, Maynooth. He studied Mathematics at the University of Durham and Medical Statistics at the University of Newcastle upon Tyne, and has worked in a number of universities, holding the Chair in Human Geography at Liverpool University before taking up his current position. His research interests are in health, crime and environmental data analysis, and in the development of spatial analytical tools, including Geographically Weighted Regression approach. He also has interests in the software tools used to develop such approaches, including R.

Lex Comber is Professor of Geographical Information Sciences at the University of Leicester. After studying for a BSc in Plant and Crop Sciences at Nottingham, he did his PhD at the Macaulay Land Use Research Institute (now the Hutton Institute) and the University of Aberdeen. His research covers all areas of spatial analyses and the application and development of quantitative geographical methods. These have been applied across topic areas that straddle both the social and environmental and include accessibility analyses, land cover/land use monitoring and handling uncertainty in geographic information and spatial data.

FURTHER RESOURCES

All of the data used in the examples in this book are provided inside R packages and so will be automatically available when the packages are installed or are collected by the code that is used. Instructions on installation of packages appears as they are introduced. In some instances data are read directly from websites into R and in these cases details are given in the text.

An annotated R script for each chapter is available at **https://study.sagepub.com/ brunsdoncomber.** The authors will make periodic updates to these as needed (for example if packages or function calls change).

This books draws heavily on the functions available in the GISTools package. For detailed information about this package go to: http://cran.r-project.org/web/ packages/GISTools/index.html

PREFACE

R has provided a freely available tool for the analysis of data for well over a decade. The original purpose of R was to provide a programming language and interactive environment for statistical data analysis. By providing a command-line focused and programmable environment for data analysis, it has proved its worth not only as a statistical analysis toolkit (in the manner of say SPSS or Minitab), but also a flexible environment for the development of new techniques. In addition, it provides a number of powerful graphical facilities.

Over recent years both of us have witnessed the increasing use of R for spatial analysis and geo-computation in the scientific activities we engage in directly. In addition we have seen the increasing use and analysis of spatial data in many other scientific and academic fields. This implies that R is now becoming an important tool for anyone who needs to work with spatial data. Although R does not offer a 'point-and-click' approach offering rapid access to a number of 'standard' GIS operations, its programmability implies that it can be used to tackle a very broad range of applications, with virtually any data format. It can be thought of as a Swiss Army Knife of spatial data handling and analysis.

Our motivation for writing this book – much of which is about using R as a tool for manipulating geographical information, and the production of maps – reflects these perceptions and the need for a text that can be used by both geographers and researchers in other areas to develop spatial analyses. For these reasons the book is structured and sequenced to provide a learning path that does not assume any prior knowledge of R, spatial analysis or GIS. Rather, as the reader progresses through the chapters, they undertake analyses and exercises that build on previously introduced concepts and tools. R provides an incredibly diverse environment within which to conduct data analyses as its functionality is constantly being expanded with the creation and sharing of new tools and functions in contributed packages. We aim to give the reader a sense of the power that R can offer – by explaining a number of geographical information based techniques and problems, and demonstrating how R may be used to address these. We are both strong believers in the principle of 'learning by doing'. We hope this approach is not only informative, but also enjoyable.

We would also like to acknowledge the help of Idris Jega Mohammed, who checked through the manuscript and examples, the reviewers of the first draft, David Unwin and Rich Harris, whose helpful and constructive comments made our task much easier, and the authors of R itself and the many packages that we use in this book.

CB, AJC

INTRODUCTION

1.1 OBJECTIVES OF THIS BOOK

This book assumes no prior knowledge of either R or spatial analysis and mapping. It provides an introduction to the use of R and the increasing number of tools that can be used for explicitly spatial analyses, geocomputation and the statistical analysis of geographical information. The text draws from a number of open source, user contributed libraries or 'packages' that support mapping and cartographic outputs arising from both raster and vector analyses. The book implicitly focuses on vector GIS as other texts cover raster with classic geostatistics (see Bivand et al., 2008), although rasters are implicitly included in some of the exercises, for example the outputs of density surfaces and some of the geographically weighted analyses as described in later chapters.

The rationale for producing this book at this time relates to a number of factors. First, the increasing use of R as an analytical tool across a range of different scientific disciplines is evident. Second, there are an increasing number of data capture devices that are GPS-enabled: smartphones, tablets, cameras, etc. This has resulted in more and more data (both formal and informal) having location attached to them. Third, there is therefore an associated increase in demand for explicitly spatial analyses of such data, in order to exploit the richness of analysis that location affords. Finally, at the time of writing, there are no books on the market that have a specific focus on spatial analysis and mapping of such data in R that do not require any prior knowledge of GIS, spatial analysis, or geocomputation. One of the few textbooks on using R for the analysis of spatial data is Bivand et al. (2008), although this is aimed at advanced users. For these reasons, what we have sought to do is to write a book with a geographical focus and (hopefully) user friendliness.

As you work through this book you will learn a number of techniques for using R directly to carry out spatial data analysis, visualisation and manipulation. Although here we focus on vector data and on social and economic applications, and the packages that this book uses have been chosen as being the most appropriate for analysing these kinds of data, R also presents opportunities for the analysis of many other kinds of spatial data – for example, relating to climate and landscape processes. While some of libraries and packages covered in this book may also be useful in the analysis of physical geographical and environmental data, there will no doubt be other packages that may also play an important role. For example, the PBSMapping package, developed by the Pacific Biological Station in Nanaimo, British Columbia, Canada, offers a number of functions that may be useful for the analysis of biogeographical data.

1.2 SPATIAL DATA ANALYSIS IN R

In recent years large amounts of spatial data have become widely available. For example, there are many governmental open data initiatives that make census data, crime data and various other data relating to social and economic processes freely available. However, there is still a need to flexibly analyse, visualise and model data of this kind in order to understand the underlying patterns and processes that the data describe. Whilst there are many software packages available that are capable of analysing spatial data, in many situations standard statistical modelling approaches are not appropriate: data observations may not be independent or the relationship between variables may vary across geographical space. For this reason many standard statistical packages provide only inadequate tools for analysis as they cannot account for the complexities of spatial processes and spatial data.

Similarly, although standard GIS packages and software provide tools for the visualisation of spatial data, their analytical capabilities are relatively limited, inflexible and cannot represent the state of the art. On the other hand, many R packages are created by experts and innovators in the field of spatial data analysis and visualisation, and as R is, in fact, a programming language it is a natural testing ground for newly developed approaches. Thus R provides arguably the best environment for spatial data analysis and manipulation. One of the key differences between a standard GIS and R is that many people view GIS as a tool to handle very large geographical databases rather than for more sophisticated modelling and analysis, and this is reflected in the evolution of GIS software. For example, R can be used as a tool to test whether an arrangement of data points is random, whereas a standard GIS may be a better tool for extracting a set of points for a particular neighbourhood from an extremely large spatial national database. We therefore do not regard R as competing with GIS; rather we see the two kinds of software as having complementary functionality.

1.3 CHAPTERS AND LEARNING ARCS

The chapters build in the complexity of the analyses they develop, and by working through the illustrative code examples you will develop sufficient skill to create your own routines, functions and programs. The book includes a mix of *embedded exercises*, where the code is provided for you to work through with extensive explanations, and *self-test questions*, which require you to develop an answer yourself. All chapters have self-test questions. In some cases these are included in an explicitly named section and in others they are embedded in the rest of the text. The final section in each chapter provides model answers to the self-test questions. Thus in contrast to the exercises, where the code is provided in the text for you to work through (i.e. for you to enter and run yourself), the self-test Questions are tasks for you to complete, mostly requiring you to write R code yourself, with answers provided in the last section of each chapter. The idea of these questions is to give you some experience with working with different kinds of data structures, functions and operations in R. There is a strong emphasis on solving problems, rather than simply working through the code. In this way, snippets of code are included in each chapter describing commands for data manipulation and analysis and to exemplify specific functionality. It is expected that you will run the R code yourself in each chapter. This can be typed directly into the R console or may be written directly into a script or document as described below. It is also possible to access the code in each chapter from the book's website (again see below). The reasons for running the code yourself are so that you get used to using the R console and to help your understanding of the code's functionality.

In various places *information boxes* (marked as I boxes) are included to develop a deeper understanding of functions and alternative approaches for achieving the same ends.

The book is aimed at both second- and third-year undergraduate and post-graduate students. Chapters 6–8 go into much more detail about specific types of spatial analysis and are extensively supported by references from the scientific literature in a way that the earlier chapters are not. For these reasons Chapters 2–5 might be considered as introductory and Chapters 6–8 might be considered as advanced. Thus the earlier chapters are suitable for an *Introduction to R* module (Chapters 2–4) or for an *Introduction to Mapping in R* module and the later ones for a module covering more *Advanced Techniques* (Chapters 6–9). The book could also be used as the basis for a *Geographical Programming* module, drawing from different chapters, especially Chapters 4 and 9, depending on the experience and technical capabilities of the student group.

The formal learning objectives of this book are:

- to apply appropriate data types, arrays, control structures, functions and packages within R code

- to introduce geographical analysis and spatial data handling in R

- to develop programming skills in R language with particular reference to current geocomputational research and applications

- to exemplify the principles of algorithm and function construction in R

- to design and construct basic graphical algorithms for the analysis and visualisation of spatial information

In terms of learning arcs, each chapter introduces a topic, has example code to run and self-test questions to work through. In a similar way, earlier chapters provide the foundations for later ones. The dependencies and prerequisites for each chapter are listed below and you should note that these are inherited (i.e. if Chapter 4 is a prerequisite then the prerequisites for Chapter 4 also are relevant):

Chapter	Prerequisite chapters	Comments
Chapter 2	None	Data types and plots – the jumping-off point for all other chapters
Chapter 3	2	The first maps and spatial data types
Chapter 4	2, 3	Coding blocks and functions
Chapter 5	2, 3	GIS-like operations in R
Chapter 6	4, 5	Cluster analysis and mapping of point data
Chapter 7	4, 5	Attribute analysis and mapping of polygon data
Chapter 8	6, 7	Analysis of geographical variation in spatial processes
Chapter 9	3, 4, 5	Spatial analysis of data from the web

1.4 THE R PROJECT FOR STATISTICAL COMPUTING

R was developed from the S language which was originally conceived at the Lucent Technologies (formerly AT&T) Bell Laboratories in the 1970s and 1980s. Douglas Martin at the company StatSci developed S into the enhanced commercial product known as S+ in the late 1980s and early 1990s (Krause and Olson, 1997). R was initially developed by Robert Gentleman and Ross Ihaka of the Department of Statistics at the University of Auckland. It is becoming widely used in many areas of scientific activity and quantitative research, partly because it is available free in source code form and also because of its extensive functionality, through the continually growing number of contributions of code and functions, in the form of R packages, which when installed can be called as libraries. The background to R, along with documentation and information about packages as well as the contributors, can be found at the R Project website http://www.r-project.org.

1.5 OBTAINING AND RUNNING THE R SOFTWARE

You should download the latest version of R in order to run the code provided in this book. At the time of writing, this is version 3.0.2 and you should ensure you have at least this version. There are 32-bit and 64-bit versions available, and we assume you have the 64-bit version. The simplest way to get R installed on your computer is to go to the download pages on the R website – a quick search for 'download R' should take you there, but if not you could try:

- http://cran.r-project.org/bin/windows/base/
- http://cran.r-project.org/bin/macosx/
- http://cran.r-project.org/bin/linux/

for Windows, Mac and Linux, respectively. The Windows and Mac versions come with installer packages and are easy to install, whilst the Linux binaries require use of a command terminal.

You may have to set a *mirror* site from which the installation files will be downloaded to your computer. Generally you should pick one that is near to you. Once you have installed the software you can run it. On a Windows computer, an R icon is typically installed on the desktop; on a Mac, R can be found in the Applications folder. Macs and Windows have slightly different interfaces, but the protocols and processes for an R session on either platform are similar.

The base installation includes many functions and commands. However, more often we are interested in using some particular functionality, encoded into packages contributed by the R developer community. Installing packages for the first time can be done at the command line in the R console using the install.packages command, as in the example below to install the GISTools library, or via the R menu items.

```
install.packages("GISTools", dependencies = T)
```

In Windows, the menu for this can be accessed by **Packages > Load Packages** and on a Mac via **Packages and Data > Package Installer**. In either case, the first time you install packages you may have to set a mirror site from which to download the packages. Once the package has been installed then the library can be called as below.

```
library(GISTools)
```

Further descriptions of packages, their installation and their data structures are given in later chapters. There are literally thousands of packages that have been contributed to the R project by various researchers and organisations. These can be located by name at http://cran.r-project.org/web/packages/available_packages_by_name.html if you know the package you wish to use. It is also possible to search the CRAN website to find packages to perform particular tasks at http://www.r-project.org/search.html. Additionally, many packages include user guides in the form of a PDF document describing the package and listed at the top of the index page of the help files for the package. The packages used in this book are:

Name	Description
datasets	A package containing a number of datasets, supplied with the standard installation of R
deldir	Functions to calculate and manipulate Delaunay triangulations and Dirichlet or Voronoi tessellations of point datasets
e1071	Functions for latent class analysis, short-time Fourier transform, fuzzy clustering, support vector machines, etc.
fMultivar	Tools for illustrating financial engineering and computational finance but also useful for spatial data
GISTools	Mapping and spatial data manipulation tools – in particular, drawing choropleth maps
gstat	Functions for spatial and spatio-temporal geostatistical modelling, prediction and simulation
GWmodel	Geographically weighted models
maptools	Functions for manipulating and reading geographic data
misc3d	Miscellaneous functions for three-dimensional (3D) plots
OpenStreetMap	Accesses high-resolution raster maps and satellite imagery from OpenStreetMap
PBSmapping	A number of GIS-like functions and public domain datasets
plyr	Functions for breaking a big problem down into manageable pieces, operating on each piece and then reassembling them
raster	Reading, writing, manipulating, analysing and modelling of gridded raster or gridded spatial data
RColorBrewer	A package providing colour palettes for shading maps and other plots
RCurl	Composition of general HTTP requests, functions to fetch uniform resource identifiers (URIs), to get and post web data
rgdal	The Geospatial Data Abstraction Library, access to projection/transformation operations
rgeos	The Geometry Engine – Open Source (GEOS), providing topology operations on geometries
rgl	3D visualisation device (OpenGL)
RgoogleMaps	Interface to query the Google server for static maps to use as background images to maps
Rgraphviz	Provides plotting capabilities for R graph objects (not available from CRAN; for download instructions, see Chapter 9)
rjson	Converts R objects into JavaScript Object Notation (JSON) objects and vice versa
sp	Classes and methods for spatial data
SpatialEpi	Performs various spatial epidemiological analyses
spatstat	A package for analysing spatial data, mainly spatial point patterns
spdep	A collection of functions and tests for evaluating spatial patterns and autocorrelation

When you install these packages it is strongly suggested you also install the dependencies – other packages required by the one that is being installed – by either checking the Install Dependencies box in the menu (on a Mac) or including `depend=TRUE` or `dep = T` in the command line (on a Mac or in Windows):

```
install.packages("GISTools", dep = TRUE)
```

Packages are occasionally completely rewritten, and this can impact on code functionality. Since we started writing this book, for example, the sp package has depreciated its `overlay` function, which has been replaced by a new function called `over`. Code using `overlay` will still work for a limited period but will be accompanied by a warning message informing the R user of the depreciation. For example, at the time of writing, having installed the `GISTools` package above, if the following is entered at the R console:

```
data(newhaven)
# the variables can be used in other operations
overlay(places, blocks)
```

it will run, returning the results, but will also generate a warning stating the function is depreciated and suggesting the function that should be used instead, in this case the sp function `overlay`. The book website will always contain working code snippets for each chapter to overcome any problems caused by function depreciation.

Such changes are only a minor inconvenience and are part of the nature of a dynamic development environment provided by R in which to do research: such changes are inevitable as packages are refined and standardised.

1.6 THE R INTERFACE

There are few pull-down menus in R, and therefore you will type command lines in what is termed a *command line interface*. Like all command line interfaces, the learning curve is steep but the interaction with the software is more detailed, which allows greater flexibility and precision in the specification of commands.

Beyond this there are further choices to be made. Command lines can be entered in two forms: directly into the *R console* window or as a series of commands into a script window. This is, by default, titled *Untitled – R Editor* in Windows or *Untitled* on a Mac.

As you work though the book, the expectation is that you run all the code that you come across. We cannot emphasise enough the importance of learning by doing – the best way to learn how to write R code is to write and enter it. Some of the code might look a bit intimidating when first viewed, especially in later chapters. However, the only really effective way to understand it is to give it a try.

It is good practice to write your code in scripts, and R includes its own editor (similar to Notepad in Windows or TextEdit on a Mac). Scripts are useful if you wish to automate data analysis, and have the advantage of keeping a saved record of the relevant R programming language commands that you use in a given piece of analysis. These can be re-executed, referred to or modified at a later date. For this reason, you should get into the habit of constructing scripts for all your analyses. Since being able to edit functions is extremely useful, both the MS Windows and Mac OSX versions of R have built-in text editors. Although they operate slightly differently, they do very similar jobs.

- To start the Windows editor with a blank document, go to **File > New Script,** and to open an existing script **File > Open Script**

- To start the Mac editor, use the menu options **File > New Document** to open a new document and **File > Open Document** to open an existing file

Once code is written into these files, they can be saved for future use; rather than copy and pasting each line of code, both installations have their own short-cut. You should highlight the code you would like to run in R and then press either:

- Ctrl-Enter for Windows or the Run toolbar button – hover your mouse over the buttons to locate it – or

- Cmd-Enter on a Mac

It is also good practice to set the working directory at the beginning of your R session. In Windows this is **File > Change dir...** and on a Mac it is **Misc > Set Working Directory**. This points the R session to the folder you choose and will ensure that any files you wish to read, write or save are placed in this directory.

Scripts can be saved by selecting **File > Save As** which will prompt you to enter a name for the R script you have just created. Chose a name (for example, 'test.R') and select save. It is good practice to use the file extension '.R'.

1.7 OTHER RESOURCES AND ACCOMPANYING WEBSITE

There are many freely available resources for R users. In order to get some practice with R we strongly suggest that you download the 'Owen Guide' (entitled *The R Guide*) and work through this up to and including Section 5. It can be accessed via `http://cran.r-project.org/doc/contrib/Owen-TheRGuide.pdf`. It does not require any additional libraries or data and provides a gentle introduction to R and its syntax.

There are many guides to the R software available on the internet. In particular, you may find some of the following links useful:

- `http://www.maths.lth.se/help/R/`

- `http://www.r-bloggers.com`

- `http://stackoverflow.com/` and specifically `http://stackoverflow.com/questions/tagged/r`

The contemporary nature of R means that much of the R development for processing geographical information is chronicled on social media sites (you can search for information on services such as Twitter, for example '#rstats') and blogs such as the R-bloggers site listed above, rather than standard textbooks. In addition to the above resources, there is a website that accompanies this book `https://study.sagepub.com/brunsdoncomber` This site contains all of the code, scripts, exercises and self-test questions contained in each chapter, and these are available to download. The scripts for each chapter allow the reader to copy and paste the code into the R console or into their own script. At the time of writing all of the code in the book is correct. However, R and its packages are occasionally updated. In most cases this is not problematic as the update almost always extends the functionality of the package without affecting the original code. However in a few instances, specific packages are completely rewritten without backward compatibility. If this happens the code on the accompanying website will be updated accordingly. You are therefore advised to check the website regularly for archival component and links to new resources.

REFERENCES

Bivand, R.S., Pebesma, E.J. and Gómez-Rubio, V.G. (2008) *Applied Spatial Data Analysis with R*. New York: Springer.

Krause, A. and Olson, M. (1997) *The Basics of S and S-PLUS*. New York: Springer.

DATA AND PLOTS

2.1 INTRODUCTION

This chapter introduces the different data types and data structures that are commonly used in R and how to visualise or 'plot' them. As you work through this book, you will gain experience of using all of these different data structures, sequentially building on ideas you have encountered previously (for example, developing your own functions). As you progress, the exercises will place more emphasis on solving problems, using and manipulating different data structures as you need them, rather than simply working through the example code. You should note the different functions called in the example code snippets that are used, such as `max`, `sqrt` and `length`. This chapter covers a lot of ground – it will:

- Review basic commands in R

- Introduce variables and assignment

- Introduce data types and classes (vectors, lists, matrices, S4, data frames)

- Describe how to test for and manipulate data types

- Introduce basic plot commands

- Describe how to read, write, load and save different data types

Chapter 1 introduced R, the reasons for using it in spatial analysis and mapping, and described how to install it. It also directed you to some of the many resources and introductory exercises describing basic operations in R. Specifically, it advised that you should work through the 'Owen Guide' (entitled *The R Guide*) up to the end of Section 5. This can be accessed via `http://cran.r-project.org/doc/contrib/Owen-TheRGuide.pdf`. This chapter assumes that you have worked your way through this introduction, which does not take long and is critical for the more specialised materials that will be introduced in the rest of this book.

2.2 THE BASIC INGREDIENTS OF R: VARIABLES AND ASSIGNMENT

The R interface can be used as a sort of calculator, returning the results of simple mathematical operations such as $(-5 + -4)$. However, it is normally convenient to *assign* values to *variables*. The variables that are created can then be manipulated or subject to further operations.

```
# examples of simple assignment
x <- 5
y <- 4
# the variables can be used in other operations
x+y
```

```
## [1] 9
```

```
# including defining new variables
z <- x + y
z
```

```
## [1] 9
```

```
# which can then be passed to other functions
sqrt(z)
```

```
## [1] 3
```

Note that in this text, R output is preceded by a double hash (##) so that it is clear that this is the output resulting from entering the R command, rather than something that should be typed in.

The snippet of code above is the first that you have come across in this book. There will be further snippets throughout each chapter. Two key points. First you are strongly advised to enter and run the code at the R prompt yourself. You may wish to write the code into a script or document as described in Chapter 1. The reasons for this are so that you get used to using the R console and to help your understanding of the code's functionality. In order to run the code in the R console, a quick way to enter it is to highlight the code (with the mouse or using the keyboard controls) and the press Ctrl-R, or Cmd-Enter on a Mac. Second, we would like to emphasise the importance of learning by doing

(Continued)

(Continued)

and getting your hands dirty. Some of the code might look a bit fearsome when first viewed, especially in later chapters, but the only really effective way to understand it is to give it a try. Remember that the code snippets are available on the book website `https://study.sagepub.com/brunsdoncomber` as scripts so that you can copy and paste these into the R console or your own script. A minor further point is that in the code comments are prefixed by # and are ignored by R when entered into the console.

The basic assignment type in R is to a *vector* of values. Vectors can have single values as in x, y and z above, or multiple values. Note the use of `c(4,5,...)` in the following to combine or *concatenate* multiple values:

```
# example of vector assignment
tree.heights <- c(4.3,7.1,6.3,5.2,3.2,2.1)
tree.heights

## [1] 4.3 7.1 6.3 5.2 3.2 2.1
```

Remember that UPPER and lower case matters to R. So `tree.heights`, `Tree.Heights` and `TREE.HEIGHTS` all refer to different variables. Make sure you type in upper and lower case exactly as it is written, otherwise you are likely to get an error.

In the example above, a vector of values have been assigned to the variable `tree.heights`. It is possible for a single assignment to refer to the entire vector, as in the code below that returns `tree.heights` squared. Note how the operation returns the square of each element in the vector.

```
tree.heights**2

## [1] 18.49 50.41 39.69 27.04 10.24 4.41
```

Other operations or functions can then be applied to these vectors variables:

```
sum(tree.heights)

## [1] 28.2
```

```
mean(tree.heights)
```

```
## [1] 4.7
```

And, if needed, the results can be assigned to yet further variables.

```
max.height <- max(tree.heights)
max.height
```

```
## [1] 7.1
```

One of the advantages of vectors and other structures with multiple data elements is that they can be subsetted. Individual elements or subsets of elements can be extracted and manipulated:

```
tree.heights
```

```
## [1] 4.3 7.1 6.3 5.2 3.2 2.1
```

```
tree.heights[1]    # first element
```

```
## [1] 4.3
```

```
tree.heights[1:3]  # a subset of elements 1 to 3
```

```
## [1] 4.3 7.1 6.3
```

```
sqrt(tree.heights[1:3]) # square roots of the subset
```

```
## [1] 2.074 2.665 2.510
```

```
tree.heights[c(5,3,2)]  # a subset of elements 5,3,2: note the ordering
```

```
## [1] 3.2 6.3 7.1
```

As well as numeric values as in the above examples, vectors can be assigned character or logical values as below. Different variables classes and types are described in more detail in the next section.

```
# examples of character variable assignment
name <- "Lex Comber"
name
```

```
## [1] "Lex Comber"

# these can be assigned to a vector of character variables

cities <- c("Leicester","Newcastle","London","Durham","Exeter")

cities

## [1] "Leicester" "Newcastle" "London" "Durham" "Exeter"

length(cities)

## [1] 5


# an example of a logical variable
northern <- c(FALSE, TRUE, FALSE, TRUE, FALSE)
northern

## [1] FALSE  TRUE FALSE  TRUE FALSE

# this can be used to subset other variables
cities[northern]

## [1] "Newcastle" "Durham"
```

As you explore the code in the text, the very strong advice of this book is that you write and develop the code using the in-built text editor in R. The scripts can be saved as .R files and code snippets can be run directly by highlighting them and then using Ctrl-R (Windows) or Cmd-Enter (Mac). Keeping your copies of your code in this way will help you keep a record of it, and will allow you to go back to earlier declarations of variables easily. A hypothetical example is shown below.

```
##### Example Script #####
## Load libraries
library(GISTools)
## Load functions
source("My.functions.R")
## load some data
```

```
my.data <- read.csv(file = "my.data.csv")
## apply a function written in My.functions.R
cube.root.func(my.data)
## apply another R function
row.tot <- rowSums(my.data)
```

2.3 DATA TYPES AND DATA CLASSES

This section introduces data classes and data types to a sufficient depth for readers of this book. However, more formal descriptions of R data objects and class can be found in the R Manual on the CRAN website under the descriptions of:

- Basic classes: `http://stat.ethz.ch/R-manual/R-devel/library/methods/html/BasicClasses.html`

- Classes: `http://stat.ethz.ch/R-manual/R-devel/library/methods/html/Classes.html`

2.3.1 Data Types in R

Data in R can be considered as being organised into a hierarchy of data types which can then be used to hold data values in different structures. Each of the types is associated with a test and a conversion function. The basic or core data types and associated tests and conversions are shown in the table below.

type	test	conversion
character	is.character	as.character
complex	is.complex	as.complex
double	is.double	as.double
expression	is.expression	as.expression
integer	is.integer	as.integer
list	is.list	as.list
logical	is.logical	as.logical
numeric	is.numeric	as.numeric
single	is.single	as.single
raw	is.raw	as.raw

You should note from the table that each type has associated with it a test is.xyz, which will return TRUE or FALSE and a conversion as xyz. Most of the exercises, methods, tools, functions and analyses in this book work with only a small subset of these data types:

- character

- numeric

- logical

These data types can be used to populate different data structures or classes, including vectors, matrices, data frames, lists and factors. The data types are described in more detail below. In each case the objects created by the different classes, conversion functions or tests are illustrated.

Characters

Character variables contain text. By default the function `character` creates a vector of whatever length is specified. Each element in the vector is equal to "" – an empty character element in the variable. The function `as.character` tries to convert its argument to character type, removing any attributes including, for example vector element names. The function `is.character` tests whether the arguments passed to it are of character type and returns TRUE or FALSE depending on whether its argument is of character type or not.

Consider the following examples of these functions and the results when they are applied to different inputs:

```
character(8)

## [1] "" "" "" "" "" "" "" ""

# conversion
as.character("8")

## [1] "8"

# tests
is.character(8)

## [1] FALSE

is.character("8")

## [1] TRUE
```

Numeric

Numeric data variables are used to hold numbers. The function `numeric` is used to create a vector of the specified length with each element equal to 0. The function `as.numeric` tries to convert (coerce) its argument to numeric type. It is identical to `as.double` and to `as.real`. The function `is.numeric` tests whether the arguments passed to it are of numeric type and returns TRUE or FALSE depending on whether its argument is of numeric type or not. Notice how the last test returns FALSE because not all the elements are numeric.

```
numeric(8)

## [1] 0 0 0 0 0 0 0 0

# conversions
as.numeric(c("1980","-8","Geography"))

## [1] 1980 -8 NA

as.numeric(c(FALSE,TRUE))

## [1] 0 1

# tests
is.numeric(c(8, 8))

## [1] TRUE

is.numeric(c(8, 8, 8, "8"))

## [1] FALSE
```

Logical

The function `logical` creates a logical vector of the specified length and by default each element of the vector is set to equal FALSE. The function `as.logical` attempts to convert its argument to be of logical type. It removes any attributes including, for example, vector element names. A range of character strings `c("T"`, `"TRUE"`, `"True"`, `"true")`, as well any number not equal to zero, are regarded as TRUE. Similarly, `c("F"`, `"FALSE"`, `"False"`, `"false")` and zero are regarded as FALSE. All others as are regarded as NA. The function `is.logical` returns TRUE or FALSE depending on whether the argument passed to it is of logical type or not.

```
logical(7)

## [1] FALSE FALSE FALSE FALSE FALSE FALSE FALSE

# conversion
as.logical(c(7, 5, 0, -4,5))

## [1]  TRUE TRUE FALSE  TRUE TRUE

# TRUE and FALSE can be converted to 1 and 0
as.logical(c(7,5,0,-4,5)) * 1

## [1] 1 1 0 1 1

as.logical(c(7,5,0,-4,5)) + 0

## [1] 1 1 0 1 1

# different ways to declare TRUE and FALSE
as.logical(c("True","T","FALSE","Raspberry","9","0", 0))

## [1]  TRUE TRUE FALSE    NA     NA     NA     NA
```

Logical vectors are very useful for indexing data, to select the data that satisfy some criteria. In spatial analysis this could be used to select database records that match some criteria. For example, consider the following:

```
data <- c(3, 6, 9, 99, 54, 32, -102)
# a logical test
index <- (data > 10)
index

## [1] FALSE FALSE FALSE  TRUE   TRUE   TRUE FALSE

# used to subset data
data[index]

## [1] 99 54 32

sum(data)

## [1] 101

sum(data[index])

## [1] 185
```

2.3.2 Data Classes in R

The different data types can be used to populate different data structures or classes. This section will describe and illustrate vectors, matrices, data frames, lists and factors – data classes that are commonly used in spatial data analysis.

Vectors

All of the commands in R in the previous subsection on data types produced vectors. Vectors are the most commonly used data structure and the standard one-dimensional R variable. You will have noticed that when you specified character or logical, etc., a vector of a given length was produced. An alternative approach is to use the function vector, which produces a vector of the length and type or mode specified. The function as.vector seeks to convert its argument into a vector of whatever mode is specified. The default is logical, and when you assign values to vectors R will seek to convert them to whichever vector mode is most convenient. The test is.vector returns TRUE if its argument is a vector of the specified class or mode with no attributes other than names, returning FALSE otherwise.

```
# defining vectors
vector(mode = "numeric", length = 8)

## [1] 0 0 0 0 0 0 0 0

vector(length = 8)

## [1] FALSE FALSE FALSE FALSE FALSE FALSE FALSE FALSE

# testing and conversion
tmp <- data.frame(a=10:15, b=15:20)
is.vector(tmp)

## [1] FALSE

as.vector(tmp)

##      a  b
## 1   10  15
## 2   11  16
## 3   12  17
## 4   13  18
## 5   14  19
## 6   15  20
```

Matrices

The function `matrix` creates a matrix from the data and parameters that are passed to it. This should normally include parameters for the number of columns and rows in the matrix. The function `as.matrix` attempts to turn its argument into a matrix, and the test `is.matrix` tests to see whether its argument is a matrix.

```
# defining matrices
matrix(ncol = 2, nrow = 0)

## [,1] [,2]

matrix(1:6)

##          [,1]
## [1,]      1
## [2,]      2
## [3,]      3
## [4,]      4
## [5,]      5
## [6,]      6

matrix(1:6, ncol = 2)

##          [,1] [,2]
## [1,]      1    4
## [2,]      2    5
## [3,]      3    6

# conversion and test
as.matrix(6:3)

##          [,1]
## [1,]      6
## [2,]      5
## [3,]      4
## [4,]      3

is.matrix(as.matrix(6:3))

## [1]  TRUE
```

> Notice how it is possible to specify empty data structures – the first line of code above produced an empty matrix with two columns and no rows. This can be very useful in some circumstances.

Matrix rows and columns can be named.

```
flow <- matrix(c(2000, 1243, 543, 1243, 212, 545,
      654, 168, 109), c(3,3), byrow=TRUE)
# Rows and columns can have names, not just 1,2,3,...
colnames(flow) <- c("Leicester", "Liverpool","Elsewhere")
rownames(flow) <- c("Leicester", "Liverpool", "Elsewhere")
# examine the matrix
flow
```

```
##                 Leicester      Liverpool      Elsewhere
## Leicester          2000           1243           543
## Liverpool          1243            212           545
## Elsewhere           654            168           109
```

```
# and functions exist to summarise
outflows <- rowSums(flow)
outflows
```

```
## Leicester  Liverpool Elsewhere
##      3786      2000       931
```

However, if the data class is not a matrix then just use names, rather than rownames or colnames.

```
z <- c(6,7,8)
names(z) <- c("Newcastle","London","Manchester")
z
```

```
## Newcastle  London  Manchester
##     6         7         8
```

R has many additional tools for manipulating matrices and performing matrix algebra functions that are not described here. However, as spatial scientists we are often interested in analysing data that has a matrix-like form, as in a data table. For example, in an analysis of spatial data in vector format, the rows in the attribute table represent specific features (such as polygons) and the columns hold information about the attributes of those features. Alternatively, in a raster analysis environment, the rows and columns may represent specific latitudes and longitudes or northings and eastings or raster cells. Methods for analysing matrices in this way will be covered in more detail in later chapters as spatial data objects (Chapter 3) and spatial analyses (Chapter 5) are introduced.

You will have noticed in the code snippets that a number of new functions are introduced. For example, early in this chapter, the function sum was used. R includes a number of functions that can be used to generate descriptive statistics such as sum, and max. You should explore these as they occur in the text to develop your knowledge of and familiarity with R. Further useful examples are in the code below and throughout this book. You could even store them in your own R script. R includes extensive help files which can be used to explore how different functions can be used, frequently with example snippets of code. An illustration of how to find out more about the sum function and some further summary functions is given below:

```
?sum
help(sum)
# Create a variable to pass to other summary functions
x <- matrix(c(3,6,8,8,6,1,-1,6,7),c(3,3),byrow=TRUE)
# Sum over rows
rowSums(x)
# Sum over columns
colSums(x)
# Calculate column means
colMeans(x)
# Apply function over rows (1) or columns (2) of x
apply(x,1,max)
# Logical operations to select matrix elements
x[,c(TRUE,FALSE,TRUE)]
# Add up all of the elements in x
sum(x)
# Pick out the leading diagonal
diag(x)
# Matrix inverse
solve(x)
# Tool to handle rounding
zapsmall(x %*% solve(x))
```

Factors

The function factor creates a vector with specific categories, defined in the levels parameter. The ordering of factor variables can be specified and an ordered function also exists. The functions as.factor and as.ordered are the coercion functions. The test is.factor returns TRUE or FALSE depending on whether their arguments is of factor type or not and is.ordered returns TRUE when its argument is an ordered factor and FALSE otherwise.

First, let us examine factors:

```
# a vector assignment
house.type <- c("Bungalow", "Flat", "Flat",
    "Detached", "Flat", "Terrace", "Terrace")
# a factor assignment
house.type <- factor(c("Bungalow", "Flat",
    "Flat", "Detached", "Flat", "Terrace", "Terrace"),
    levels=c("Bungalow","Flat","Detached","Semi","Terrace"))
house.type
```

```
## [1] Bungalow Flat  Flat  Detached Flat  Terrace  Terrace
## Levels: Bungalow  Flat  Detached  Semi  Terrace
```

```
# table can be used to summarise
table(house.type)
```

```
## house.type
## Bungalow Flat Detached Semi Terrace
##        1    3        1    0       2
```

```
# 'levels' control what can be assigned
house.type <- factor(c("People Carrier", "Flat",
    "Flat", "Hatchback", "Flat", "Terrace", "Terrace"),
    levels=c("Bungalow","Flat","Detached","Semi","Terrace"))
house.type
```

```
## [1] <NA>    Flat    Flat    <NA>    Flat    Terrace    Terrace
## Levels: Bungalow Flat Detached Semi Terrace
```

Factors are useful for categorical or classified data – that is, data values that must fall into one of a number of predefined classes. It is obvious how this might be relevant to geographical analysis, where many features represented in spatial data are labelled using one of a set of discrete classes. Ordering allows inferences about preference or hierarchy to be made (lower–higher, better–worse, etc.) and this can be used in data selection or indexing (as above) or in the interpretation of derived analyses.

Ordering

There is no concept of ordering in factors. However, this can be imposed by using the `ordered` function.

```
income <-factor(c("High", "High", "Low", "Low",
    "Low", "Medium", "Low", "Medium"),
    levels=c("Low", "Medium", "High"))
income > "Low"

## [1] NA NA NA NA NA NA NA NA

# 'levels' in 'ordered' defines a relative order
income <-ordered (c("High", "High", "Low", "Low",
    "Low", "Medium", "Low", "Medium"),
    levels=c("Low", "Medium", "High"))
income > "Low"

## [1] TRUE   TRUE FALSE FALSE FALSE   TRUE FALSE   TRUE
```

Thus we can see that ordering is implicit in the way that the levels are specified and allows other, ordering related functions to be applied to the data.

The functions `sort` and `table` are new functions. In the above code relating to factors, the function `table` was used to generate a tabulation of the data in `house.type`. It provides a count of the occurrence of each level in `house.type`. The command `sort` orders a vector or factor. You should use the help in R to explore how these functions work and try them with your own variables. For example:

```
sort(income)
```

Lists

The `character`, `numeric` and `logical` data types and the associated data classes described above all contain elements that must all be of the same basic type. Lists do not have this requirement. Lists have slots for different elements and can be considered as an ordered collection of elements. A list allows you to gather a variety of different data types together in a single data structure and the nth element of a list is denoted by double square brackets.

```
tmp.list <- list("Lex Comber",c(2005, 2009), "Lecturer",
    matrix(c(6,3,1,2), c(2,2)))
tmp.list
```

```
## [[1]]
## [1] "Lex Comber"
##
## [[2]]
## [1] 2005 2009
##
## [[3]]
## [1] "Lecturer"
##
## [[4]]

##      [,1] [,2]
## [1,]   6    1
## [2,]   3    2
```

```
# elements of the list can be selected
tmp.list[[4]]
```

```
##      [,1] [,2]
## [1,]   6    1
## [2,]   3    2
```

From the above it is evident that the function `list` returns a list structure composed of its arguments. Each value can be tagged depending on how the argument was specified. The conversion function `as.list` attempts to coerce its argument to a list. It turns a factor into a list of one-element factors and drops attributes that are not specified. The test `is.list` returns TRUE if and only if its argument is a list. These are best explored through some examples; note that `list` items can be given names.

```
employee <- list(name="Lex Comber", start.year = 2005,
    position="Professor")
employee
```

```
## $name
## [1] "Lex Comber"
##
## $start.year
## [1] 2005
```

```
##
## $position
## [1] "Professor"
```

Lists can be joined together with append, and lapply applies a function to each element of a list.

```
append(tmp.list, list(c(7,6,9,1)))
```

```
## [[1]]
## [1] "Lex Comber"
##
## [[2]]
## [1] 2005 2009
##

## [[3]]
## [1] "Lecturer"
##
## [[4]]
##      [,1] [,2]
## [1,]   6    1
## [2,]   3    2
##
## [[5]]
## [1] 7 6 9 1
```

```
# lapply with different functions
lapply(tmp.list[[2]], is.numeric)
```

```
## [[1]]
## [1] TRUE
##
## [[2]]
## [1] TRUE
```

```
lapply(tmp.list, length)
```

```
## [[1]]
## [1] 1
##
## [[2]]
## [1] 2
```

```
##
## [[3]]
## [1] 1
##
## [[4]]
## [1]  4
```

Note that the `length` of a matrix, even when held in a list, is the total number of elements.

Defining your own classes

In R it is possible to define your own data type and to associate it with specific behaviours, such as its own way of printing and drawing. For example, you will notice in later chapters that the `plot` function is used to draw maps for spatial data objects as well as conventional graphs. Suppose we create a list containing some employee information.

```
employee <- list(name="Lex Comber", start.year = 2005,
    position="Professor")
```

This can be assigned to a new class, called `staff` in this case (it could be any name but meaningful ones help).

```
class(employee) <- "staff"
```

Then we can define how R treats that class in the form <existing function>.<class>; to change, for example, how it is printed. Note how the existing function for printing is modified by the new class definition:

```
print.staff <- function(x) {
    cat("Name: ",x$name, "\n")
    cat("Start Year: ",x$start.year, "\n")
    cat("Job Title: ",x$position, "\n")}
# an example of the print class
print(employee)

## Name:  Lex Comber
## Start Year:  2005
## Job Title:  Professor
```

You can see that R knows to use a different `print` function if the argument is a variable of class `staff`. You could modify how your R environment treats existing classes in the same way, but do this with caution. You can also 'undo' the class assigned by using unclass and the print.staff function can be removed permanently by using rm(print.staff):

```
print(unclass(employee))

## $name
## [1] "Lex Comber"
##
## $start.year
## [1] 2005
##
## $position
## [1] "Professor"
```

Classes in lists

Variables can be assigned to new or user-defined class objects. The example below defines a function to create a new staff object.

```
new.staff <- function(name,year,post) {
   result <- list(name=name, start.year=year, position=post)
   class(result) <- "staff"
   return(result)}
```

A list can then be defined, which is populated using that function as in the code below (note that functions will be dealt with more formally in later chapters).

```
leics.uni <- vector(mode='list',3)
# assign values to elements in the list
leics.uni[[1]] <- new.staff("Fisher, Pete", 1991,
    "Professor")
leics.uni[[2]] <- new.staff("Comber, Lex", 2005,
    "Lecturer")
leics.uni[[3]] <- new.staff("Burgess, Robert", 1998, "VC")
```

And the list can be examined:

```
leics.uni
## [[1]]
## Name:  Fisher,  Pete
## Start Year:  1991
```

```
## Job Title:  Professor
##
## [[2]]
## Name:  Comber,  Lex
## Start Year:  2005
## Job Title:  Lecturer
##
## [[3]]
## Name:  Burgess,  Robert
## Start Year:  1998
## Job Title:  VC
```

2.3.3 Self-Test Questions

In the next pages there are a number of self-test questions. In contrast to the previous sections where the code is provided in the text for you to work through (i.e. you to enter and run it yourself), the self-test questions are tasks for you to complete, mostly requiring you to write R code. Answers are provided at the end of this chapter. The self-test questions relate to the main data types that have been introduced: factors, matrices, lists (named and unnamed) and classes.

Factors

Recall from the descriptions above that factors are used to represent categorical data – where a small number of categories are used to represent some characteristic in a variable. For example, the colour of a particular model of car sold by a showroom in a week can be represented using factors:

```
colours <- factor(c("red","blue","red","white",
    "silver","red","white","silver",
    "red","red","white","silver","silver"),
    levels=c("red","blue","white","silver","black"))
```

Since the only colours this car comes in are red, blue, white, silver and black, these are the only levels in the factor.

Self-Test Question 1. Suppose you were to enter:

```
colours[4] <- "orange"
colours
```

What would you expect to happen? Why?

Next, use the `table` function to see how many of each colour were sold. First reassign the colours, as you may have altered this variable in the previous self-test question. You can find previously used commands using the up and down arrows on your keyboard.

```
colours <- factor(c("red","blue","red","white",
    "silver", "red", "white", "silver",
    "red","red","white","silver","silver"),
    levels=c("red","blue","white","silver","black"))
table(colours)
```

```
## colours
##     red blue white silver black
##       5    1     3      4     0
```

Note that the result of the `table` function is just a standard vector, but that each of its elements is named – the names in this case are the levels in the factor. Now suppose you had simply recorded the colours as a character variable, in `colours2` as below, and then computed the table:

```
colours2 <-c("red","blue","red","white",
    "silver","red","white","silver",
    "red","red","white","silver")
# Now, make the table
table(colours2)
```

```
## colours2
##   blue red  silver white
##      1   5       3     3
```

Self-Test Question 2. What two differences do you notice between the results of the two `table` expressions?

Now suppose we also record the type of car – it comes in saloon, convertible and hatchback types. This can be specified by another factor variable called `car.type`:

```
car.type <- factor(c("saloon","saloon","hatchback",
    "saloon","convertible","hatchback","convertible",
    "saloon", "hatchback","saloon", "saloon",
    "saloon", "hatchback"),
    levels=c("saloon","hatchback","convertible"))
```

The table function can also work with two arguments:

```
table(car.type, colours)
```

```
##                colours
##  car.type      red blue white silver black
##     saloon      2    1    2     2     0
##     hatchback   3    0    0     1     0
##     convertible 0    0    1     1     0
```

This gives a two-way table of counts – that is, counts of red hatchbacks, silver saloons and so on. Note that the output this time is a matrix. For now enter:

```
crosstab <- table(car.type,colours)
```

to save the table into a variable called crosstab to be used later on.

Self-Test Question 3. What is the difference between table(car.type,colours) and table(colours,car.type)?

Finally in this section, ordered factors will be considered. Suppose a third variable about the cars is the engine size, and that the three sizes are 1.1 litres, 1.3 litres and 1.6 litres. Again, this is stored in a variable, but this time the sizes are ordered. Enter:

```
engine <- ordered(c("1.1litre","1.3litre","1.1litre",
     "1.3litre","1.6litre","1.3litre","1.6litre",
     "1.1litre ","1.3litre","1.1litre", "1.1litre",
     "1.3litre","1.3litre"),
     levels=c("1.1litre","1.3litre","1.6litre"))
```

Recall that with ordered variables, it is possible to use comparison operators >, <, >= and <=. For example:

```
engine > "1.1litre"
## [1] FALSE TRUE FALSE TRUE TRUE TRUE TRUE FALSE TRUE FALSE FALCE
## [12] TRUE TRUE
```

Self-Test Question 4. Using the engine, car.type and colours variables, write expressions to give the following:

- The colours of all cars with engines with capacity greater than 1.1 litres.
- The counts of types (hatchback, etc.) of all cars with capacity below 1.6 litres.
- The counts of colours of all hatchbacks with capacity greater than or equal to 1.3 litres.

Matrices

Recall that in the previous section you created a variable called `crosstab` – and that this was a matrix. In the section on matrices, a number of functions were shown that could be applied to matrices:

```
dim(crosstab)  # Matrix dimensions

## [1] 3 5

rowSums(crosstab)  # Row sums

##       saloon      hatchback      convertible
##          7              4               2

colnames(crosstab)  # Column names

## [1] "red"     "blue"     "white"     "silver"     "black"
```

Another important tool for matrices is the `apply` function. This applies a function to either the rows or columns of a matrix giving a single-dimensional list as a result. A simple example finds the largest value in each row:

```
apply(crosstab,1,max)

##     saloon     hatchback     convertible
##        2            3              1
```

In this case, the function `max` is applied to each row of `crosstab`. The 1 as the second argument specifies that the function will be applied row by row. If it were 2 then the function would be column by column:

```
apply(crosstab,2,max)

##     red     blue     white     silver     black
##      3       1         2          2          0
```

A useful function is `which.max`. Given a list of numbers, it returns the index of the largest one. For example:

```
example <- c(1.4,2.6,1.1,1.5,1.2)
which.max(example)

## [1] 2
```

so that in this case the second element is the largest.

Self-Test Question 5. What happens if there is more than one number taking the largest value in a list? Either use the help facility or experimentation to find out.

Self-Test Question 6. `which.max` can be used in conjunction with `apply`. Write an expression to find the index of the largest value in each row of `crosstab`.

The function `levels` returns the levels of a variable of type `factor` in character form. For example:

```
levels(engine)
```

```
## [1] "1.1litre" "1.3litre" "1.6litre"
```

The order they are returned in is that specified in the original `factor` assignment and the same order as row or column names produced by the `table` function. This means that it can be used in conjunction with `which.max` when applied to matrices to obtain the row or column names instead of an index number:

```
levels(colours)[which.max(crosstab[,1])]
```

```
## [1] "blue"
```

Alternatively, the same effect can be achieved by the following:

```
colnames(crosstab)[which.max(crosstab[,1])]
```

```
## [1] "blue"
```

You should unpick these last two lines of code to make sure you understand what each element is doing.

```
colnames(crosstab)
```

```
## [1]  "red"    "blue"    "white"    "silver"    "black"
```

```
crosstab[,1]
```

```
##         saloon  hatchback  convertible
##              2          3            0
```

```
which.max(crosstab[,1])
```

```
## hatchback
##         2
```

More generally, a function could be written to apply this operation to any variable with names:

```
# Defines the function
which.max.name <- function(x) {
    return(names(x)[which.max(x)])}
# Next, give the variable 'example' names for the values
names(example) <- c("Leicester","Nottingham",
    "Loughborough","Birmingham","Coventry")
example
```

```
## Leicester  Nottingham  Loughborough  Birmingham  Coventry
##       1.4         2.6           1.1         1.5       1.2
```

```
which.max.name(example)
```

```
## [1] "Nottingham"
```

Self-Test Question 7. Finally, `which.max.name` could be applied (using `apply`) to a matrix, to find the row name with the largest value, for each of the columns, or vice versa. For the car sales matrix, this would give you the best-selling colour for each car type (or vice versa). Write the `apply` expression for each of these.

Note that in the last code snippet, a `function` was defined called `which.max.name`. You have been using functions, but these have all been existing ones as defined in R until now. Functions will be thoroughly dealt with in Chapter 4, but you should note two things about them at this point. First is the form:

```
function name <- function(function inputs) {
  variable <- function actions
  return(variable)
}
```

Second are the syntactic elements of the curly brackets { } that bound the code and the `return` function that defines the value to be returned by the function.

Lists

From the text in this chapter, recall that lists can be named and unnamed. Here we will only consider the named kind. Lists may be created by the `list` function. To create a list variable enter:

```
var <- list(name1=value1, name2=value2,...)
```

Note that the above is just a template used as an example – entering it into R will give an error as there are no variables called value1, value2, etc., and the dots . . . in this context are not valid R syntax.

Self-Test Question 8. Suppose you wanted to store both the row- and column-wise apply results (from Question 7) into a list called most.popular with two named elements called colour (containing the most popular colour for each car type) and type (containing the most popular car type for each colour). Write an R expression that shows the best-selling colour and car types into a list.

Classes

The objective of this task is to create a class based on the list created in the last section. The class will consist of a list of most popular colours and car types, together with a third element containing the total number of cars sold (called total). Call this class sales.data. A function to create a variable of this class, given colours and car.type, is below:

```
new.sales.data <- function(colours, car.type) {
    xtab <- table(car.type,colours)
    result <- list(colour=apply(xtab,1,which.max.name),
        type=apply(xtab,2,which.max.name),
        total=sum(xtab))
    class(result) <- "sales.data"
    return(result)}
```

This can be used to create a sales.data object which has the colours and car.type variables assigned to it via the function:

```
this.week <- new.sales.data(colours,car.type)
this.week

## $colour
##       saloon  hatchback  convertible
##        "red"      "red"      "white"
##
## $type
##            red        blue       white      silver       black
## "hatchback"    "saloon"    "saloon"    "saloon"    "saloon"
##
## $total
## [1] 13
##
## attr(,"class")
## [1] "sales.data"
```

In the above code, a new variable called `this.week` of class `sales.data` is created. Following the ideas set out in the preceding section, it is now possible to create a `print` function for variables of class `sales.data`. This can be done by writing a function called `print.sales.data` that takes an input or argument of the `sales.data` class.

Self-Test Question 9. Write a print function for variables of class `sales.data`. This is a difficult problem and should be tackled by those with previous programming experience. Others can try it now, but should return to it after the functions have been formally introduced in the next chapter.

2.4 PLOTS

There are a number of plot routines and packages in R. In this section some basic plot types will be introduced, followed by some more advanced plotting commands and functions. The aim of this section is to give you an understanding of how the basic plot types can be used as building blocks in more advanced plotting routines that are called in later chapters to display the results of spatial analysis.

2.4.1 Basic Plot Tools

The most basic plot is the scatter plot. Figure 2.1 was created from the function `rnorm` which generates a set of random numbers.

```
x1 <- rnorm(100)
y1 <- rnorm(100)
plot(x1,y1)
```

The generic `plot` function creates a graph of two variables that are plotted on the x-axis and the y-axis. The default settings for the `plot` function produce a

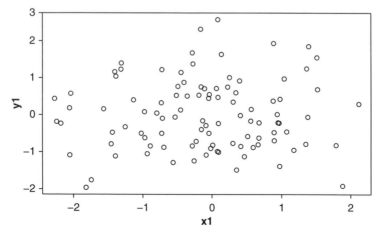

Figure 2.1 A basic scatter plot

scatter plot, and you should note that by default the axes are labelled with expressions passed to the plot function. Many parameters can be set for plot either by defining the plot environment (described later) or when the plot is called. For example, the option col specifies the plot colour and pch the plot character:

```
plot(x1,y1,pch=16, col='red')
```

Other options include different types of plot: type = 'l' produces a line plot of the two variables, and again the col option can be used to specify the line colour and the option lwd specifies the plot line width. You should run the code below to produce different line plots:

```
x2 <- seq(0,2*pi,len=100)
y2 <- sin(x2)
plot(x2,y2,type='l')
plot(x2,y2,type='l', lwd=3, col='darkgreen')
```

You should examine the help for the plot command (reminder: type ?plot at the R prompt) and explore different plot types that are available. Having called a new plot as in the above examples, other data can be plotted using other commands: points, lines, polygons, etc. You will see that plot by default assumes the plot type is point unless otherwise specified. For example, in Figure 2.2 the line data described by x2 and y2 are plotted, after which the points described by x2 and y2r are added to the plot.

```
plot(x2,y2,type='l', col='darkgreen', lwd=3,
ylim=c(-1.2,1.2))
y2r <- y2 + rnorm(100,0,0.1)
points(x2,y2r, pch=16, col='darkred')
```

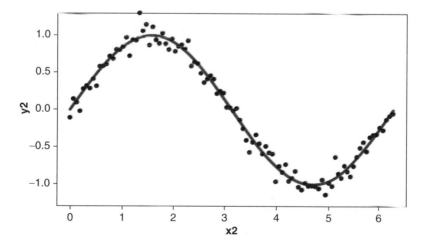

Figure 2.2 A line plot with points added

In the above code, the `rnorm` function creates a vector of small values which are added to `y2` to create `y2r`. The function `points` adds points to an existing plot. Many other options for plots can be applied here. For example, note the `ylim` option. This sets the limits on the *y*-axis, and `xlim` does the same for the *x*-axis. You should apply the commands below to the plot data.

```
y4 <- cos(x2)
plot(x2, y2, type='l', lwd=3, col='darkgreen')
lines(x2, y4, lwd=3, lty=2, col='darkblue')
```

Notice that, similar to `points`, the function `lines` adds lines to an existing plot. Note also the `lty` option: this specifies the type of line (dotted, simple, etc.) and is described in the plot parameters below.

You should examine the different types (and other plot parameters) in `par`. Enter `?par` for the help page to see the full list of different plot parameters. One of these, `mfrow`, is used below to set a combined plot of one row and two columns. This needs to be reset or the rest of your plots will continue to be printed in this way. To do this enter:

```
par(mfrow = c(1,2))
# reset
par(mfrow = c(1,1))
```

The function `polygon` adds a polygon to the plot. The option `col` sets the polygon fill colour. By default a black border is drawn; however, including the parameter `border = NA` would result in no border being drawn. In Figure 2.3 two different plots of the same data illustrate the application of these parameters.

```
x2 <- seq(0,2*pi,len=100)
y2 <- sin(x2)
y4 <- cos(x2)
# specify the plot order: see ?par for more information
par(mfrow = c(1,2))
# plot #1
plot(y2,y4)
polygon(y2,y4,col='lightgreen')
# plot #2: this time with 'asp' to set the aspect ratio
of the axes
plot(y2,y4, asp=1, type='n')
polygon(y2,y4,col='lightgreen')
```

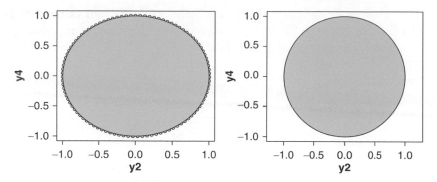

Figure 2.3   Points with polygons added

The parameter `asp` fixes the aspect ratio, in this case to 1 so that the x and y scales are the same, and `type = 'n'` draws the plot axes to correct scale (i.e. of the y2 and y4 data) but adds no lines or points.

So far the plot commands have been used to plot pairs of *x* and *y* coordinates in different ways: points, lines and polygons (this may suggest different vector types in a GIS for some readers). We can extend these to start to consider geographic coordinates more explicitly with some geographic data. You will need to install the GISTools package, which may involve setting a mirror site as described in Chapter 1. The first time you use any package in R it needs to be downloaded before it is installed.

```
install.packages("GISTools", depend = T)
```

Then you can call the package in the R console:

```
library(GISTools)
```

You will see some messages when you load the package, letting you know that the packages that GISTools makes use of have also been loaded automatically. The code below loads a number of datasets with the `data(georgia)` command. It then selects the first element from the `georgia.polys` dataset and assigns it to a variable called `appling`. This contains the coordinates of the outline of Appling County in Georgia. It then plots this to generate Figure 2.4. You only need to *install* a package onto your computer the first time you use it. Once it is installed it can simply be called. That is, there is no need to download it again, you can simply enter `library(package)`.

```
# library(GISTools)
data(georgia)
# select the first element
appling <- georgia.polys[[1]]
```

```
# set the plot extent
plot(appling, asp=1, type='n', xlab="Easting",
ylab="Northing")
# plot the selected features with hatching
polygon(appling, density=14, angle=135)
```

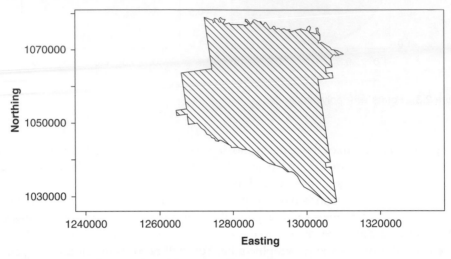

Figure 2.4 Appling County plotted from coordinate pairs

There are a number of things to note in this bit of code.

1. data(georgia) loads three datasets: georgia, georgia2 and georgia.polys.

2. The first element of georgia.polys contains the coordinates for the outline of Appling County.

3. Polygons do not have to be regular: they can, as in this example, be geographical zones. The code assigns the coordinates to a variable called appling and the variable is a two-column matrix.

4. Thus, with an x and y pairing, the following plot commands all work with data in this format: plot, lines, polygon, points.

5. As before, the plot command in the code below has the type = 'n' parameter and asp fixes the aspect ratio. The result is that that the *x* and *y* scales are the same but the command adds no lines or points.

2.4.2 Plot Colours

Plot colours can be specified as red, green and blue (RGB) values: that is, three values in the ranges 0 to 1. Having run the code above, you should have a variable called appling in your workspace. Now try entering the code below:

```
plot(appling, asp=1, type='n', xlab="Easting",
ylab="Northing")
polygon(appling, col=rgb(0,0.5,0.7))
```

A fourth parameter can be added to rgb to indicate transparency as in the code below, where the range is 0 to 1 for invisible to opaque.

```
polygon(appling, col=rgb(0,0.5,0.7,0.4))
```

Text can also be added to the plot and its placement in the plot window specified. The cex parameter (for character *ex*pansion) determines the size of text. Note that parameters like col also work with text and that HTML colours also work, such as "B3B333". The code below generates two plots. The first plots a set of random points and then plots appling with a transparency shading over the top. The second plots appling, but with some descriptive text. The result of applying these plot commands should look like Figures 2.5 and 2.6.

```
# set the plot extent
plot(appling, asp=1, type='n', xlab="Easting", ylab="Northing")
# plot the points
points(x = runif(500,126,132)*10000,
    y = runif(500,103,108)*10000, pch=16, col='red')
# plot the polygon with a transparency factor
polygon(appling, col=rgb(0,0.5,0.7,0.4))
```

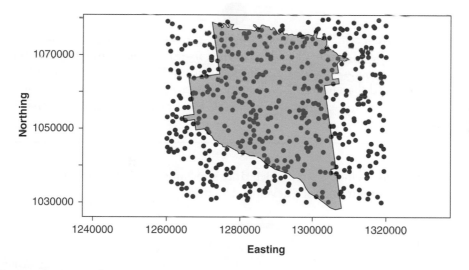

Figure 2.5 Appling County with transparency

```
plot(appling, asp=1, type='n', xlab="Easting",
    ylab="Northing")
polygon(appling, col="#B3B333")
# add text, specifying its placement, colour and size
text(1287000,1053000, "Appling County",cex=1.5)
text(1287000,1049000, "Georgia",col='darkred')
```

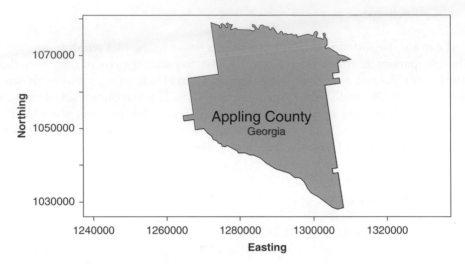

Figure 2.6 Appling County with text

In the above code, the coordinates for the text placement needed to specified. The function `locator` is very useful in this context: it can be used to determine locations in the plot window. Enter `locator()` at the R prompt, and then left-click in the plot window at various locations. When you right-click, the coordinates of these locations are returned to the R console window.

Other plot tools include `rect`, which draws rectangles. This is useful for placing map legends as your analyses develop. The three code blocks below produce the plot in Figure 2.7.

```
plot(c(-1.5,1.5),c(-1.5,1.5),asp=1, type='n')
# plot the green/blue rectangle
rect(-0.5,-0.5,0.5,0.5, border=NA, col=rgb(0,0.5,0.5,0.7))
```

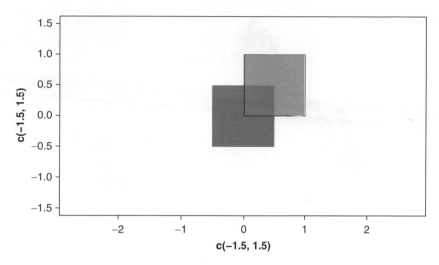

Figure 2.7 Plotting rectangles

```
# then the second one
rect(0,0,1,1, col=rgb(1,0.5,0.5,0.7))
```

The command image plots tabular and raster data as shown in Figure 2.8. It has default colour schemes, but other colour palettes exist. This book strongly recommends the use of the RColorBrewer package, which is described in more detail in Chapter 3, but an example of its application is given below:

```
# load some grid data
data(meuse.grid)
# define a SpatialPixelsDataFrame from the data
mat = SpatialPixelsDataFrame(points = meuse.grid[c("x", "y")],
    data = meuse.grid)
# set some plot parameters (1 row, 2 columns)
par(mfrow = c(1,2))
# set the plot margins
par(mar = c(0,0,0,0))
# plot the points using the default shading
image(mat, "dist")
# load the package
library(RColorBrewer)
# select and examine a colour palette with 7 classes
greenpal <- brewer.pal(7,'Greens')
# and now use this to plot the data
image(mat, "dist", col=greenpal)
```

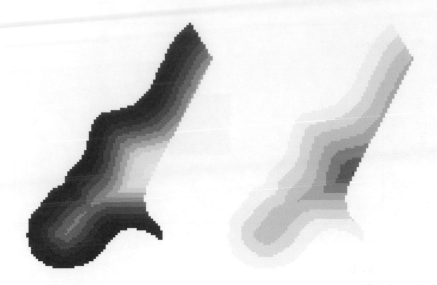

Figure 2.8   Plotting raster data

```
# reset par
par(mfrow = c(1,1))
```

You should note that the par(mfrow = c(1,2)) results in one row and two columns and that it is reset in the last line of code.

The command contour(mat, "dist") will generate a contour plot of the matrix above. You should examine the help for contour. A nice example of its use can be found in code in the help page for the volcano dataset that comes with R. Enter the following in the R console:

```
?volcano
```

2.5 READING, WRITING, LOADING AND SAVING DATA

There are a number of ways of getting data in and out of R, and three are briefly considered here: reading and writing text files, R data files and spatial data.

2.5.1 Text Files

Consider the appling data variable above. This is a matrix variable, containing two columns and 125 rows. You can examine the data using dim and head:

```
# display the first six rows
head(appling)
# display the variable dimensions
dim(appling)
```

You will note that the data fields (columns) are not named. However, these can be assigned.

```
colnames(appling) <- c("X", "Y")
```

The data can be written into a comma-separated variable file using the command `write.csv` and then read back into a different variable, as follows:

```
write.csv(appling, file = "test.csv")
```

This writes a .csv file into the current working directory. If you open it using a text editor or spreadsheet software, you will see that it has three columns, X and Y as expected plus the index for each record. This is because the default for `write.csv` includes `row.names = TRUE`. Again examine the help file for this function.

```
write.csv(appling, file - "test.csv", row.names = F)
```

R also allows you to read .csv files using the `read.csv` function. Read the file you have created into a variable:

```
tmp.appling <- read.csv(file = "test.csv")
```

Notice that in this case what is read from the .csv file is assigned to the variable `tmp.appling`. Try reading this file without assignment. The default for `read.csv` is that the file has a header (i.e. the first row contains the names of the columns) and that the separator between values in any record is a comma. However, these can be changed depending on the nature of the file you are seeking to load into R. A number of different types of files can be read into R. You should examine the help files for reading data in different formats. Enter `??read` to see some of these listed. You will note that `read.table` and `write.table` require more parameters to be specified than `read.csv` and `write.csv`.

2.5.2 R Data Files

It is possible to save variables that are in your workspace to a designated file. This can be loaded at the start of your next session. For example, if you have been running the code as introduced in this chapter you should have a number of variables, from x at the start to `engine` and `colours` and the `appling` data above.

You can save this *workspace* using the drop-down menus in the R interface or using the `save` function. The R interface menu route saves everything that is present in your workspace – as listed by `ls()` – whilst the `save` command allows you to specify what variables you wish to save.

```
# this will save everything in the workspace
save(list = ls(), file = "MyData.RData")
# this will save just appling
save(list = "appling", file = "MyData.RData")
# this will save appling and georgia.polys
save(list = c("appling", "georgia.polys"), file =
    "MyData.RData")
```

You should note that the .RData file binary format is very efficient at storing data: the `appling` `.csv` file used 4 kb of memory, whilst the .RData file used only 2 kb. Similarly, .RData files can be loaded into R using the menu in the R interface or loaded at the command line at the R console:

```
load("MyData.RData")
```

This will load the variables in the .RData file into the R console.

2.5.3 Spatial Data Files

Very often we have data that is in a particular format, such as *shapefile* format. R has the ability to load many different spatial data formats.

Consider the `georgia` dataset that was loaded earlier. This can be written out as a shapefile in the following way:

```
data(georgia)
writePolyShape(georgia, "georgia.shp",)
```

You will see that a shapefile has been written into your current working directory, with its associated supporting files (.dbf, etc.) that can be recognised by other applications (QGIS, etc.). Similarly, this can be read into R and assigned to a variable, provided that a package calling the `writePolyShape` and `readShapePoly` functions in `maptools` such as `GISTools` has been loaded into R:

```
new.georgia <- readShapePoly("georgia.shp")
```

You should examine the `readShapeLines, readShapePoints, readShapePoly` functions and their associated `write` functions. You should also note that R is able to read and write other proprietary spatial data formats, which you should be able to find through a search of the R help system or via an internet search engine.

ANSWERS TO SELF-TEST QUESTIONS

Q1. orange is not one of the factor's levels, so the result is NA.

```
colours[4] <- "orange"
colours

## [1] red blue red <NA> silver red white silver red red
## [11] white silver silver
## Levels: red blue white silver black
```

Q2. There is no count for 'black' in the character version – table does not know that this value exists, since there is no levels information. Also the order of colours is alphabetical in the character version. In the factor version, it is based on that specified in the factor function.

Q3. The first variable is tabulated along the rows, the second along the columns.

Q4. Colours of all cars with engines with capacity greater than 1.1 litres:

```
# Undo the colour[4] <- "orange" line used above
colours <- factor(c("red","blue","red","white",
    "silver","red","white","silver",
    "red","red","white","silver"),
levels=c("red","blue","white","silver","black"))
colours[engine > "1.1litre"]

## [1] blue  white  <NA>  red  white  red  silver  <NA>
## Levels: red blue white silver black
```

Counts of types of all cars with capacity below 1.6 litres:

```
table(car.type[engine < "1.6litre"])

##
##    saloon  hatchback  convertible
##         7          4            0
```

Counts of colours of all hatchbacks with capacity greater than or equal to 1.3 litres:

```
table(colours[(engine >= "1.3litre") & (car.type ==
"hatchback")])


##
##    red   blue   white   silver   black
##     2      0       0        0       0
```

Q5. The index returned corresponds to the *first* number taking the largest value.
Q6. An expression to find the index of the largest value in each row of `crosstab` using `which.max` and `apply`.

```
apply(crosstab,1,which.max)

##   saloon   hatchback   convertible
##       1          1            3
```

Q7. `apply` functions to return the best-selling colour and car type.

```
apply(crosstab,1,which.max.name)

##   saloon   hatchback   convertible
##    "red"       "red"       "white"

apply(crosstab,2,which.max.name)

##           red        blue       white        silver       black
## "hatchback"    "saloon"    "saloon"    "saloon"    "saloon"
```

Q8. An R expression that shows the best-selling colour and car types into a list.

```
most.popular <- list(colour=apply(crosstab,1,which.max.name),
     type=apply(crosstab,2,which.max.name))
most.popular

##    $colour
##          saloon   hatchback   convertible
##           "red"       "red"       "white"
##
##    $type
##               red        blue       white       silver       black
##    "hatchback"    "saloon"    "saloon"    "saloon"    "saloon"
```

Q9. A print function for variables of the class `data.frame`.

```
print.sales.data <- function(x) {
    cat("Weekly Sales Data:\n")
    cat("Most popular colour:\n")
    for (i in 1:length(x$colour)) {
      cat(sprintf("%12s:%12s\n",names(x$colour)[i],
      x$colour[i]))}
    cat("Most popular type:\n")
    for (i in 1:length(x$type)) {
      cat(sprintf("%12s:%12s\n",names(x$type)[i],
      x$type[i]))}
    cat("Total Sold = ",x$total)
}

this.week

## Weekly Sales Data:
## Most popular colour:
##       saloon:         red
##    hatchback:         red
##  convertible:       white
## Most popular type:
##          red:   hatchback
##         blue:      saloon
##        white:      saloon
##       silver:      saloon
##        black:      saloon
## Total Sold = 13
```

Although the above is one *possible* solution to the question, it is not unique. You may decide to create a very different-looking `print.sales.data` function. Note also that although until now we have concentrated only on `print` functions for different classes, it is possible to create class-specific versions of *any* function.

HANDLING SPATIAL DATA IN R

3.1 OVERVIEW

The aim of this chapter is provide an introduction to the mapping and geographical data handling capabilities of R. It explicitly focuses on developing building blocks for the spatial data analyses in later chapters. These extend the mapping functionality that was briefly introduced in the previous chapter and that will be extended further in Chapter 5. It includes an introduction to the `GISTools` package and its functions, describes methods for producing choropleth maps – from basic to quite advanced outputs – and introduces some methods for generating descriptive statistics. These skills are fundamental to the analyses that will be developed in later in this book. This chapter will:

- Introduce the `GISTools` package
- Describe how to compile maps based on multiple layers
- Describe how to set different shading schemes
- Describe how to plot spatial data with different parameters
- Describe how to develop basic descriptive statistical analyses of spatial data

3.2 INTRODUCTION: GISTools

The previous chapters introduced some basic analytical and graphical techniques using R. However, few of these were particularly geographical. A number of packages are available in R that allow sophisticated visualisation, manipulation and analysis of spatial data. Some of this functionality will be demonstrated in this chapter in conjunction with some mapping tools and specific data types to create different examples of mapping in R. Remember that a package in R is a set of pre-written functions (and possibly data items as well) that are not available when you initially start R running, but can be loaded from the R library at the command line. To illustrate these techniques, the chapter starts by developing some elementary maps, building to more sophisticated mapping.

3.2.1 Installing and Loading `GISTools`

You will use different methods and tools contained within the `GISTools` package to draw maps and to handle spatial information. You should have installed the `GISTools` package onto your computer as you ran the code in Chapter 2 using the `install.packages` command. Once you have downloaded and installed a package on your computer, you can simply load the package when you use R subsequently. To load `GISTools` into the R session that you have just started, simply enter:

```
library(GISTools)
```

It is possible to inspect the functionality and tools available in `GISTools` or any other package by examining the documentation:

```
help(GISTools)
```

or

```
?GISTools
```

This provides a general description of the package. At the bottom of the help window, there is a hyperlink to the index which, if you click on it, will open a page with a list of all the tools available in the package. The CRAN website also has full documentation for each package – for `GISTools`, see `http://cran.r-project.org/web/packages/GISTools/index.tml`.

3.2.2 Spatial Data in `GISTools`

`GISTools`, similar to many other R packages, comes with a number of embedded datasets that can be loaded from the command line after the package is installed. Two datasets will be used in this chapter: polygon and line data for New Haven, Connecticut, and counties in the state of Georgia, both in the USA. The New Haven data include crime statistics, roads, census blocks (including demographic information), railway lines and place names. The data come from two sources, both of which have made the data freely available. The crime data are obtained from the New Haven Crime Log website (`http://www.newhavencrimelog.org`) provided by the *New Haven Independent* newspaper (`http://www.newhavenindependent.org`) – the data may be extracted from the HTML source code of the crime map web pages. The remaining data are obtained from the University of Connecticut's Map and Geographical Information Center (MAGIC: `http://magic.lib.uconn.edu/`). These data can be downloaded in MapInfo MIF or ESRI E00 formats, and with a public domain program called `ogr2ogr` it is possible to convert them into ESRI Shapefiles. The Georgia data include outlines of counties in Georgia (from `http://www.census.gov/geo/`) with a number of attributes relating to the 1990 census including population (`TotPop90`), the percentage of the population that are rural (`PctRural`), that have a college degree (PctBach), that are elderly (PctEld), that are foreign born (PctFB), that are classed as being in poverty (PctPov), that are black (PctBlack) and the median income of the county (MedInc). The two datasets are shown in Figure 3.1.

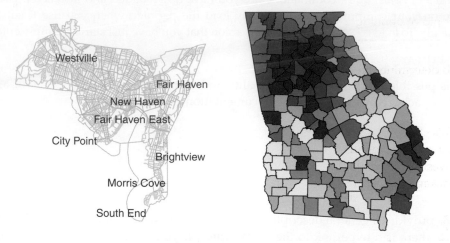

Figure 3.1   The New Haven census blocks with roads in blue, and the counties in the state of Georgia shaded by median income

The first thing you should do with any dataset is examine it. For spatial data, this often means a visual examination of its spatial properties and perhaps a more formal consideration of its attributes. Initially you will use the New Haven datasets to draw your first map in R. Load the New Haven data:

```
data(newhaven)
```

To examine the data that have been loaded enter:

```
ls()
```

```
## [1] "blocks"  "breach"  "burgres.f"   "burgres.n"
## [5] "famdisp" "places"  "roads"       "tracts"
```

This gives the printout above (blocks, breach, roads,...) showing all of the datasets that are loaded. A number of these, including the data called roads, are geographical data. Enter:

```
plot(roads)
```

and a map of roads in New Haven appears.

The `plot` command has been used earlier for graphics – but now, after loading the `GISTools` package, R has learned a new plot method to apply when the term between the brackets refers to geographical data. This is an example of defining and using classes in R as described in Chapter 2.

To determine the `class` of the `roads` dataset, enter:

```
class(roads)
```

This shows that roads is a variable of class `SpatialLinesDataFrame`, defined in the `sp` package that was automatically loaded in with `GISTools`. You should investigate the class of `blocks`, `tracts` and `breach` in the same way. The `sp` package defines a number of classes as summarised in the table below.

Without Attributes	With attributes	ArcGIS Equivalent
`SpatialPoints`	`SpatialPointsDataFrame`	Point shapefiles
`SpatialLines`	`SpatialLinesDataFrame`	Line shapefiles
`SpatialPolygons`	`SpatialPolygonsDataFrame`	Polygon shapefiles

So, for example, the `breach` data are a `SpatialPoints` class that simply describes locations, with no attributes, whereas the `blocks` data are of the `SpatialPolygonsDataFrame` class as they include some census variables associated with each census block. Thus spatial data with attributes defined in this way hold their attributes in the `data.frame` and you can see this by looking at the first few lines of the `blocks` `data.frame` using the `head` function:

```
head(data.frame(blocks))
```

This prints the first six lines of attributes associated with the census blocks data. A formal consideration of spatial attributes and how to analyse and map them is given later in this chapter. The census blocks in New Haven can be plotted:

```
plot(blocks)
```

Now suppose we want to plot another variable with the census blocks which shows the roads for the area. Entering:

```
plot(roads)
```

will draw a map of the roads. However, one problem is that this has now overwritten the blocks that were drawn before. To stop this from happening, an extra parameter called add can be included in the second plot call to ensure that the first set of data that was plotted is not overwritten. This overlays (rather than overwrites) the information. The add=TRUE part sets a parameter in the plot command to the logical value TRUE, instructing R not to overwrite, but to add the new information to the existing plot. A number of other parameters can also be included. For example, enter:

```
par(mar = c(0,0,0,0))
plot(blocks)
plot(roads, add=TRUE, col="red")
```

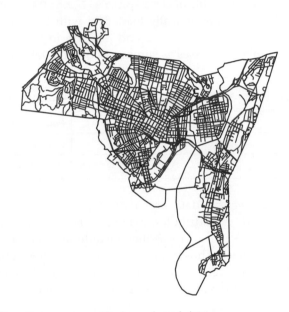

Figure 3.2　The New Haven census blocks and road data

The first line plots the blocks data. Again, because there are no other parameters, this starts a new plot. The next line adds the roads data, but the extra parameter tells R to draw them in red. Note that where quotes are needed these can be either single or double quotes, but not mixed and not formatted into curly quotes. Your map should look like the one in Figure 3.2.

The plot commands above generates maps of the census blocks and the roads in New Haven, regardless of whether the data describe area or linear features. Those familiar with GIS will recognise these as two of the commonly referred to vector features often cited in a GIS context of 'points, lines and areas'. In R, the command plot can also be used to plot point features. For example:

```
plot(blocks)
plot(breach, col = "red", add = TRUE)
```

This draws a map of locations where breaches of the peace have occurred in New Haven, overlaying the census blocks. Note that the default plot character is a cross and that some areas have a greater density of incidents than others. Remember from Chapter 2 that pch can be used to change the plot character for graphs. It can be used in the same way to map point spatial data. You should experiment with different pch and colour settings to get the best visualisation of the breaches of the peace and the census blocks data together. For example:

```
plot(blocks, lwd = 0.5, border = "grey50")
plot(breach, col = "red", pch = 1, add = TRUE)
```

It is possible to display a list of colours by entering:

```
colors()
```

And remember that help for plot describes many plot options, including different plot characters.

3.2.3 Embollishing the Map

You have now drawn your first maps in R showing the roads, breaches of peace and census blocks in New Haven. However, maps generally need more information than this. In particular, someone who had no prior knowledge of New Haven may not realise the geographical extent (in miles or kilometres) of the area. Assuming you still have the map window from the previous section, you can add a scale using the map.scale command. This command has a large number of parameters. Enter:

```
map.scale(534750,152000,miles2ft(2),"Miles",4,0.5)
```

A scale bar is drawn (overplotted) on the map. The first two parameters are the location at which the scale bar appears, in the coordinate system of the map. Currently, this is in US survey feet, using the State Plane Coordinate System for Connecticut. The coordinates specify the centre of the scale. The third parameter is the length (in projected map units) of the scale. In this case it is 2 miles. Since this distance also has to be specified in the coordinate system of the map, this quantity must be converted into feet, using the miles2ft function. The fourth parameter is a text string specifying the name of the units for the scale (miles in this case). The fifth parameter gives the number of gradations in the scale, and the sixth gives the fraction of the units that each gradation on the scale represents. Here, there are four gradations, and each one represents 0.5 miles.

A second embellishment is a north-pointing arrow. To add this, enter:

```
north.arrow(534750,154000,miles2ft(0.25),col= "lightblue")
```

This adds (overplots) the north arrow to the map. Again, the first two parameters here specify the location of the arrow: they give the coordinates, in map units, of the centre of the base of the arrow. The third parameter specifies the length of the arrow's base (here 0.25 miles in map units) and the `col` parameter specifies the colour that the arrow is filled with. If left unspecified, the arrow will be filled in white. Remember the `locator()` function introduced in Chapter 2 – this can be very useful for determining where to place items such scale bars and north arrows in plot windows. A final decoration to the map is a map title. Suppose the map is to be called 'New Haven, CT.'. Then enter the code below to add the title to the map.

```
title('New Haven, CT.' )
```

It should now look like the map in Figure 3.3.

Figure 3.3 An embellished map of the New Haven census blocks and breaches of the peace

3.2.4 Saving Your Map

Having created a map in a window on the screen, you may now want to save the map for either printing, or incorporating in a document. There are a number of ways that this can be done. The simplest is to right-click with the mouse on the map window, select **copy** or **copy image to clipboard** (Mac) or **Copy as metafile** or **Copy as bitmap** (Windows), and then paste it into a word-processing document (for example, one being created in either OpenOffice or MS Windows). Another is to highlight the window and to use **File** > **Save as** to save the map as an image file, with a name that you give it. However, it is also possible to save images by using the R commands that were used to create the map. This takes more initial effort, but has the advantage that it is possible to make minor changes (such as altering the position of the scale, or drawing the census block boundaries in a different colour) and to easily rerun the code. Finally, it is also possible to save your map in a number of file formats, such as PDF or PNG.

One way to create a file of commands is to edit a text file with a name ending in .R – note the capital letter. In R, open a new document on a Windows machine by going to File > New script and **File** > **New script,** or on a Mac by selecting **File** > **New Document**. Then type in the following:

```
# load package and data
library(GISTools)
data(newhaven)
# plot spatial data
plot(blocks)
plot(roads,add=TRUE,col= 'red')
# embellish the map
map.scale(534750,152000,miles2ft(2),  "Miles",4,0.5)
north.arrow(530650,154000,miles2ft(0.5),col= 'lightblue')
title('New Haven, CT')
```

Save the file as 'newhavenmap.R' in the directory in which you started up R.

When you start an R session you should set the working directory to be the folder that you wish to use to write and read data to and from, to store your command files, such as the `newhavenmap.R` file, and any workspace files or .RData files that you save. In Windows this is **File** > **Change dir...**, and on a Mac it is **Misc** > **Set Working Directory**.

Now, go back to the R command line and enter:

```
source("newhavenmap.R")
```

and your map will be redrawn. The file contains all of the commands to draw the map, and 'sourcing' it makes R run through these in sequence. Suppose you now wish to redraw the map, but with the roads drawn in blue, rather than red. In the file editor, go to the second line, and edit the line to become:

```
plot(roads,add=TRUE,col= 'blue')
```

and save the file again. Re-entering source ("newhavenmap.R") now draws the map, but with the roads drawn in blue. Another parameter sometimes used in map drawing is the line width parameter, lwd. This time, edit the first plot command in the file to become:

```
plot(blocks, lwd=3)
```

and re-enter the source command. The map is redrawn with thicker boundaries around the census blocks. The col and lwd parameters can of course be used in combination – edit the file again, so that the second line becomes:

```
plot(roads,add=TRUE,col= "red",lwd=2)
```

and source the file again. This time the roads are thicker, and drawn in red. Another advantage of saving command files, as noted earlier, is that it is possible to place the graphics created into various graphics file formats. To create a PDF, for example, the command:

```
pdf(file= 'map.pdf')
```

can be placed before the first line containing a plot command in the newhavenmap.R file. This tells R that after this command, any graphics will not be drawn on the screen, but instead written to the file map.pdf (or whatever name you choose for the file). When you have written all of the commands you need to create your map, then enter:

```
dev.off()
```

which is short for device off, and tells R to close the PDF file, and go back to drawing graphics in windows on the screen in the future. To test this out, insert a new first line at the beginning of newhavenmap.R and a new last line at the end. Then re-source the file. This time, no new graphics are drawn but you have now created a set of commands to write the graphic into a PDF file called map.pdf. This file will be created in the folder in which you are working. To check that this has worked, open your working directory folder in Windows Explorer, Mac Finder, etc., and there should be a file called map.pdf. Click on it and whatever PDF reader you use should open, and your map displayed as a PDF file. This file can be incorporated into presentations, word-processing documents and so on. A similar command, for producing PNG files, is:

```
png(file= 'map.png')
```

which writes all subsequent R graphics into a PNG file, until a `dev.off()` is issued. To test this, replace the first line of `newhavenmap.R` with the above command, and re-source it from the R command line. A new file will appear in the folder called `map.png` which may be incorporated into documents as with the PDF file.

3.3 MAPPING SPATIAL OBJECTS

3.3.1 Introduction

The first part of this chapter has outlined basic commands for plotting data and for producing maps and graphics using R. This next section will now concentrate on developing and expanding these basic techniques, will introduce some new plot parameters and will show you how to extract and download Google Maps data as background context. As you develop more sophisticated analyses in later sections you may wish to return to some of the examples used in this section. It will develop mapping of vector spatial data (points, lines and areas) and will also introduce some new R commands and techniques to help put all of this together. To begin with, you will need some predetermined data and, as ever, you may wish to think about creating a workspace folder in which you can store any results you generate.

3.3.2 Data

In this section you will practise your mapping and plotting techniques. The code in this section will examine the georgia dataset, select a subset of specific counties and display these using an OpenStreetMap backdrop. You will need to make use of the `GISTools` package to draw maps and handle spatial information.

You should start a new R session or clear your workspace to remove all the variables and datasets you have created and opened using the previous code and commands. You can clear your workspace via the menu **Misc > Remove all objects** (on a Mac, select **Workspace > Clear Workspace**) or by entering:

```
rm(list=ls())
```

Then you should make sure the `GISTools` package and the georgia datasets are loaded by entering:

```
library(GISTools)
data(georgia)
```

Check that the data has loaded correctly using `ls()`. There should be three Georgia datasets: `georgia`, `georgia2` and `georgia.polys`.

3.3.3 Plotting Options

A number of plot parameters exist in addition to the ones that have previously been used, including different window sizes, multiple plots in the same window, polygon or area shading, hatching, boundary thickness, boundary colour and labelling. Many of these plot parameters are described in the help for par. First, plot georgia with a single shade and a background colour:

```
plot(georgia, col = "red", bg = "wheat")
```

It is also possible to generate an outline of the area using the gUnaryUnion function as in the code below, with the results shown in Figure 3.4. The manipulation of spatial data using overlay, union and intersection functions will be covered in more depth in Chapter 5 later in this book.

```
# do a merge
georgia.outline <- gUnaryUnion(georgia, id = NULL)
# plot the spatial layers
plot(georgia, col = "red", bg = "wheat", lty = 2,
    border = "blue")
plot(georgia.outline, lwd = 3, add = TRUE)
# add titles
title(main = "The State of Georgia", font.main = 2,
    cex.main = 1.5, sub = "and its counties",
    font.sub = 3, col.sub = "blue")
```

The State of Georgia

and its counties

Figure 3.4   An example of applying different plot parameters

In the above code there are two plot commands: the first plots the georgia data-set, specifying a dashed blue line to show the county boundaries, a red colour for the objects and a map background colour of wheat. The second overlays the out-line created by the union operation with a thicker line width, before the title and subtitle are added. The plot window can be expanded to include multiple plots using the mfrow plot parameter. This takes as its arguments the number of rows and the number of columns. Note in the code below the explicit call to create two maps in the plot window and their order using par(mfrow=c(1,2)) and to adjust the plot margins (mar) to accommodate the plots.

```
# set some plot parameters
par(mfrow=c(1,2))
par(mar = c(2,0,3,0))
# 1st plot
plot(georgia, col = "red", bg = "wheat")
title("georgia")
# 2nd plot
plot(georgia2, col = "orange", bg = "lightyellow3")
title("georgia2")
# reset par(mfrow)
par (mfrow=c(1,1))
```

Thus different plot parameters can be used for different subsets of the data such that they are plotted in ways that are different from the default. Note that the parameters can be manually reset for plot windows that are open, for example by entering par(mfrow=c(1,1)), or the defaults are reset when a new window is opened.

Sometimes we would like to label the features in our maps. Have a look at the names of the counties in the georgia dataset. These are held in the 13th attribute column and names(georgia) will return a list of the names of all attributes:

```
data.frame(georgia)[,13]
```

It would be useful to display these on the map, and this can be done using the pointLabel function in the maptools package that is loaded with GISTools. Notice the col is set to NA. The result is shown in Figure 3.5.

```
# assign some coordinates
Lat <- data.frame(georgia)[,1]    #Y or North/South
Lon <- data.frame(georgia)[,2]    #X or East/West
# assign some label
Names <- data.frame(georgia)[,13]
# set plot parameters, plot and label
par(mar = c(0,0,0,0))
plot(georgia, col = NA)
pl <- pointLabel(Lon, Lat, Names, offset = 0, cex =.5)
```

Figure 3.5 Adding feature labels to the map

Perhaps we are interested in a specific sub-region of the data, for example the area to the east of the state covered by the counties of Jefferson, Jenkins, Johnson, Washington, Glascock, Emanuel, Candler, Bulloch, Screven, Richmond and Burke. A subset of these counties can be selected and plotted in the following way.

```
# the county indices below were extracted from the data.
frame
county.tmp <- c(81, 82, 83, 150, 62, 53, 21, 16, 124,
    121, 17)
georgia.sub <- georgia[county.tmp,]
```

and then plotted:

```
par(mar = c(0,0,3,0))
plot(georgia.sub, col = "gold1", border = "grey")
```

```
plot(georgia.outline, add = TRUE, lwd = 2)
title("A subset of Georgia", cex.main = 2, font.main = 1)
pl <- pointLabel(Lon[county.tmp], Lat[county.tmp],
                 Names[county.tmp], offset = 3, cex = 1.5)
```

Notice how the `county.tmp` variable is used to index the `georgia` data. It is possible to select individual areas or polygons from spatial datasets using the bracket notation as used in matrices and vectors.

Finally, we can bring the different spatial data that have been created together in a single map. You should note that the plot window extent is set by the first plot call and when subsequent plots are 'added' (overplotted), then only the portions of them within that window are displayed.

```
plot(georgia, border = "grey", lwd = 0.5)
plot(georgia.sub, add = TRUE, col = "lightblue")
plot(georgia.outline, lwd = 2, add = TRUE)
title("Georgia with a subset of counties")
```

3.3.4 Adding Context

Finally, a map with context may be more informative. Fortunately at the time of writing this can be done by adding OpenStreetMap tiles.[1] This requires some additional packages to be downloaded and installed in R and a connection to the internet:

```
install.packages(c("OpenStreetMap"),depend=T)
library(OpenStreetMap)
```

The approach is to define the area of interest, to download and plot the map tile from OpenStreetMap and then to plot your data over the tiles. In this case the area for the background map data is defined from the Georgia subset, as created above, which is used to identify the data to download from OpenStreetMap. The results of the code below are shown in Figure 3.6. Note the `spTransform` function in the last line of the code. This transforms the `georgia.sub` data to the same projection as the OpenStreetMap data layer.

```
# define upper left, lower right corners
ul <- as.vector(cbind(bbox(georgia.sub)[2,2],
    bbox(georgia.sub)[1,1]))
```

---

1 At the time of writing there can be some compatibility issues with the rJava package required by OpenStreetMap. These relate to the use of 32-bit and 64-bit programes, especially on Windows PCs. If you experience problems installing OpenStreetMap, then, it is suggested that you use the 32-bit version of R, which is also installed as part of R for Windows.

```
lr <- as.vector(cbind(bbox(georgia.sub)[2,1],
    bbox(georgia.sub)[1,2]))
# download the map tile
MyMap <- openmap(ul,lr,9, 'mapquest')
# now plot the layer and the backdrop
par(mar = c(0,0,0,0))
plot(MyMap, removeMargin=FALSE)
plot(spTransform(georgia.sub, osm()), add = TRUE, lwd = 2)
```

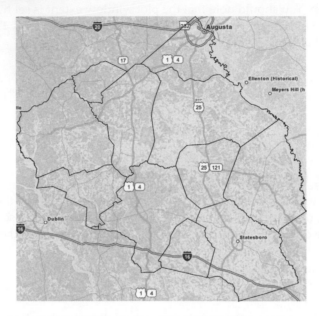

Figure 3.6 A subset of Georgia with an OpenStreetMap backdrop

Google Maps can also be downloaded and used as context as in Figure 3.7. Again, this requires packages to be downloaded and installed and a connection to the internet.

```
install.packages(c("RgoogleMaps", "PBSmapping"), depend=T)
```

Then the area for the background map data is defined to identify the tiles to be downloaded from Google Maps. Some of the plotting commands are specific to the packages installed. Note the first step to convert the subset to `PolySet` format and the last line that defines a polygon plot over Google Maps:

```
# load the package
library(RgoogleMaps)
library(PBSmapping)
```

```
# convert the subset
shp <- SpatialPolygons2PolySet(georgia.sub)
# determine the extent of the subset
bb <- qbbox(lat = shp[,"Y"], lon = shp[,"X"])
# download map data and store it
MyMap <- GetMap.bbox(bb$lonR, bb$latR, destfile = "DC.jpg")
# now plot the layer and the backdrop
par(mar = c(0,0,0,0))
PlotPolysOnStaticMap(MyMap, shp, lwd=2,
    col = rgb(0.25,0.25,0.25,0.025), add = F)
# reset the plot margins
par(mar=c(5,4,4,2))
```

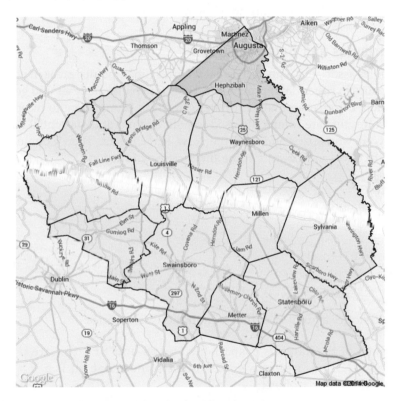

Figure 3.7 A subset of Georgia with a Google Maps backdrop

3.4 MAPPING SPATIAL DATA ATTRIBUTES

3.4.1 Introduction

This section describes some approaches for displaying spatial data attributes. Some of these ideas and commands have already been used in the proceding illustrations, but this section provides a more formal and comprehensive description.

All of the maps that you have generated thus far have simply displayed data (for example, the roads in New Haven and the counties in Georgia). This is fine if the aim is simply to map the locations of different features. However, we are often interested in identifying and analysing the properties or attributes associated with different spatial features. The New Haven and Georgia datasets introduced above both contain areas or regions within them. In the case of the New Haven these are the census reporting areas (census blocks or tracts), and in Georgia the counties within the state. These areas have census attributes which provide popu-lation census information for each spatial unit. These attributes are held in the data frame of the spatial object. For example, in the code above you examined the data frame of the Georgia dataset and listed the attributes of individual objects within the dataset. Figure 3.1 actually maps the median income of each county in Georgia, although this code was not shown.

3.4.2 Attributes and Data Frames

The attributes associated with individual features (lines, points, areas in vector data and cell values in raster data) provide the basis for spatial analyses and geographic investigation. Before examining attributes directly, it is important to reconsider the data structures that are commonly used to hold and manipulate spatial data in R.

Clear your workspace and load the New Haven data. Then examine in turn blocks, breach and tracts using the summary function:

```
# load & list the data
data(newhaven)
ls()
# have a look at the attributes
summary(blocks)
summary(breach)
summary(tracts)
```

You should notice a number of things from these summaries:

- That each of the datasets is spatial: blocks and tracts are SpatialPolygonsDataFrame objects and breach is a SpatialPoints object;

- That blocks and tracts have *data frames* attached to them that contain attributes whose values are summarised by the summary function;

- That breach does not have any attributes (i.e. it has no *data frame*), it just records locations.

The data frame of these spatial objects needs to accessed in order to examine, manip-ulate or classify the attribute data. Each row in the data frame contains attribute values associated with one of the spatial objects – polygons in `blocks` – and each column describes the values associated with a particular attribute for all of the objects. Accessing the data frame allows you to read, alter or compute new attributes. Entering

```
data.frame(blocks)
```

prints all of the attribute information for each census block in New Haven in R console window, whilst

```
head(data.frame(blocks))
```

prints out the first six rows. The attributes can be individually identified using their names. To see the list of column names enter:

```
colnames(data.frame(blocks))
```

One is called `P_VACANT` and describes the percentage of households that are unoccupied (i.e. vacant) in each of the blocks. To access the variable itself, enter:

```
data.frame(blocks)$P_VACANT
```

The $ operator works as it would on a standard data frame to access individual variables (columns) in the data frame. For the data frame of spatial objects a shorthand exists to access this variable. Enter:

```
blocks$P_VACANT
```

A third option is to attach the data frame. Enter:

```
attach(data.frame(blocks))
```

All of the attribute variables now appear as ordinary R variables. For example, to draw a histogram of the percentage vacant housing for each block, enter:

```
hist(P_VACANT)
```

Finally, it is good practice to detach any objects that have been attached after you have finished using them. It is possible to attach many data frames simultaneously, and this can lead to problems if you are not careful. Enter:

```
detach(data.frame(blocks))
```

You can try a similar set of commands with the `tracts` data, but the `breach` dataset has no attributes: it simply records the locations of breaches of the peace. However, the breaches of the peace data can be used to create a raster dataset:

```
# use kde.points to create a kernel density surface
breach.dens = kde.points(breach,lims=tracts)
summary(breach.dens)
```

The `breach.dens` dataset is of class `SpatialPixelsDataFrame` and similarly its attributes are held in a *data frame* which can be examined:

```
head(data.frame(breach.dens))
```

Notice that this has three attributes: the kernel density estimation and two locational attributes that describe the x and y locations. Other raster formats include `SpatialGridDataFrame` into which `SpatialPixelsDataFrame` objects can be coerced:

```
# use 'as' to coerce this to a SpatialGridDataFrame
breach.dens.grid <- as(breach.dens, "SpatialGridDataFrame")
summary(breach.dens.grid)
```

3.4.3 Mapping Polygons and Attributes

A *choropleth* is a thematic map in which areas are shaded in proportion to their attributes. The `GISTools` package includes a choropleth mapping function. Enter:

```
choropleth(blocks, blocks$P_VACANT)
```

This produces a map of the census block in New Haven, shaded by the proportions of vacant properties. Adding a legend to the map allows the map to be interpreted in terms of the levels of vacancy associated with each of the different colour shades in the map. The `choro.legend` command requires information about the variables and the shading scheme used in the map. The shading scheme is a list of class interval boundaries for the quantity being mapped, together with the colour that is used to shade each class interval. There is always one more colour than there are class interval boundaries. In R, shading schemes can be assigned to the variable, and this is passed on to `choro.legend`, and sometimes other functions. In the simplest use of the `choropleth` function, the shading scheme is computed automatically from the variable that is passed to it to be mapped, using a function called `auto.shading`. To compute the shading scheme for `P_VACANT` and store it in a variable called `vacant.shades`, enter

```
vacant.shades = auto.shading(blocks$P_VACANT)
```

and have a look at what is created by entering:

```
vacant.shades
```

You will notice that the `auto.shading` command creates a list with two elements: `$breaks` and `$cols`. These respectively describe the break points between classes and the shading colours used. This information about the shading scheme used can be passed on to `choro.legend`:

```
choro.legend(533000,161000,vacant.shades)
```

This places a legend in the plot window at the coordinates specified by the first two arguments, using the shading scheme specified by the third. The default shading scheme (`auto.shading`) returns five classes, but it is possible to use more. Enter:

```
# set the shading
vacant.shades = auto.shading(blocks$P_VACANT,n=7)
# plot the map
choropleth(blocks,blocks$P_VACANT,shading=vacant.shades)
choro.legend(533000,161000,vacant.shades)
```

The first line of code above firstly derives a shading scheme with seven class intervals (n=7), the next draws the choropleth map – the new argument here is `shading=vacant.shades`, which tells the map-drawing routine to use this shading scheme rather than the default. The final line adds the legend to the map, as before.

It is also possible to alter the colours used in a shading scheme. The default colour scheme uses increasing intensities of red. Graduated lists of colours like this are generated using the `RColorBrewer` package, which is automatically loaded with `GISTools`. This package makes use of a set of colour palettes designed by Cynthia Brewer and intended to optimise the perceptual difference between each shade in the palette, so that visually each shading colour is distinct even when converted to a greyscale. The palettes available in this package are displayed with the command:

```
display.brewer.all()
```

This displays the various colour palettes and their names in a plot window. To generate a list of colours from one of these palettes, for example, enter the following:

```
brewer.pal(5,'Blues')
```

```
## [1] "#EFF3FF" "#BDD7E7" "#6BAED6" "#3182BD" "#08519C"
```

This is a list of colour codes used by R to specify the palette. The arguments to `brewer.pal` specify that a five-stage palette based on shades of blue is required. The output of `brewer.pal` can be fed into `auto.shading` to give alternative colours in shading schemes. For example, enter the code below and a choropleth map shaded in green is displayed with its legend (see Figure 3.8). The `cols` argument in `auto.shading` specifies the new colours in the shading scheme.

```
vacant.shades = auto.shading(blocks$P_VACANT,
    cols=brewer.pal(5,"Greens"))
choropleth(blocks, blocks$P_VACANT,shading=vacant.shades)
choro.legend(533000,161000,vacant.shades)
```

A final adjustment to the `auto.shading` command is to change the way the class interval boundaries are computed. As a default, they are based on quantiles of the attribute being mapped, but they can be changed to equal-sized intervals or standard deviations. For example, specifying the option `cutter=rangeCuts` to the `auto.shading` function changes the mapped class intervals as in Figure 3.8 (right).

```
vacant.shades = auto.shading(blocks$P_VACANT, n=5,
    cols=brewer.pal(5,"Blues"), cutter=rangeCuts)
choropleth(blocks,blocks$P_VACANT,shading=vacant.shades)
choro.legend(533000,161000,vacant.shades)
```

In summary, the `choropleth` function maps attributes held in `SpatialPolygons DataFrame` data variables. It automatically shades the variables using five intervals

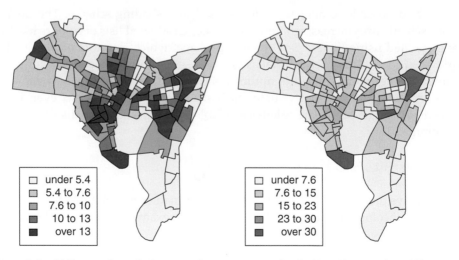

Figure 3.8 Different choropleth maps of vacant properties in New Haven using different shades and cutters

and the 'Reds' palette from the RColorBrewer package. The shading colours, their number and the way the intervals between them are determined can all be adjusted. In order to better understand how these functions operate together you should examine the different functions. Enter:

```
choropleth
```

The function code detail is displayed in the R console window. You will see that choropleth calls the auto.shading function if no shading parameter is specified. Enter:

```
auto.shading
```

Notice that this in turn specifies a number of default parameters (two digits, five colours and the RColorBrewer 'Reds' palette) and calculates the class intervals using quantiles. In addition to using the R help system to understand functions, examining functions in this way can also provide you with insight into their operation.

3.4.4 Mapping Points and Attributes

Point data can be mapped in R as well as polygons and lines. In the New Haven crime dataset, the point locations of reports of breach of the peace events are available. These events are essentially public disorder incidents, on many occasions requiring police intervention. The data are stored in a variable called breach. Plotting this variable works in the same way as plotting polygons or lines, using the plot command:

```
plot(breach)
```

This plots the locations of each of the breach of the peace incidents with a + symbol. Usually it is more helpful to plot these on top of another map. As with the roads data earlier, this can be done with the add option:

```
plot(blocks)
plot(breach, add=TRUE)
```

The pch argument (plot character) allows the plotting symbol to be altered. Entering pch='@', for example, replaces the plot symbol with an @ sign:

```
plot(blocks)
plot(breach,add=TRUE,pch='@')
```

Also, as well as text characters, there are a number of special plotting symbols that can be used. A list of plot character options can be found on the help pages for points (enter ?points) and are denoted by numbers. These are specified by entering things like pch=16 and so on. Try entering

```
plot(blocks)
plot(breach,add=TRUE,pch=16)
```

and

```
plot(blocks)
plot(breach,add=TRUE,pch=1,col='red')
```

In the last example, you can see that the col option specifying the colour of the plot symbols also works with point data.

If you have very dense point data then one point may obscure another. Adding some transparency to the points can help visualise dense point data. The add. alpha function adds transparency to colour palettes. For example, to add transparency to the Brewer 'Reds' palette, enter:

```
# examine the Brewer "Reds" colour palette
brewer.pal(5, "Reds")
# then add a 50% transparency
add.alpha(brewer.pal(5, "Reds"),.50)
```

This prints out a list of five red colours with a transparency term added to them. One of these can be used to display the breaches of the peace as in Figure 3.9, where the density of points is shown more clearly shown.

```
par(mar= c(0,0,0,0))
# plot the blocks and then the breaches of the peace
plot(blocks, lwd = 0.7, border = "grey40")
plot(breach,add=TRUE, pch=1, col= "#DE2D2680")
```

Commonly, point data come in a tabular format rather than as an R spatial object (i.e. of class sp) with attributes that include the latitude and longitude or easting and northing of the individual data points. For example, the quakes dataset is included as part of R. It provides the locations of 1000 seismic events (earthquakes) near Fiji. To load and examine the data enter:

```
# load the data
data(quakes)
# look at the first 6 records
head(quakes)
```

Figure 3.9 Breaches of the peace with a transparency added to the colour

You will see that the dataset comes with a number of attributes: `lat`, `long`, `depth`, `mag` and `stations`. Here you will use the lat and long attributes to create a spatial points dataset, and because we want to include the attributes this will be a `SpatialPointsDataFrame` object. The results of running the code below are shown in Figure 3.10, which shows the spatial context of the data in the Pacific Ocean, to the north of New Zealand.

```
# define the coordinates
data(quakes)
coords.tmp <- cbind(quakes$long, quakes$lat)
# create the SpatialPointsDataFrame
quakes.spdf <- SpatialPointsDataFrame(coords.tmp,
    data = data.frame(quakes))
# set the plot parameters to show 2 maps
par(mar = c(0,0,0,0))
```

```
par(mfrow=c(1,2))
# 1st plot with default plot character
plot(quakes.spdf)
# then with a transparency term
plot(quakes.spdf, pch = 1, col = '#FB6A4A80')
# reset par(mfrow)
par(mfrow=c(1,1))
```

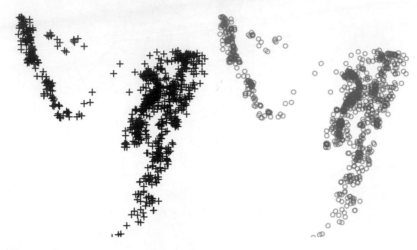

Figure 3.10   Two plots of the Fiji quake data

```
##Not Run##
# you could load the 'maps' package for some context
# install.packages("maps", dep = T)
# library(maps)
# map('world2', fill = F, add = TRUE)
##End Not Run##
```

The last bit of code nicely illustrates how to create a spatial dataset in R. Essentially the sequence is:

- Define the coordinates for the spatial object;
- Assign these to a SpatialPoints, SpatialLines or SpatialPolygons object;
- If the object has attributes, then the dataframe needs to be specified for the SpatialPointsDataFrame, SpatialLinesDataFrame or SpatialPolygonsDataF object.

You should examine the help for these classes of objects. Points just need coordinate pairs, but polygons and lines need lists of coordinates for each object.

```
help("SpatialPolygons-class")
```

This can be illustrated using the `georgia.polys` dataset:

```
data(georgia)
# select the polys of interest
tmp <- georgia.polys[c(1,3,151,113)]
# convert to Polygon and the Polygons object
t1 <- Polygon(tmp[1]); t1 <- Polygons(list(t1), "1")
t2 <- Polygon(tmp[2]); t2 <- Polygons(list(t2), "2")
t3 <- Polygon(tmp[3]); t3 <- Polygons(list(t3), "3")
t4 <- Polygon(tmp[4]); t4 <- Polygons(list(t4), "4")
# create a SpatialPolygons object
tmp.Sp <- SpatialPolygons(list(t1,t2,t3,t4), 1:4)
plot(tmp.Sp, col = 2:5)
# create an attribute
names <- c("Appling", "Bacon", "Wayne", "Pierce")
# now create an SPDF object
tmp.spdf <- SpatialPolygonsDataFrame(tmp.Sp,
    data=data.frame(names))
# plot the data to examine (code not run)
# data.frame(tmp.spdf)
# plot(tmp.spdf, col = 2:5)
```

Note the use of the semi-colon (;) to combine commands on the same line. Note also the way that t1, t2, etc. are created and then overwritten.

You will have noticed that the quakes dataset has an attribute describing the magnitude of each earthquake. We can visualise the magnitudes in a number of ways – for example, by using choropleth (which will take any sp spatial dataset), by selecting data according to different criteria and then plotting these in particular ways, or by plotting all the data points but specifying the size of each data point to be proportional to the attribute magnitude. These are shown in the code blocks below and in the results in Figures 3.11 and 3.12. As a reminder, when you run this code and the other code in this book, you should try manipulating and changing the parameters that are used to explore different mapping approaches. First, choropleth and different sizes of plot characters can be used to indicate the magnitude of the variable being considered (Figure 3.11):

```
# set some plot parameters
par(mfrow=c(2,2))
par(mar = c(0,0,0,0)) # set margins
## 1. Plot using choropleth
choropleth(quakes.spdf, quakes$mag)
```

```
## 2. Plot with a different shading scheme & pch
shades = auto.shading(quakes$mag,n=6,
    cols=brewer.pal(6,'Greens'))
choropleth(quakes.spdf, quakes$mag, shades, pch = 1)
## 3. Plot with a transparency
shades$cols <- add.alpha(shades$cols, 0.5)
choropleth(quakes.spdf, quakes$mag, shading = shades,
pch = 20)
## 4. Plot character size determined by attribute magnitude
tmp <- quakes$mag      # assign magnitude to tmp
tmp <- tmp - min(tmp) # remove minimum
tmp <- tmp / max(tmp) # divide by maximum
plot(quakes.spdf, cex = tmp*3, pch = 1, col = '#FB6A4A80')
```

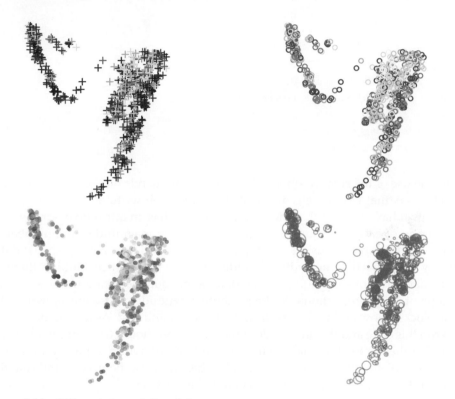

Figure 3.11   Different choropleth point maps

Next a threshold can be used to define classes in a number of different ways. The plots in Figure 3.12 map these classes using different pot characters and colours.

```
# Set the plot parameters
par(mfrow=c(1,2))
par(mar = c(0,0,0,0))
## 1. Apply a threshold to categorise the data
tmp2 <- cut(quakes$mag, fivenum(quakes$mag), include.lowest = T)
class <- match(tmp2,levels(tmp2))
# specify 4 plot characters to use
pch.var <- c(0,1,2,5)
# Plot the classes
plot(quakes.spdf, pch = pch.var[class], cex = 0.7,
    col = "#252525B3")
## 2. Thresholds for classes can be specified
# logical operations help to define 3 classes
# note the terms such as '+ 0' convert TRUE / FALSE to numbers
index.1 <- (quakes$mag >= 4 & quakes$mag < 5) + 0
index.2 <- (quakes$mag >=5 & quakes$mag < 5.5) * 2
index.3 <- (quakes$mag >=5.5) * 3
class <- index.1 + index.2 + index.3
# specify 3 plot colours to use
col.var <- (brewer.pal(3, "Blues"))
plot(quakes.spdf, col = col.var[class], cex = 1.4, pch = 20)
# reset par(mfrow)
par(mfrow=c(1,1))
```

Figure 3.12 Different ways of classifying and mapping point attributes

The code used above includes logical operators and illustrates how they can be used to select elements that satisfy some condition. These can be used singularly or in combination to select in the following way:

```
data <- c(3, 6, 9, 99, 54, 32, -102)
index <- (data == 32 | data <= 6)
data[index]

## [1]    3   6   32 -102
```

These are described in greater detail in Chapter 4.

Finally, it is possible to use the `PlotOnStaticMap` function from the `RgoogleMaps` package to plot the earthquake locations with some context from Google Maps. This is similar to Figure 3.6, which mapped a subset of Georgia counties against an OpenStreetMap backdrop, except that this time points rather than polygons are being displayed and different Google Maps backdrops are used as context, as in Figures 3.13 and 3.14.

```
library(RgoogleMaps)
Lat <- as.vector(quakes$lat)
Long <- as.vector(quakes$long)
MyMap <- MapBackground(lat=Lat, lon=Long, zoom = 10)
# note the use of the tmp variable defined earlier to set
# the cex value
PlotOnStaticMap(MyMap,Lat,Long,cex=tmp+0.3,pch=1,
    col= '#FB6A4A80')
```

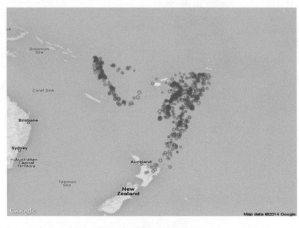

Figure 3.13 Plotting points with a Google Maps context

```
MyMap <- MapBackground(lat=Lat, lon=Long, zoom = 10,
    maptype = "satellite")
PlotOnStaticMap(MyMap,Lat,Long,cex=tmp+0.3,pch=1,
    col='#FB6A4A80')
```

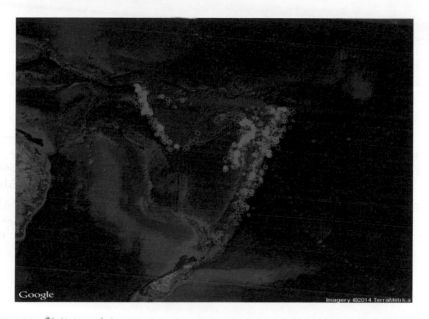

Figure 3.14 Plotting points with Google satellite image context

3.4.5 Mapping Lines and Attributes

This section considers line data spatial objects. These can be defined in a number of ways and typically describe different network features such as roads. In the example below, a subset of the roads in New Haven is extracted. This involves defining a polygon to clip the road data and converting it to a SpatialPolygonsDataFrame object before doing so.

```
data(newhaven)
# 1. create a clip area
xmin <- bbox(roads)[1,1]
ymin <- bbox(roads)[2,1]
xmax <- xmin + diff(bbox(roads)[1,]) / 2
ymax <- ymin + diff(bbox(roads)[2,]) / 2
xx = as.vector(c(xmin, xmin, xmax, xmax, xmin))
yy = as.vector(c(ymin, ymax, ymax, ymin, ymin))
# 2. create a spatial polygon from this
crds <- cbind(xx,yy)
```

```
Pl <- Polygon(crds)
ID <- "clip"
Pls <- Polygons(list(Pl), ID=ID)
SPls <- SpatialPolygons(list(Pls))
df <- data.frame(value=1, row.names=ID)
clip.bb <- SpatialPolygonsDataFrame(SPls, df)
# 3. clip out the roads and the data frame
roads.tmp <- gIntersection(clip.bb, roads, byid = T)
tmp <- as.numeric(gsub("clip", "", names(roads.tmp)))
tmp <- data.frame(roads)[tmp,]
# 4. finally create the SLDF object
roads.tmp <- SpatialLinesDataFrame(roads.tmp,
    data = tmp, match.ID = F)
```

Having prepared the roads data subset in this way, a number of methods for mapping spatial lines can be illustrated. These include maps based on classes and continuous variables or attributes contained in the data frame. As before, we can start with a straightforward map which is then embellished in different ways: shading by road type (the AV_LEGEND attribute) and line thickness defined by road segment length (the attribute LENGTH_MI). The maps are shown in Figure 3.15.

```
par(mfrow=c(1,3)) # set plot order
par(mar = c(0,0,0,0)) # set margins
# 1. simple map
plot(roads.tmp)
# 2. mapping an attribute variable
road.class <- unique(roads.tmp$AV_LEGEND)
# specify a shading scheme from the road types
shades <- rev(brewer.pal(length(road.class), "Spectral"))
tmp <- roads.tmp$AV_LEGEND
index <- match(tmp, as.vector(road.class))
plot(roads.tmp, col = shades[index], lwd = 3)
# 3. using an attribute to specify the line width
plot(roads.tmp, lwd = roads.tmp$LENGTH_MI * 10)
# reset par(mfrow)
par(mfrow=c(1,1))
```

3.4.6 Mapping Raster Attributes

The spatial object type considered in this section relates to raster data. Earlier in this chapter a simple raster dataset was created using a kernel density function. This generated a SpatialPixelsDataFrame object which was converted to a SpatialGridDataFrame object. In this section the Meuse dataset, included as part of the sp package, will be used to illustrate how raster attributes can be mapped.

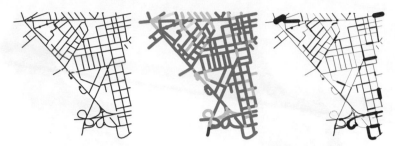

Figure 3.15 A subset of the New Haven roads data, plotted in different ways: simple; shaded using an attribute; line width based on an attribute

Load the meuse.grid data and examine its properties using the class and summary functions.

```
data(meuse.grid)
class(meuse.grid)
summary(meuse.grid)
```

You should notice that meuse.grid is a data.frame object and that it has seven attributes, including an easting (x) and a northing (y). These are described in the meuse.grid help pages (enter ?meuse.grid). The spatial properties of the dataset can be examined by plotting the easting and northing attributes:

```
plot(meuse.grid$x, meuse.grid$y, asp = 1)
```

And it can be converted to a SpatialPixelsDataFrame object (enter ? SpatialPixelsDataFrame for a description of this type of object):

```
meuse.grid = SpatialPixelsDataFrame(points =
    meuse.grid[c("x", "y")], data = meuse.grid)
```

It is possible to map different attributes held in the data.frame of the SpatialPixelsDataFrame object. Essentially these work by specifying the raster dataset and the attribute to be mapped. You should note that the raster datasets passed to image and spplot can be SpatialGridDataFrame or SpatialPixelsDataFrame objects. A number of examples of mapping routines with different shading schemes using image (Figure 3.16) and using spplot (Figure 3.17) are shown below. You may have to close the plot window after the first raster plot before entering the code for the second.

```
par(mfrow=c(1,2)) # set plot order
par(mar = c(0.25, 0.25, 0.25, 0.25)) # set margins
# map the dist attribute using the image function
image(meuse.grid, "dist", col = rainbow(7))
image(meuse.grid, "dist", col = heat.colors(7))
```

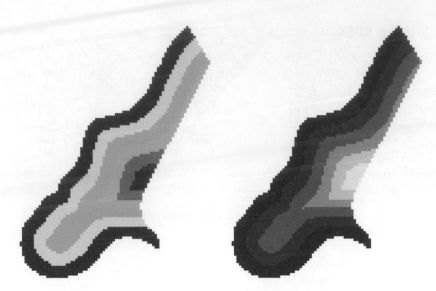

Figure 3.16 Maps of the Meuse raster data using the `image` function

```
# using spplot from the sp package
par(mar = c(0.25, 0.25, 0.25, 0.25)) # set margins
p1 <- spplot(meuse.grid, "dist",
    col.regions=terrain.colors(20))
# position in c(xmin, ymin, xmax, ymax)
print(p1, position = c(0,0,0.5,0.5), more = T)
p2 <- spplot(meuse.grid, c("part.a", "part.b", "soil",
    "ffreq"), col.regions=topo.colors(20))
print(p2, position = c(0.5,0,1,0.5), more = T)
```

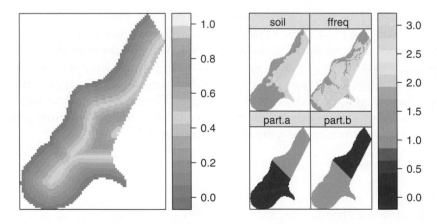

Figure 3.17 Maps of the Meuse raster data using the `spplot` function

3.5 SIMPLE DESCRIPTIVE STATISTICAL ANALYSES

The final section of this chapter before the self-test questions describes how to develop some basic descriptive statistical analyses of attributes held in R data.frame objects. These are intended to provide an introduction to methods for analysing the properties of spatial data attributes which will be extended in more formal treatments of statistical and spatial analyses in later chapters. This section first describes approaches for examining the properties of data variables using histograms and box-plots, and then extends this to consider some simple ways of analysing data variables in relation to each other using scatter plots and simple regressions, before showing how mosaic plots can be used to visualise relationships between variables.

3.5.1 Histograms and Boxplots

You should make sure the New Haven data is loaded. There are number of ways of generating simple summaries of any variable. The function table can be used to summarise the counts of categorical or discrete data, and hist, summary and fivenum provide summaries of continuous variables. You should use these to explore the $P_VACANT variable in blocks. For example, typing hist(blocks$P_ VACANT) will draw a histogram of the percentage vacant housing for each census block in New Haven. Similarly, typing summary(blocks$P_VACANT) or fivenum(blocks$P_VACANT) will produce other summaries of the distribution of the variable. As with all plot functions, it is possible to adjust the histogram bin sizes and the plot labels as in the example below.

```
data(newhaven)
hist(blocks$P_VACANT, breaks = 20, col = "cyan",
    border = "salmon",
    main = "The distribution of vacant property
    percentages",
    xlab = "percentage vacant", xlim = c(0,40))
```

A further way to provide visual descriptive summaries of variables is to use box-and-whisker plots (or boxplots) via the boxplot function. This can be used to display a single variable or multiple variables together. In order to illustrate this the blocks dataset can be split into high- and low-vacancy areas based on whether the proportion of properties vacant is greater than 10%.

```
index <- blocks$P_VACANT > 10
high.vac <- blocks[index,]
low.vac <- blocks[!index,]
```

Then boxplot can be used to visualise the differences between these two subsets in terms of the distribution of owner occupancy and the proportion of different ethnic groups, as in Figure 3.18.

```
# set plot parameters and shades
cols = rev(brewer.pal(3, "Blues"))
par(mfrow = c(1,2))
par(mar = c(2.5,2,3,1))
# attach the data frame
attach(data.frame(high.vac))
# create a boxplot of 3 variables
boxplot(P_OWNEROCC,P_WHITE,P_BLACK,
    names=c("OwnerOcc", "White", "Black"),
    col=cols, cex.axis = 0.7, main = "High Vacancy")
# detach the data frame
detach(data.frame(high.vac))
# do the same for the second boxplot & variables
attach(data.frame(low.vac))
boxplot(P_OWNEROCC,P_WHITE,P_BLACK,
    names=c("OwnerOcc","White", "Black"),
    col=cols, cex.axis = 0.7, main = "Low Vacancy")
```

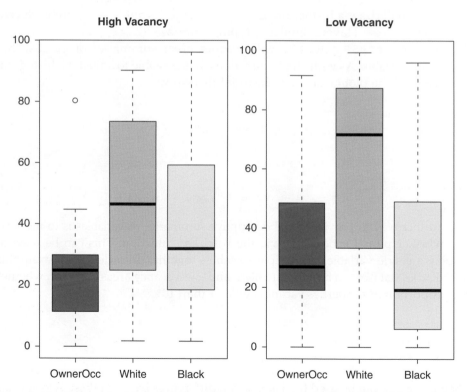

Figure 3.18 Box-and-whisker plots of the `blocks` dataset split into high- and low-vacancy areas

```
detach(data.frame(low.vac))
# reset par(mfrow)
par(mfrow=c(1,1))
# reset the plot margins
par(mar=c(5,4,4,2))
```

3.5.2 Scatter Plots and Regressions

The differences in the two subgroups suggest that there may be some statistical association between the amount of vacant properties and the proportions of different ethnic groups, typically due to well-known socio-economic inequalities and power imbalances. First, we can plot the data to see if we can visually identify any trends:

```
plot(blocks$P_VACANT/100, blocks$P_WHITE/100)
plot(blocks$P_VACANT/100, blocks$P_BLACK/100)
```

The scatter plots suggest that there *may* be a negative relationship between the proportion of white people in a census block and the proportion of vacant properties and that there *may* be a positive association with the proportion of black people. It is difficult to be confident in these statements, but can be examined more formally by using a simple regression model as estimated by the lm function and then plotting the coefficient estimates or slopes:

```
# assign some variables
p.vac <- blocks$P_VACANT/100
p.w <- blocks$P_WHITE/100
p.b <- blocks$P_BLACK/100
# fit regressions
mod.1 <- lm(p.vac ~ p.w)
mod.2 <- lm(p.vac ~ p.b)
```

The function lm is used in R to fit regression models (lm stands for 'linear models'). The models to be fitted are specified in a special notation in R. Effectively a model description is an R variable of its own. Although we do not go into detail about the modelling language in this book, more can be found in, for example, de Vries and Meys (2012: Chapter 15); for now, it is sufficient to know that the R notation $y \sim x$ suggests the model $y = ax + b$. The notation is sufficiently rich to allow the specification of very broad set of linear models.

The coefficients can be inspected and it is evident that the proportion of white people is a weak negative predictor of the proportion of vacant properties in a census block and that the proportion of black people is a weak positive predictor.

Specifically, the model suggests relationships that indicate that the amount of vacant properties in a census block decreases by 1% for each 3.5% increase in the proportion of white people and that it increases by 1% for each 3.7% increase in the proportion of black people in the census block. However, when a multi-variate analysis model is computed neither are found to be significant predictors of vacant properties. The models can be examined using the summary command:

```
summary(mod.1)

##
## Call:
## lm(formula = p.vac ~ p.w)
##
## Residuals:
##      Min       1Q    Median       3Q       Max
## -0.1175  -0.0373  -0.0120   0.0171   0.2827
##
## Coefficients:
##                 Estimate  Std. Error  t value  Pr(>|t|)
## (Intercept)      0.1175      0.0109     10.75  <2e-16 ***
## p.w             -0.0355      0.0172     -2.06    0.042 *
## ---
## Signif. codes:
## 0 '***' 0.001 '**' 0.01 '*' 0.05 '.' 0.1 ' ' 1
##
## Residual standard error: 0.062 on 127 degrees of freedom
## Multiple R-squared: 0.0323,Adjusted R-squared: 0.0247
## F-statistic: 4.24 on 1 and 127 DF, p-value: 0.0415

# not run below
# summary(mod.2)
# summary(lm(p.vac ~ p.w + p.b))
```

The trends can be plotted with the data as in Figure 3.19.

```
# define a factor for the jitter function
fac = 0.05
# define a colour palette
cols = (brewer.pal(6, "Spectral"))
# plot the points with small random term added
# this is to help show densities
# 1st properties vacant against p.w
plot(jitter(p.vac, fac), jitter(p.w, fac),
    xlab= "Proportion Vacant",ylab = "Proprtion White /
    Black", col = cols[1], xlim = c(0, 0.8))
```

```
# then properties vacant against p.b
points(jitter(p.vac, fac), jitter(p.b, fac), col = cols[6])
# fit some trend lines from the 2 regression model coefficients
abline(a = coef(mod.1)[1], b= coef(mod.1)[2],
       lty = 1, col = cols[1]); #white
abline(a = coef(mod.2)[1], b= coef(mod.2)[2],
       lty = 1, col = cols[6]); #black
# add some legend items
legend(0.71, 0.19, legend = "Black", bty = "n", cex = 0.8)
legend(0.71, 0.095, legend = "White", bty = "n", cex = 0.8)
```

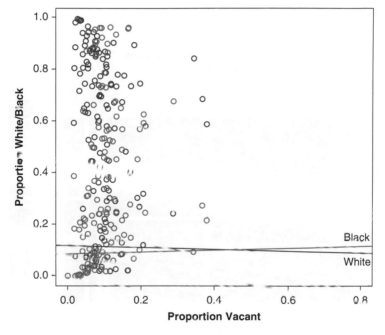

Figure 3.19 Plotting regression coefficient slopes

3.5.3 Mosaic Plots

For data where there is some kind of true or false statement, mosaic plots can be used to generate a powerful visualisation of the statistical properties and relationships between variables. What they seek to do is to compare crosstabulations of counts (hence the need for true or false statements) against a model where proportionally equal counts are expected, in this case of vacant housing across ethnic groups. The mosaic plot in Figure 3.20 shows that the distribution of census blocks with vacancy levels higher than 10% is *not* evenly distributed amongst different ethnic groups: the tiles in the mosaic plot have areas proportional to the counts (in this case the number of people affected) and their colours show which groups are under- or over-represented, when compared against a model of expected equality. The blue tiles show combinations of property vacancy and ethnicity that are higher than would be expected, with the tiles shaded deep blue corresponding to combinations whose residuals are greater than +4, when compared to the model, indicating a much greater frequency in those cells than would be found if the model of equality were true. The tiles shaded deep red correspond to the residuals less than 4, indicating much lower frequencies than would be expected. Thus the white ethnic group is significantly more strongly associated with areas where vacant properties make up less than 10%, and the other ethnic groups are significantly more strongly associated with areas where vacant properties make up less than 10%, than would be expected in a model of equal distribution.

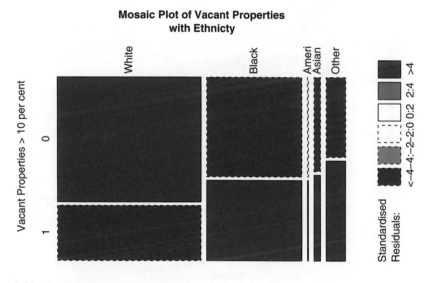

Figure 3.20 An example of a mosaic plot

```
# populations of each group in each census block
pops <- data.frame(blocks[,14:18]) * data.frame(blocks)[,11]
pops <- as.matrix(pops/100)
colnames(pops) <- c("White", "Black", "Ameri", "Asian",
    "Other")
# a true / false for vacant properties
vac.10 <- (blocks$P_VACANT > 10) + 0
# the crosstabulations
mat.tab <- xtabs(pops ~vac.10)
```

```
# mosaic plot
ttext = sprintf("Mosaic Plot of Vacant Properties
                with ethnicty")
mosaicplot(t(mat.tab),xlab='',
            ylab= 'Vacant Properties > 10 percent',
            main=ttext,shade=TRUE,las=3,cex=0.8)
```

3.6 SELF-TEST QUESTIONS

This chapter has introduced a number of commands and functions for mapping spatial data and visualising spatial data attributes. The questions in this section present a series of tasks for you to complete that build on the methods illustrated in the preceding sections. The answers at the end of the chapter present snippets of code that will complete the tasks but, as ever, you may find that your code differs from the answers provided. This is to be expected and is not something that should concern you as there are usually many ways to achieve the same objectives. The tasks seek to extend the mapping that you should have already done (as a reminder, the expectation is that you run the code embedded in the text throughout the book), and in places greater detail and explanation of the specific techniques is given. Four general areas are covered:

- Plots and maps: working with map data
- Misrepresentation of continuous variables: using different cut functions for choropleth mapping
- Selecting data: creating variables and subsetting data using logical statements
- Re-projections: transforming data using spTransfrom

Self-Test Question 1. Plots and maps: working with map data
Your task is to write code that will produce a map of the counties in Georgia, shaded in a colour scheme of your choice but using 11 classes describing the distribution of median income in thousands of dollars (this is described by the MedInc attribute in the data frame). The maps should include a legend and the code should write the map to a TIFF file, with a resolution of 300 dots per inch and a map size of 7 × 7 inches.

```
# Hints
display.brewer.all() # to show the Brewer palettes
?locator # to identify coordinates in the plot window
cex = 0.75        # sets the character size in choro.legend
# Tools
library(GISTools) # for the mapping tools
```

```
data(georgia)        # to load the Georgia data
choropleth()         # to create the maps
choro.legend()       # to display the legend
```

Self-Test Question 2. Misrepresentation of continuous variables: using different cutters for choropleth mapping

It is well known that it is very easy to *lie with maps* (see Monmonier, 1996). One of the very commonly used tricks for misrepresenting the spatial distribution of phenomena relates to the inappropriate categorisation of continuous variables. Your task in this exercise is produce three maps that represent the same feature, and in so doing you will investigate the impact of different *cut* functions when used to generate maps.

Write code to create three maps in the same window of the numbers of houses in the New Haven census blocks. Apply different cut functions to divide the HSE_UNITS in the blocks dataset into five classes in different ways based on quantiles, absolute ranges, and standard deviations. You need not add legends, scale bars, etc. but should include map titles.

```
# Hints
?auto.shading     # the help for autoshading tool
?par                    # the help for plot parameters
par(mfrow = c(1,2)) # set the plot order to be 1 row & 2 columns
# run the code below to specify a 10 by 8 inch plot window
if (.Platform$GUI == "AQUA") {
    quartz(w=10,h=8)  } else {
    x11(w=10,h=8)  }
# Tools
library(GISTools)        # for the mapping tools
data(newhaven)           # to load the New Haven data
```

Self-Test Question 3. Selecting data: creating variables and subsetting data using logical statements.

In the previous sections on mapping polygon attributes and mapping lines, different methods for selecting or subsetting the spatial data were introduced. These applied an overlay of spatial data using the gIntersection function to select roads within the extent of a SpatialPolygons object, and a series of logical operators were used to select and classify earthquake locations that satisfied specific criteria. Additionally, logical operators were introduced in the previous chapter. When applied to a variable they return true or false statements or, more correctly, logical data types. In this exercise, the objective is to create a secondary attribute and then to use a logical statement to select data objects when applied to the attribute you create.

A company wishes to market a product to the population in rural areas. They have a model that says that they will sell one unit of their product for every 20 people in rural areas that are visited by one of their sales team, and they would like to know which counties have a rural population density of 20 people per square kilometre. Using the Georgia data, you should develop some code that selects counties based on a rural population density measure. You will need to calculate for each county a *rural population density* score and map the counties in Georgia that have a score of greater than 20 rural people per square kilometre.

```
# Hints
locator()           # to identify locations in the plot window
rect()              # to draw a rectangle for a legend
legend()            # to indicate the rural and non-rural areas
help("!")           # to examine logic operators
# Tools
library(GISTools)   # for the mapping tools
data(georgia)       # use georgia2 as it has a geographic projection
library(rgeos)      # you may need to use install.packages()
gArea()             # a function in rgeos
```

Self-Test Question 4. Re-projections: transforming data using spTransfrom
Spatial data come with projections, which define an underlying geodetic model over which the spatial data are projected. Different spatial datasets need to be aligned over the same projection for the spatial features they describe to be compared and analysed together. National grid projections typically represent the world as a flat surface and allow distance and area calculations to be made, which cannot be done using models that use degrees and minutes. World geodetic systems such as WGS84 provide a standard model provide standard reference system. In the provious exercise you worked with the georgia2 dataset which is projected in metres, whereas georgia is projected in degrees in WGS84. A range of different projects are described in formats for different packages and software are described at the Spatial Reference website.[2] A typical re projection would be something like

```
new.spatial.data <- spTransform(old.spatial.data,
    new.Projection)
```

You should note that data need to have a projection in order to be transformed. Projections can be assigned if you know what the projection is. Recall the code from earlier in this chapter using the Fiji earthquake data:

---

2 http://www.spatialreference.org

```
library(GISTools)
library(rgdal)
data(quakes)
coords.tmp <- cbind(quakes$long, quakes$lat)
# create the SpatialPointsDataFrame
quakes.spdf <- SpatialPointsDataFrame(coords.tmp,
    data = data.frame(quakes))
```

You can examine the projection properties of this `SpatialPointsDataFrame` object by entering:

```
summary(quakes.spdf)
```

You will see that the `Is projected` and `proj4string` properties are empty. These can be populated if you know the spatial reference system and then the data can be transformed.

```
proj4string(quakes.spdf) <- CRS("+proj=longlat +ellps=WGS84")
```

The objective of this exercise is to re-project the New Haven `blocks` and `breach` datasets from their original reference system to WGS84. Recall that at the start of this chapter the description of these datasets was that they had a local projections system, using the State Plane Coordinate System for Connecticut, in US survey feet. You should transform the breaches of the peace and the census blocks data to latitude and longitude using the `CRS` statement above and the `spTransfrom` function in the `rgdal` package. Then, having transformed the datasets, you should extend the context mapping that used the `RgoogleMaps` package in earlier sections to map the locations of the breaches of peace and the census blocks with a Google Maps backdrop.

```
# Hints
# use the help and the example code they include
?PlotOnStaticMap # for the points
?PlotPolysOnStaticMap # for the census block
# adjust the polygon shading using rgb and transparency
?rgb
# Tools
library(GISTools) # for the mapping tools
library(rgdal) # this has the spatial reference tools
library(RgoogleMaps)
library(PBSmapping)
data(newhaven) # for the breach point dataset
```

ANSWERS TO SELF-TEST QUESTIONS

Q1. Plots and maps: working with map data

```
# load the data and the package
library(GISTools)
data(georgia)
# open the tif file and give it a name
tiff("Quest1.tiff", width=7,height=7,units='in',res=300)
# define the shading scheme
shades <- auto.shading(georgia$MedInc/1000,n=11,
    cols=brewer.pal(11, "Spectral"))
# plot the map
choropleth(georgia,georgia$MedInc/1000,shading=shades)
# add the legend & keys
choro.legend(-81.7, 35.1, shades,
      title ="Median Income (1000s $)", cex = 0.75)
# close the file
dev.off()
```

Your map should look something like Figure 3.21:

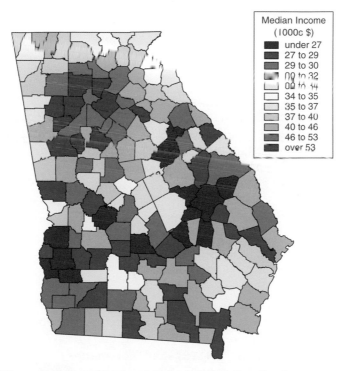

Figure 3.21 The map produced by the code for Self-Test Question 1

Q2. Misrepresentation of continuous variables: using different cutters for choropleth mapping

```
# Code
library(GISTools)
data(newhaven)
attach(data.frame(blocks))
# 1. Initial investigation
# You could start by having a look at the data
hist(HSE_UNITS, breaks = 20)
# You should notice that it has a normal distribution
# but with some large outliers
# have a look at the impacts of different cut schemes
quantileCuts(HSE_UNITS, 5)
rangeCuts(HSE_UNITS, 5)
sdCuts(HSE_UNITS, 5)
# 2. Do the task
# define the plot window
if (.Platform$GUI == "AQUA") {
  quartz(w=10,h=6) } else {
    x11(w=10,h=6) }
# set the plot parameters
par(mar = c(0.25,0.25,2, 0.25))
par(mfrow = c(1,3))
par(lwd = 0.7)
# a) mapping classes defined by quantiles
shades <- auto.shading(HSE_UNITS, cutter = quantileCuts,
    n = 5, cols = brewer.pal(5, "RdYlGn"))
choropleth(blocks,HSE_UNITS,shading=shades)
choro.legend(533000,161000,shades)
title("Quantile Cuts", cex.main = 2)
# b) mapping classes defined by absolute ranges
shades <- auto.shading(HSE_UNITS, cutter = rangeCuts,
  n = 5, cols = brewer.pal(5, "RdYlGn"))
choropleth(blocks,HSE_UNITS,shading=shades)
choro.legend(533000,161000,shades)
title("Range Cuts", cex.main = 2)
# c) mapping classes defined by standard deviations
shades <- auto.shading(HSE_UNITS, cutter = sdCuts,
  n = 5, cols = brewer.pal(5, "RdYlGn"))
choropleth(blocks,HSE_UNITS,shading=shades)
choro.legend(533000,161000,shades)
```

```
title("St. Dev. Cuts", cex.main = 2)
# 3. Finally detach the data frame
detach(data.frame(blocks))
# reset par(mfrow)
par(mfrow=c(1,1))
```

Your map should look something like Figure 3.22:

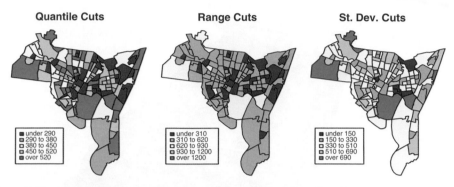

Figure 3.22 The map produced by the code for Self-Test Question 2

Q3. Selecting data: creating variables and subsetting data using logical statements

```
# attach the data frame
attach(data.frame(georgia2))
# calculate rural population
rur.pop <- PctRural * TotPop90 / 100
# calculate county areas in km^2
areas <- gArea(georgia2, byid = T)
areas <- as.vector(areas / (1000* 1000))
# calculate rural density
rur.pop.den <- rur.pop/areas
# detach the data frame
detach(data.frame(georgia2))
# select counties with density > 20
index <- rur.pop.den > 20
# plot them
plot(georgia2[index,], col = "chartreuse4")
# plot the non-rural counties
plot(georgia2[!index,], col = "darkgoldenrod3", add = TRUE)
# add some fancy bits
title("Counties with a rural population density
      of >20 people per km^2", sub = "Georgia, USA")
rect(850000, 925000, 970000, 966000, col = "white")
legend(850000, 955000, legend = "Rural",
```

```
    bty = "n", pch = 19,         col = "chartreuse4")
legend(850000, 975000, legend = "Not Rural",
    bty = "n", pch = 19,         col = "darkgoldenrod3")
```

Your map should look something like Figure 3.23:

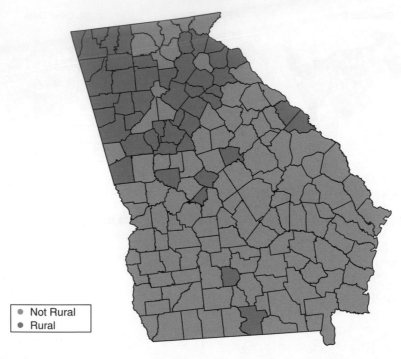

**Counties with a rural population density
of >20 people km^2**

● Not Rural
● Rural

Figure 3.23 The map produced by the code for Self-Test Question 3

Q4. Re-projections: transforming data using `spTransfrom`

```
library(GISTools)  # for the mapping tools
library(rgdal)     # this has the spatial reference tools
library(RgoogleMaps)
library(PBSmapping)
data(newhaven)
# define a new projection
newProj <- CRS("+proj=longlat +ellps=WGS84")
# transform blocks and breach
breach2 <- spTransform(breach, newProj)
blocks2 <- spTransform(blocks, newProj)
# extract coordinates to pass to Google
coords <- coordinates(breach2)
```

```
Lat <- coords[,2]
Long <- coords[,1]
# download map
MyMap <- MapBackground(lat=Lat, lon=Long, zoom = 20)
# convert polys to PBS format
shp <- SpatialPolygons2PolySet(blocks2)
# plot polys on map with shading
PlotPolysOnStaticMap(MyMap, shp, lwd=0.7,
        col = rgb(0.75,0.25,0.25,0.15), add = F)
# now plot points
PlotOnStaticMap(MyMap,Lat,Long,pch=1,col='red', add = TRUE)
```

Your map should look something like Figure 3.24:

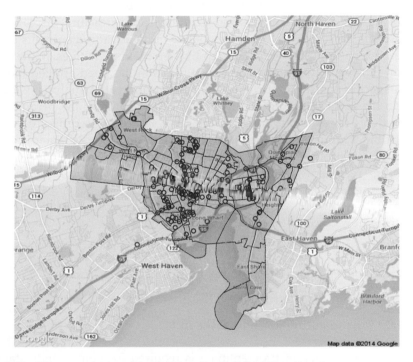

Figure 3.24   The map produced by the code for Self-Test Question 4

REFERENCES

de Vries, A. and Meys, J. (2012) *R for Dummies*. Chichester: John Wiley & Sons.

Monmonier, M. (1996) *How to Lie with Maps*, 2nd edn. Chicago: University of Chicago Press.

PROGRAMMING IN R

4.1 OVERVIEW

As you have been working through the code and exercises in this book you have applied a number of different tools and techniques for extracting, displaying and analysing data. In places you have used some quite advanced snippets of code. However, this has all been done in a step-by-step manner, with each line of code being run individually, and the occasional function has been applied individually to a specific dataset or attribute. Quite often in spatial analysis, we would like to do the same thing repeatedly, but adjusting some of the parameters on each iteration – for example, applying the same algorithm to different data, different attributes, or using different thresholds. The aim of this chapter is to introduce some basic programming principles and routines that will allow you to do many things repeatedly in single block of code. This is the basics of writing computer programs. This chapter will:

- Describe how to combine commands into loops

- Describe how to control loops using `if`, `else`, `repeat`, etc.

- Describe logical operators to index and control

- Describe how to create functions, test them and to make them universal

- Explain how to automate short tasks in R

No previous knowledge of programming is required for you to understand the content of this chapter. Different concepts will be introduced with worked examples, supported by snippets of code, and by working through these, at the end of this chapter you should understand key principles of programming and be able to apply these to spatial information processing problems. If you have no previous experience of programming *do not worry*. By developing basic competence in R, you will get used to using code blocks or groups of commands, sometimes combined into functions. If you have experience in programming in another language, then this chapter will serve to introduce the R syntax.

4.2 INTRODUCTION

In spatial data analysis and mapping, we frequently want to apply the same set of commands over and over again, to cycle through data or lists of data and do things to data depending on whether some condition is met or not, and so on. These types of repeated actions are supported by *functions*, *loops* and *conditional statements*. A few simple examples serve to illustrate how R programming combines these ideas through functions with conditional commands, loops and variables.

For example, consider the following variable `tree.heights`:

```
tree.heights <- c(4.3,7.1,6.3,5.2,3.2)
```

We may wish to print out the first element of this variable if it has a value less than 6: this is a *conditional command* as the operation (in this case to print something) is carried out conditionally (i.e. if the condition is met):

```
tree.heights

## [1] 4.3 7.1 6.3 5.2 3.2

if (tree.heights[1] < 6) { cat('Tree is small\n') } else
  { cat('Tree is large\n')}

## Tree is small
```

Alternatively, we may wish to examine all of the elements in the variable `tree.heights` and, depending on whether each individual value meets the condition, perform the same operation. We can carry out operations repeatedly using a *loop* structure as below. Notice the construction of the `for` loop in the form `for(variable in sequence) {R expression}`.

```
for (i in 1:3) {
    if (tree.heights[i] < 6) { cat('Tree',i,' is small\n') }
    else { cat('Tree',i, 'is large\n')} }

## Tree 1 is small
## Tree 2 is large
## Tree 3 is large
```

A third situation is where we wish to perform the same set of operations, group of conditional or looped commands over and over again, perhaps to different data. We can do this by grouping code and defining our own *functions*:

```
assess.tree.height <- function(tree.list, thresh)
    { for (i in 1:length(tree.list))
    { if(tree.list[i] < thresh) {cat('Tree',i, ' is small\n')}
    else { cat('Tree',i, ' is large\n')}
    }
}
assess.tree.height(tree.heights, 6)

## Tree 1 is small
## Tree 2 is large
## Tree 3 is large
## Tree 4 is small
## Tree 5 is small

tree.heights2 <- c(8,4.5,6.7,2,4)
assess.tree.height(tree.heights2, 4.5)

## Tree 1 is large
## Tree 2 is large
## Tree 3 is large
## Tree 4 is small
## Tree 5 is small
```

Notice how the code in the function `assess.tree.height` above modifies the original loop: rather than `for(i in 1:3)` it now uses the length of the variable `1:length(tree.list)` to determine how many times to loop through the data. Also a variable `thresh` was used for whatever threshold the user wishes to specify.

The sections in this chapter develop more detailed ideas around functions, loops and conditional statements, and the testing and debugging of functions, in order to support automated analyses in R.

4.3 BUILDING BLOCKS FOR PROGRAMS

In the examples above a number of programming concepts were introduced. Before we start to develop these more formally into functions, it is important to explain these *ingredients* in a bit more detail.

4.3.1 Conditional Statements

Conditional statements test to see whether some *condition* is TRUE or FALSE, and if the answer is TRUE then some specific actions are undertaken. Conditional statements are composed of `if` and `else`.

The if statement is followed by a *condition*, an expression that is evaluated, and then a *consequent*, to be executed if the condition is TRUE. The format of an if statement is:

If–condition–consequent

Actually this could be read as 'if the condition is true then the consequent is...'. The components of a conditional statement are:

- the condition, an R expression that is either TRUE or FALSE

- the consequent, any valid R statement which is only executed if the condition is TRUE

For example, consider the simple case below where the value of x is changed and the same condition is applied. The results are different (in the first case a statement is printed to the console, in the second it is not), because of the different values assigned to x.

```
x <- -7
if (x < 0) cat("x is negative")

## x is negative

x <- 8
if (x < 0) cat("x is negative")
```

Frequently if statements also have an *alternative consequent* that is executed when the condition is FALSE. Thus the format of the *conditional statement* is expanded to

If–condition–consequent–else–alternative

Again, this could be read as 'if the condition is true then do the consequent; or, if the condition is not true then do the alternative'. The components of a conditional statement that includes an alternative are:

- The *condition*, an R expression that is either TRUE or FALSE;

- The *consequent* and *alternative*, which can be any valid R statements;

- The *consequent* is executed if the *condition* is TRUE;

- The *alternative* is executed if the *condition* is FALSE.

The example is expanded below to accommodate the alternative:

```
x <- -7
if (x < 0) cat("x is negative") else cat("x is positive")

## x is negative

x <- 8
if (x < 0) cat("x is negative") else cat("x is positive")

## x is positive
```

The condition statement is composed of one or more *logical operators*, and in R these are defined as follows:

Logical operator	Description
==	Equal
!=	Not equal
>	Greater than
<	Less than
>=	Greater than or equal
<=	Less than or equal
!	Not (goes in front of other expressions)
&	And (combines expressions)
|	Or (combines expressions)

In addition, R contains a number of *logical functions* which can also be used to evaluate conditions. A sample of these are listed below, but many others exist.

Logical function	Description
any(x)	TRUE if any in a vector of conditions x is true
all(x)	TRUE if all of a vector of conditions x is true
is.numeric(x)	TRUE if x contains a numeric value
is.character(x)	TRUE if x contains a character value
is.logical(x)	TRUE if x contains a true or false value

There are quite a few more is-type functions (i.e. logical evaluation functions) that return TRUE or FALSE statements that can be used to develop conditional tests. To explore these enter:

```
??is.
```

The examples below illustrate how the logical tests all and any may be incorporated into conditional statements:

```
x <- c(1,3,6,8,9,5)
if (all(x > 0)) cat("All numbers are positive")

## All numbers are positive

x <- c(1,3,6,-8,9,5)
if (any(x > 0)) cat("Some numbers are positive")

## Some numbers are positive

any(x==0)

## [1] FALSE
```

4.3.2 Code Blocks

Frequently we wish to execute a group of consequent statements together if, for example, some condition is TRUE. Groups of statements are called *code blocks*, and in R are contained by { and }. The examples below show how code blocks can be used if a condition is TRUE to execute consequent statements and can be expanded to execute alternative statements if the Condition is FALSE.

```
x <- c(1,3,6,8,9,5)
if (all(x > 0)) {
    cat("All numbers are positive\n")
    total <- sum(x)
    cat("Their sum is",total) }

## All numbers are positive
## Their sum is          32
```

The curly brackets are used to group the consequent statements: that is, they contain all of the actions to be performed if the condition is met is TRUE and all of the alternative actions if the condition is not met (i.e. is FALSE):

```
if condition { consequents } else { alternatives }
```

These are illustrated in the code below:

```
x <- c(1,3,6,8,9,-5)
if (all(x > 0)) {
    cat("All numbers are positive\n")
    total <- sum(x)
    cat("Their sum is",total) } else {
    cat("Not all numbers are positive\n")
    cat("This is probably an error\n")
    cat("as numbers are rainfall levels") }


## Not all numbers are positive
## This is probably an error
## as numbers are rainfall levels
```

4.3.3 Functions

Section 4.2 included a function called `assess.tree.height`. The format of a function is:

```
function name <- function(argument list) { R
expression }
```

The R expression is usually a code block and in R the code is contained by curly brackets or braces: { and }. Wrapping the code into a `function` allows it to be used without having to retype the code each time you wish to use it. Instead, once the function has been defined and compiled, it can be called repeatedly and with different arguments or parameters. Notice in the function below that there are a number of sets of containing brackets { } that are variously related to the function, the consequent and the alternative.

```
mean.rainfall <- function(rf)
{ if (all(rf> 0))               #open Function
  { mean.value <- mean(rf)        #open Consequent
    cat("The mean is ",mean.value)
  } else                          #close Consequent
    { cat("Warning: Not all values are positive\n") #open Alternative
    }                             #close Alternative
  }                               #close Function
mean.rainfall(c(8.5,9.3,6.5,9.3,9.4))

## The mean is  8.6
```

More commonly functions are defined that do something to the input specified in the *argument list* and return the result, either to a variable or to the console window, rather than just printing something out. This is done using return() within the function. Its format is

```
return( R expression )
```

Essentially what this does if it is used in a function is to make R expression the value of the function. In the following the mean.rainfall function now returns the mean of the data passed to it, and this can be assigned to another variable:

```
mean.rainfall2 <- function(rf) {
if (all(rf> 0)) {
    return( mean(rf))} else {
    return(NA)}
    }
mr <- mean.rainfall2(c(8.5,9.3,6.5,9.3,9.4))
mr

## [1] 8.6
```

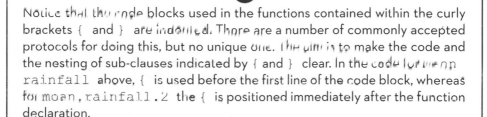

Notice that the code blocks used in the functions contained within the curly brackets { and } are indented. There are a number of commonly accepted protocols for doing this, but no unique one. The aim is to make the code and the nesting of sub-clauses indicated by { and } clear. In the code for mean rainfall above, { is used before the first line of the code block, whereas for mean.rainfall.2 the { is positioned immediately after the function declaration.

It is possible to declare variables inside functions, and you should note that these are distinct from external variables with the same name. Consider the internal variable rf in the mean.rainfall2 function above. Because this is a variable that is *internal* to the function, it only exists *within* the function and will not alter any *external* variable of the same name. This is illustrated in the code below.

```
rf <- "Tuesday"
mean.rainfall2(c(8.5,9.3,6.5,9.3,9.4))

## [1] 8.6

rf

## [1] "Tuesday"
```

4.3.4 Loops and Repetition

Very often, we would like to run a code block a certain number of times, for example for each record in a data frame or a spatial data frame. This is done using `for` loops. The format of a loop is:

```
for( 'loop variable' in 'list of values' ) do R expression
```

Again, typically code blocks are used as in the example of a `for` loop:

```
for (i in 1:5) {
    i.cubed <- i * i * i
    cat("The cube of",i, "is",i.cubed, "\n")}

## The cube of 1 is 1
## The cube of 2 is 8
## The cube of 3 is 27
## The cube of 4 is 64
## The cube of 5 is 125
```

When working with a data frame and other tabular-like data structures, it is common to want to perform a series of R expressions on each row, on each column or on each data element. In a `for` loop the `'list of values'` can be a simple sequence of 1 to n ($1:n$), where n is related to the number of rows or columns in a dataset of the data or the length of the input variable as in the `assess.tree.height` function above.

However, there are many other situations when a different `'list of values'` is required. The function `seq` is a very useful helper function that generates number sequences. It has the following formats:

```
seq(from, to, by = step value)
```

or

```
seq(from, to, length = sequence length)
```

In the example below, it is used to generate a sequence of 0 to 1 in steps of 0.25:

```
for (val in seq(0,1,by=0.25)) {
    val.squared <- val * val
    cat("The square of",val, "is",val.squared, "\n")}

## The square of 0 is 0
## The square of 0.25 is 0.0625
```

```
## The square of 0.5 is 0.25
## The square of 0.75 is 0.5625
## The square of 1 is 1
```

Conditional loops are very useful when you wish to run a code block until a certain condition is met. In R these are specified using the repeat and break functions. Here is an example:

```
i <- 1; n <- 654
repeat{
    i.squared <- i * i
    if (i.squared > n) break
    i <- i + 1 }
cat("The first square number exceeding",n, "is ",i.squared,
"\n")
```

```
## The first square number exceeding 654 is 676
```

Notice in the above example that the first line of the code makes two state-ments separated by a semi-colon ';' Although it is possible to link many lines in this way, it is advisable to do this only occasionally and to link only simple snippets of code as above.

Finally, it is possible to include loops in functions as in the following example with a conditional loop:

```
first.bigger.square <- function(n) {
    i <- 1
    repeat{
      i.squared <- i * i
      if (i.squared > n) break
      i <- i + 1 }
    return(i.squared)}
first.bigger.square(76987)
```

```
## [1] 77284
```

4.3.5 Debugging

As you develop your code and compile it into functions, especially initially, you will probably encounter a few teething problems: hardly any function of reasonable size works first time! There are two general kinds of problem:

- The function crashes (i.e. it throws up an error)

- The function does not crash, but returns the wrong answer

Usually the second kind of error is the worst. *Debugging* is the process of finding the problems in the function. A typical approach to debugging is to 'step' through the function line by line and in so doing find out where a crash occurs, if one does. You should then check the values of variables to see if they have the values they are supposed to. R has tools to help with this.

To debug a function

- Enter debug(function name)

- Then call the function

For example, enter:

```
debug(mean.rainfall2)
```

Then just use the function you are trying to debug and R goes into 'debug mode':

```
mean.rainfall2(c(8.5,9.3,6.5,9.3,9.4))
```

```
## [1] 8.6
```

You will notice that the prompt becomes Browse> and the line of the function about to be executed is listed. You should note a number of features associated with debug:

- Entering a return executes it, and debug goes to next line

- Typing in a variable lists the value of that variable

- R can 'see' variables that are specific to the function

- Typing in any other command executes that command

When you enter c the return runs to the end of a loop/function/block. Typing in Q exits the function.

To return to normal

- Enter undebug(function name)

A final comment is that learning to write functions and programming is a bit like learning to drive – you may 'pass the test' but you will become a good driver by spending time behind the wheel. Similarly, the best way to learn to write functions is to practise, and the more you practise the better you will get at programming. You should try to set yourself various function writing tasks and examine the functions that are introduced throughout this book. Most of the commands that you use in R are functions that can themselves be examined: entering them without any brackets afterwards will reveal the blocks of code they use. Have a look at the ifelse function by entering at the R prompt:

```
ifelse
```

This allows you to examine the code blocks, the control, etc. in existing functions.

4.4 WRITING FUNCTIONS

4.4.1 Introduction

In this section you will gain some initial experience in writing functions that can be used in R, using a number of coding illustrations. You should enter the code blocks for these, compile them and then run them with some data to build up your experience. Unless you already have experience in writing code, this will be your first experience of programming. This section contains a series of specific tasks for you to complete in the form of self-test questions. The answers to the questions are provided in the final section of the chapter.

In the preceding section, the basic idea of writing functions was described. You can write functions directly by entering them at the R command line:

```
cube.root <- function(x) {
    result <- x ^ (1/3)
    return(result)}
cube.root(27)

## [1] 3
```

Note that ^ means 'raise to the power' and recall that a number to the power of one third is its cube root. The cube root of 27 is 3, since 27 = 3 × 3 × 3, hence the answer printed out for cube.root(27). However, entering functions from the command line is not always very convenient:

- If you make a typing error in an early line of the definition, it is not possible to go back and correct it

- You would have to type in the definition every time you used R

A more sensible approach is to type the function definition into a text file. If you write this definition into a file – calling it, say, `functions.R` – then you can load this file when you run R, without having to type in the whole definition. Assuming you have set R to work in the directory where you have saved this file, just enter:

```
source("functions.R")
```

This has the same effect of entering the entire function at the command line. In fact any R commands in a file (not just function definitions) will be executed when the `source` function is used. Also, because the function definition is edited in a file, it is always possible to return to any typing errors and correct them – and if a function contains an error, it is easy to correct this and just redefine the function by re-entering the command above. The built-in R editor for writing and saving code was introduced in Chapter 1.

Open a text-editing window. In the new window, enter in the code for the program:

```
cube.root <- function(x)  {
    result <- x ^ (1/3)
    return(result) }
```

Then use **Save As** to save the file as `functions.R` in the directory you are working in. In R you can now use `source` as described:

```
source('functions.R')
cube.root(343)
cube.root(99)
```

Note that you can type in several function definitions in the same file. For example, underneath the code for the `cube.root` function, you should define a function to compute the area of a circle. Enter:

```
circle.area <- function(r)  {
    result <- pi * r ^ 2
    return(result) }
```

If you save the file, and enter `source('functions.R')` to R again then the function `circle.area` will be defined as well as `cube.root`. Enter:

```
source('functions.R')
cube.root(343)
circle.area(10)
```

4.4.2 Data Checking

One issue when writing functions is making sure that the data that have been given to the function are the right kind. For example, what happens when you try to compute the cube root of a negative number?

```
cube.root(-343)
```

```
## [1] NaN
```

That probably wasn't the answer you wanted. NaN stands for 'not a number', and is the value returned when a mathematical expression is numerically indeterminate. In this case, this is actually due to a shortcoming with the ^ operator in R, which only works for positive base values. In fact –7 is a perfectly valid cube root of –343, since $(-7) \times (-7) \times (-7) = -343$. In fact we can state a conditional rule:

- If $x \geq 0$: Calculate the cube root of x normally

- Otherwise: Use cube.root(-x)

That is, for cube roots of negative numbers, work out the cube root of the positive number, then change it to negative. This can be dealt with in an R function by using an if statement:

```
cube.root <    function(x) {
    if (x >= 0) {
        result <- x ^ (1/3) } else {
        result <- -(-x) ^ (1/3) }
    return(result)}
```

Now you should go back to the text editor and modify the code in functions.R to reflect this. You can do this by modifying the original cube.root function. You can now save this edited file, and use source to reload the updated function definition. The function should work with both positive and negative values.

```
cube.root(3)
```

```
## [1] 1.442
```

```
cube.root(-3)
```

```
## [1] -1.442
```

Next, try debugging the function – since it is working properly, you will not (hopefully!) find any errors, but this will demonstrate the debug facility. Enter:

```
debug(cube.root)
```

at the R command line (not in the file editor!). This tells R that you want to run cube.root in debug mode. Next, enter:

```
cube.root(-50)
```

at the R command line and see how repeatedly pressing the return key steps you through the function. Note particularly what happens at the if statement.

At any stage in the process you can type an R expression to check its value. When you get to the if statement enter:

```
x > 0
```

at the command line and press return to see whether it is true or false. Checking the value of expressions at various points when stepping through the code is a good way of identifying potential bugs or glitches in your code. Try running through the code for a few other cube root calculations, by replacing –50 above with different numbers, to get used to using the debugging facility. When you are finished, enter

```
undebug(cube.root)
```

at the R command line. This tells R that you are ready to return cube.root to running in normal mode. For further details about the debugger, at the command line enter:

```
help(debug)
```

4.4.3 More Data Checking

In the previous section, you saw how it was possible to check for negative values in the cube.root function. However, other things can go wrong. For example, try entering:

```
cube.root("Leicester")
```

This will cause an error to occur and to be printed out by R. This is not surprising because cube roots only make sense for numbers, not character variables. However, it might be helpful if the cube root function could spot this and print a warning explaining the problem, rather than just crashing with a fairly obscure error message such as the one above, as it does at the moment. Again, this can be dealt with using an **if** statement. The strategy to handle this is:

- If x is numerical: Compute its cube root

- If x is not numerical: Print a warning message explaining the problem

Checking whether a variable is numerical can be done using the `is.numeric` function:

```
is.numeric(77)
is.numeric("Lex")
is.numeric("77")
v <- "Two Sevens Clash"
is.numeric(v)
```

The function could be rewritten to make use of `is.numeric` in the following way:

```
cube.root <- function(x) {
   if (is.numeric(x)) {
      if (x >= 0) { result <- x^(1/3) }
      else { result <- -(-x)^(1/3) }
      return(result) }
   else {
      cat("WARNING: Input must be numerical, not character\n")
      return(NA) }
}
```

Note that here there is an `if` statement inside another `if` statement – this is an example of a 'nested' code block. Note also that when no proper result is defined, it is possible to return the value NA instead of a number (NA = 'not available'). Finally, recall that the \n in cat tells R to add a carriage return (new line) when printing out the warning. Try updating your cube root function in the editor with this latest definition, and then try using it (in particular with character variables) and stepping through it using debug.

An alternative way of dealing with cube roots of negative numbers is to use the R functions `sign` and `abs`. The function `sign(x)` returns a value of 1 if x is positive, –1 if it is negative, and 0 if it is zero. The function `abs(x)` returns the value of x without the sign, so for example `abs(-7)` is 7, and `abs(5)` is 5. This means that you can specify the core statement in the cube root function without using an `if` statement to test for negative values, as:

```
result <- sign(x)*abs(x)^(1/3)
```

This will work for both positive and negative values of x.

Self-Test Question 1. You should define a new function `cube.root.2` that uses this way of computing cube roots – and also include a test to make sure x is a numerical variable, and print out a warning message if it is not.

4.4.4 Loops Revisited

In this section, you will revisit the idea of looping in function definitions. There are two main kinds of loops in R: **deterministic** and **conditional** loops. The former is executed a fixed number of times, specified at the beginning of the loop. The latter is executed until a specific condition is met.

Conditional loops

A very old example of a conditional loop is *Euclid's algorithm*. This is a method for finding the *greatest common divisor* (GCD) of a pair of numbers. The GCD of a pair of numbers is the largest number that divides exactly (i.e. with remainder zero) into each number in the pair. The algorithm is set out below:

1. Take a pair of numbers a and b – let the *dividend* be max(a, b), and the *divisor* be min(a, b).

2. Let the *remainder* be the arithmetic remainder when the dividend is divided by the divisor.

3. Replace the dividend with the divisor.

4. Replace the divisor with the remainder.

5. If the remainder is not equal to zero, repeat from step 2 to here.

6. Once the remainder is zero, the GCD is the dividend.

Without considering in depth the reasons why this algorithm works, it should be clear that it makes use of a conditional loop. The test to see whether further looping is required occurs in step 5 above. It should also be clear that the divisor, dividend and remainder are all variables. Given these observations, we can turn Euclid's algorithm into an R function:

```
gcd <- function(a,b)
{
    divisor <- min(a,b)
    dividend <- max(a,b)
    repeat
        { remainder <- dividend %% divisor
            dividend <- divisor
```

```
            divisor <- remainder
            if (remainder == 0) break
        }
    return(dividend)
}
```

The one unfamiliar thing here is the `%%` symbol. This is just the remainder operator – the value of x `%%` y is the remainder when x is divided by y.

Using the editor, create a definition of this function, and read it in to R. You can put the definition into `functions.R`. Once the function is defined, it may be tested:

```
gcd(6,15)
gcd(25,75)
gcd(31,33)
```

Self-Test Question 2. Try to match up the lines in the function definition with the lines in the description of Euclid's algorithm. You may also find it useful to step through an example of gcd in debug mode.

Deterministic loops

As described in earlier chapters, the form of a deterministic loop is

```
for (<VAR> in <Item1>:<Item2>)
    {
    ... code in loop...
    }
```

where <VAR> refers to the looping variable. It is common practice to refer to <VAR> in the code in the loop. <Item1> and <Item2> refer to the range of values over which <VAR> loops. For example, a function to print the cube roots of numbers from 1 to n takes the form:

```
cube.root.table <- function(n)
    {
    for (x in 1:n)
        {
        cat("The cube root of ", x, " is", cube.root(x), "\n")
        }
    }
```

Self-Test Question 3. Write a function to compute and print out `GCD(x,60)` for x in the range 1 to n. (ii) Write another function to compute and print out `GCD(x,y)` for x in the range 1 to n1 and y in the range 1 to n2. In this exercise you will need to nest one deterministic loop inside another one.

Self-Test Question 4. Modify the `cube.root.table` function so that the loop variable runs from 0.5 in steps of 0.5 to n. The key to this is provided in the descriptions of loops in the sections above.

4.4.5 Further Activity

You will notice that in the previous example, the output is rather messy, with the cube roots printing to several decimal places – it might look neater if you could print to fixed number of decimal places. In the function `cube.root.table` replace the `cat...` line with

```
cat(sprintf("The cube root of %4.0f is %8.4f \n",x,cube.root(x)))
```

Then enter `help(sprintf)` and try to work out what is happening in the code above.

4.5 WRITING FUNCTIONS FOR SPATIAL DATA

The sections on plotting and graphics in Chapter 2 outlined a number of techniques for visualising data using R, and Chapter 3 introduced some basic techniques for analysing and displaying spatial data. The exercises in this section apply some of the techniques from Chapters 2 and 3, in conjunction with writing functions and using spatial data. In so doing, these exercises show you how to create some elementary maps in R using functions rather than line by line coding. They also outline some new R commands and techniques to help put all of this together. These exercises and examples applying functions give a flavour of how R can be used to handle geographical data, and in particular how graphics can be produced.

To begin with, you will load the `GISTools` package and the `georgia` data. However, before doing this and running the code below you need to check that you are in the correct working directory. You should already be in the habit of doing this at the start of every R session. Also, if this is not a fresh R session then you should clear the workspace of any variables and functions you have created. Recall from Chapter 3 that this can be done through the menu **Misc > Remove all objects** in Windows (or **Workspace > Clear Workspace** on a Mac) or by entering:

```
rm(list = ls())
```

Then load the `GISTools` package and the `georgia` datasets:

```
library(GISTools)
data(georgia)
```

One of the variables is called `georgia.polys`. There are two ways to confirm this. A new one is to type `ls()` into R. This function tells R to list all currently defined variables:

```
ls()
## [1] "georgia"       "georgia.polys" "georgia2"
```

The other way of checking that `georgia.polys` now exists is just to type it in to R and see it printed out.

```
georgia.polys
```

What is actually printed out has been excluded here, as it would go on for pages and pages. However, the content of the variable will now be explained. `georgia.polys` is a variable of type `list`, with 159 items in the list. Each item is a matrix of *k* rows and 2 columns. The two columns correspond to *x* and *y* coordinates describing a polygon made from *k* points. Each polygon corresponds to one of the 159 counties that make up the state of Georgia in the United States. To check this quickly, enter the code below to produce Figure 4.1.

```
plot(georgia.polys[[1]],asp=1,type='l')
```

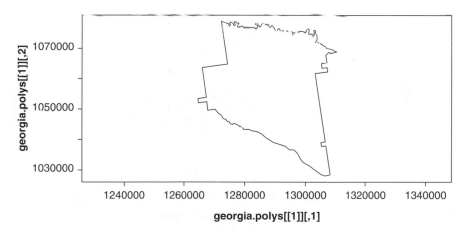

Figure 4.1 The plot produced by `plot(georgia.polys[[1]],asp=1,type='l')`

The above will not win any prizes for cartography – but it should be recognisable as Appling County, as featured in earlier chapters. In this case, the polygons are ordered alphabetically by county name and Appling happens to come first.

4.5.1 Drawing Polygons in a List

Having loaded the variable `georgia.polys`, which is a list of polygons, it would be useful to draw all of these – essentially making a map of all of the counties in Georgia. Recall that the function `polygon` draws polygons, but that it adds the polygon to an existing graph. To create the background graph, you need to use the `plot` function with the `'n'` option. A good bounding box for the whole of Georgia is

Corner	South-West	North-East
Easting	939,220 m	1,419,420 m
Northing	905,510 m	1,405,900 m

So first draw a blank plot with these limits. Then add the outlines of each of the polygons in the list. The simplest way to do this is to use `lapply` to apply the `polygon` function to each polygon in the list `georgia.polys` as in the code to below to produce Figure 4.2:

```
plot(c(939200,1419420),c(905510,1405900),asp=1,type='n')
lapply(georgia.polys,polygon)
```

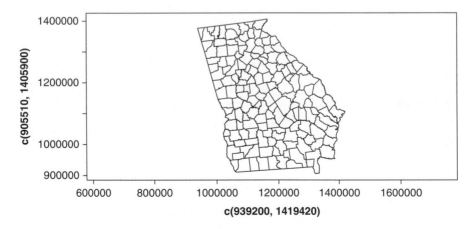

Figure 4.2 Plotting using the `lapply` function

What you will have noticed is that although this has worked, using the function caused a lot of things to be printed out. This is because `lapply` returns a list of the same length as the input list, with each element in the list corresponding to the result of applying the input function to each element in the input list. However, in this instance the function `polygon` doesn't return a value. As a result, each element in the output of `lapply` contains the value `NULL`, signifying an empty list. What you see printed out is a list of 159 `NULL` values, one for each county polygon. Since this isn't very helpful here, you can use the `invisible` function. This basically overrides the standard option of printing out the result of an expression. To do this, just enter:

```
plot(c(939200,1419420),c(905510,1405900),asp=1,type='n')
invisible(lapply(georgia.polys,polygon))
```

This has the same effect as before, but doesn't print out the result, just the map.

Self-Test Question 5. Write a function to take a polygon list, such as `georgia.polys`, and draw a map in the same way as the above example. Call it `draw.polys`. One thing you may want to adjust is the labelling on the axes. At the moment they are labelled by default with the expressions passed in the call to `plot`. In fact, it might be better to just have a blank window – basically we are trying to plot a map, not a graph!

Entering the code below will give an entirely blank window – in effect this is a graph with all of the usual annotation switched off, and the various options `xlab`, `ylab`, `xaxt`, `yaxt` and `bty` switch off displays of axes, labels and the box around the graph:

```
plot(c(939200,1419420),c(905510,1405900),asp=1,
     type='n',xlab='',ylab='',xaxt='n',yaxt='n',bty='n')
```

Write the `draw.polys` function to use these options to create a blank window, and then plot the polygons.

4.5.2 Automatically Choosing the Bounding Box

The last result (particularly the output from the self-test question) looked more like a proper map. However, you needed to rely on a bounding box that was supplied earlier in the text. It would be useful to be able to work out the bounding box automatically given the polygon list. The R functions `min` and `max` find the largest and smallest values in a list of numbers. These can be used, on an individual polygon in the list, to find the extreme north, south, east and west coordinates. For example the code below finds the most eastern point on the boundary of polygon 1:

```
poly1 <- georgia.polys[[1]]
min(poly1[,1])
```

```
## [1] 1264520
```

The other extremes can be found by the following expressions:

Extreme point	Most northern	Most southern
R Expression	max(poly1[,2])	min(poly1[,2])
Extreme point	Most eastern	Most western
R Expression	min(poly1[,1])	max(poly1[,1])

One of these expressions could be applied to every polygon in the list to get a list of the most eastern point in each polygon. Firstly, define a most.eastern function to return the most eastern point of a polygon:

```
most.eastern <- function(poly) {return(min(poly[,1]))}
```

Next, use lapply to apply it to each polygon in the list:

```
most.eastern.list <- lapply(georgia.polys,most.eastern)
```

If you type in most.eastern.list you will see the result is a list of 159 items. Each one is the most eastern point of the corresponding polygon. In fact, there is a shorter way of doing this:

```
most.eastern.list <- lapply(georgia.polys,
    function(poly) {return(min(poly[,1]))} )
```

In this version, the function most.eastern is replaced with the definition of the function. Assuming you do not want to make use of the function again, this is a quicker way of doing things. Since the function never gets given a name, this is referred to as an *anonymous function*. In fact, you can make this even shorter. Since the function body only has one line, you don't actually need to enclose it in curly brackets { and } – and you can write the whole thing on a single line:

```
most.eastern.list <- lapply(georgia.polys,
    function(poly) return(min(poly[,1])) )
```

Now if you apply unlist to this list this will return a basic vector of 159 most eastern points. Finally, you can apply min to this – this gives you the most eastern point of *all* the polygons in the list.

```
min(unlist(most.eastern.list))
```

```
## [1] 939221
```

It is possible to combine all of these operations into a new function called `most.eastern.point` and then to test it:

```
# Function definition
most.eastern.point <- function(polys) {
        # Most eastern points
        most.eastern.list <- lapply(polys,
                function(poly) return(min(poly[,1])))
                # Return the smallest
                return(min(unlist(most.eastern.list)))}
# Test it
most.eastern.point(georgia.polys)

## [1] 939221
```

Self-Test Question 6. Write similar functions for the most western, most northern and most southern points in the polygon list.

You can test the functions you create with the code below, assuming you have used similar naming conventions:

```
c(most.eastern.point(georgia.polys),
    most.western.point(georgia.polys))
c(most.southern.point(georgia.polys),
    most.northern.point(georgia.polys))
```

Self-Test Question 7. Use these functions to update the `draw.polys` function to automatically work out the map window.

4.5.3 Shaded Maps

In this section, you will extend the methods above to produce shaded maps, rather than plain ones. To do this, you will need to create a new `factor` variable. First, make sure the `georgia` datasets are still loaded. As a reminder, three variables are loaded – `georgia`, `georgia2` and `georgia.polys`:

```
data(georgia)
```

Next, a factor variable called `classifier` will be created with two levels, `urban` and `rural`, that will be used to apply an urban/rural classification for each of the counties in Georgia. This is based on whether or not more than 50% of the population live in a rural area. Have a look at the `georgia` attributes and the rural descriptor `PctRural` by entering:

```
names(georgia)
georgia$PctRural
```

Now create the `classifier` variable:

```
classifier <- factor(ifelse(georgia$PctRural > 50,
    "rural","urban"))
```

You should examine this variable and note the use of the `factor` function and the `ifelse` function. This is new and combines both `if` and `else` statements. You should explore this in the help file.

Now, create a vector of colours, to shade in the map. To show the rural areas in dark green and the urban areas in yellow, the first step is to create a vector of appropriate colours. Define a character vector called `fill.cols` with the same length as the number of polygons, initially just containing empty strings:

```
fill.cols <- vector(mode="character",
    length=length(classifier))
```

Then set the elements in `fill.cols` that correspond to rural counties with the value **"darkgreen"**, and those corresponding to urban areas with the value **"yellow"**:

```
fill.cols[classifier=="urban"] <- "yellow"
fill.cols[classifier=="rural"] <- "darkgreen"
```

To draw the map, it is necessary to draw each polygon in the list `georgia.polys` with the colour given in the corresponding element in `fill.cols`. Note that this is possible because the `georgia` and `georgia.polys` datasets are similarly ordered. The `lapply` function can't be used here, as it can only apply functions to single elements in a list – and here we need an additional argument to give the colour. Fortunately there is also another function, `mapply` (the 'm' stands for multivariate), that handles this situation. This takes the form:

```
mapply(<function>,<1st arguments list>,<2nd
arguments list>,...)
```

Note that this is in a different order to `lapply`. In this case, the '1st argument list' is the polygon list, and the second argument is the list of colours. Assuming you have successfully defined the functions required for Self-Test Question 6, enter the code below to produce Figure 4.3.

```
# NB. ew is east/west, ns is north/south
# apply functions to determine bounding coordinates
ew <- c(most.eastern.point(georgia.polys),
        most.western.point(georgia.polys))
ns <- c(most.southern.point(georgia.polys),
        most.northern.point(georgia.polys))
# set the plot parameters
par(mar = c(0,0,0,0))
plot(ew,ns,asp=1,
        type='n',xlab='',ylab='',xaxt='n',yaxt='n',bty='n')
invisible(mapply(polygon,georgia.polys,col=fill.cols))
```

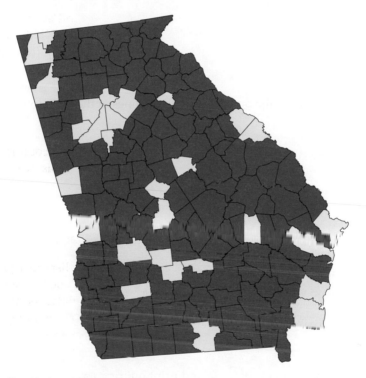

Figure 4.3 Rural/urban areas in Georgia

Self-Test Question 8. Repeat the above, but using different densities of hatching instead of colour shading, to show the rural areas. For information, you can create a vector with numeric variables, instead of characters, by using:

```
hatching <- vector(mode="numeric",
    length=length(georgia.polys))
```

You should note that a density of zero in the polygon command implies no hatching.

ANSWERS TO SELF-TEST QUESTIONS

Q1. A new cube.root function:

```
cube.root.2 <- function(x)
  { if (is.numeric(x))
    { result <- sign(x)*abs(x)^(1/3)
        return(result)
    } else
    { cat("WARNING: Input must be numerical, not character\n")
      return(NA)  }
}
```

Q2. Match up the lines in the gcd function to the lines in the description of Euclid's algorithm:

```
gcd <- function(a,b)
  {
    divisor <- min(a,b) # line 1
    dividend <- max(a,b) # line 1
    repeat #line 5
      { remainder <- dividend %% divisor #line 2
        dividend <- divisor # line 3
        divisor <- remainder # line 4
        if (remainder == 0) break #line 6
      }
    return(dividend)
}
```

Q3. (i) Here is a function to compute and print out gcd(x,60):

```
gcd.60 <- function(a)
  {
  for(i in 1:a)
  { divisor <- min(i,60)
      dividend <- max(i,60)
        repeat
        { remainder <- dividend %% divisor
                dividend <- divisor
```

```
            divisor <- remainder
            if (remainder == 0) break
      }
   cat(dividend, "\n")
    }
   }
```

Alternatively, you could nest the predefined gcd function inside the modified one:

```
gcd.60 <- function(a)
  {for(i in 1:a)
    { dividend <- gcd(i,60)
      cat(i, ":", dividend, "\n")
    }
  }
```

(ii) Here is a function to compute and print out gcd(x,y):

```
gcd.all <- function(x,y)
  { for(n1 in 1:x)
    { for(n2 in 1:y)
      { dividend <- gcd(n1, n2)
        cat("when x is",n1, "& y is",n2, "dividend=",dividend, "\n")
      }
    }
  }
```

Q4. The obvious solution to this is:

```
cube.root.table <- function(n)
  { for (x in seq(0.5, n, by = 0.5))
    { cat("The cube root of ",x, " is",
        sign(x)*abs(x)^(1/3), "\n")}
  }
```

However, this will not work when negative values are passed to it: seq cannot create the array. The function can be modified to accommodate sequences running from 0.5 to both negative and positive values of n:

```
cube.root.table <- function(n)
  { if (n > 0 ) by.val = 0.5
    if (n < 0 ) by.val = -0.5
```

```
    for (x in seq(0.5, n, by = by.val))
    { cat("The cube root of ",x, " is",
      sign(x)*abs(x)^(1/3), "\n") }
}
```

Q5. Write the `draw.polys` function:

```
draw.polys <- function(poly.list)
    { plot(c(939200,1419420),c(905510,1405900),asp=1,
      type='n',xlab='',ylab='',xaxt='n',yaxt='n',bty='n')
    invisible(lapply(poly.list,polygon))
    }
# Test it
draw.polys(georgia.polys)
```

You might also want to add a test as to whether the input to the function is actually a list and report an error if it is not – you can do the test with the `is.list` function.

Q6. The function definitions and tests are given below:

```
# The function definitions
most.western.point <- function(polys) {
    most.western.list <- lapply(georgia.polys,
        function(poly) return(max(poly[,1])))
    return(max(unlist(most.western.list)))}
#
most.southern.point <- function(polys) {
    most.southern.list <- lapply(georgia.polys,
        function(poly) return(min(poly[,2])))
    return(min(unlist(most.southern.list)))}
#
most.northern.point <- function(polys) {
    most.northern.list <- lapply(georgia.polys,
        function(poly) return(max(poly[,2])))
    return(max(unlist(most.northern.list)))}
# Test the functions
c(most.eastern.point(georgia.polys),
  most.western.point(georgia.polys))

## [1] 939221 1419424

c(most.southern.point(georgia.polys),
  most.northern.point(georgia.polys))

## [1] 905508 1405900
```

Note that the last two expressions could be used as the arguments in `plot` to set the map window. This can be used in the next answer.

Q7. Combine the various functions to update the `draw.polys` function to automatically work out the map window.

```
# NB. ew = east/west ns=north/south
draw.polys <- function(poly.list) {
    ew <- c(most.eastern.point(poly.list),
            most.western.point(poly.list))
    ns <- c(most.southern.point(poly.list),
            most.northern.point(poly.list))
    plot(ew,ns,asp=1,
         type='n',xlab='',ylab='',xaxt='n',yaxt='n',bty='n')
    invisible(lapply(poly.list,polygon))  }
#
# Test it - it should look the same as before!
#
draw.polys(georgia.polys)
```

Q8. This is one possibility – it only hatches urban counties:

```
hatch.densities <- vector(mode="numeric",length=length(georgia.polys))
hatch.densities[classifier=="urban"] <- 40
hatch.densities[classifier=="rural"] <- 0
# This assumes ew and ns were defined earlier
plot(ew,ns,asp=1,
     type='n',xlab='',ylab='',xaxt='n',yaxt='n',bty='n')
invisible(mapply(polygon,georgia.polys,density=hatch.densities))
```

USING R AS A GIS

5.1 INTRODUCTION

In GIS and spatial analysis, we are often interested in finding out how the information contained in one spatial dataset relates to that contained in another. The kinds of questions we may be interested in include:

- How does X interact with Y?
- How many X are there in different locations of Y
- How does the incidence of X relate to the rate of Y?
- How many of X are found within a certain distance of Y?
- How does process X vary with Y spatially?

X and Y may be diseases, crimes, pollution events, attributed census areas, environmental factors, deprivation indices or any other geographic process or phenomenon that you are interested in understanding. Answering such questions using a spatial analysis frequently requires some initial data pre-processing and manipulation. This might be to ensure that different data have the same spatial extent, describe processes in a consistent way (for example, to compare land cover types from different classifications), are summarised over the same spatial framework (for example, census reporting areas), are of the same format (raster, vector, etc.) and are projected in the same way (the latter was introduced in Chapter 3).

This chapter uses worked examples to illustrate a number of fundamental and commonly applied spatial operations on spatial datasets. Many of these form the basis of most GIS software. The datasets may be ones you have read into R from shapefiles or ones that you have created in the course of your analysis. Essentially, the operations illustrate different methods for extracting information from one spatial dataset based on the spatial extent of another. Many of these are what are frequently referred to as *overlay* operations in GIS software such as ArcGIS or QGIS, but here are extended to include a number of other types of data manipulation. The sections below describe the following operations:

- Intersections to clip one dataset to the extent of another
- Creating buffers around features
- Merging the features in a spatial dataset
- Point-in-polygon and area calculations
- Creating distance attributes
- Combining spatial data and attributes
- Converting between raster and vector

As you work through the example code in this chapter a number of self-test questions are introduced. Some of these go into much greater detail and complexity than in earlier chapters and are accompanied with extensive direction for you to work through and follow.

The `GISTools` and `rgeos` packages have a number of functions for performing overlay and other spatial operations on spatial datasets which create new data, information or attributes. In many cases, it is up to the analyst (you!) to decide the order of operations in a particular analysis and, depending on your objectives, a given operation may be considered as a pre-processing step or as an analytical one. For example, calculating distances, areas, or point-in-polygon counts prior to a statistical test may be pre-processing steps prior to the actual data analysis or used as the actual analysis itself. The key feature of these operations is that they create new data or information.

5.2 SPATIAL INTERSECTION OR CLIP OPERATIONS

The GISTools package comes with dataset describing tornados in the USA. Load the package and this data into a new R session:

```
library(GISTools)
data(tornados)
```

You will see that four datasets are now loaded: `torn`, `torn2`, `us_states` and `us_states2`. The `torn` and `torn2` data describe the locations of tornados recorded between 1950 and 2004, and the `us_states` and `us_states2` datasets are spatial data describing the states of the USA. Two of these are in WGS84 projections (`torn` and `us_states`) and two are projected in a GRS80 datum (`torn2` and `us_states2`).

We can plot these and examine the data as in Figure 5.1.

```
# set plot parameters and initial plot for map extent
par(mar=c(0,0,0,0))
plot(us_states)
```

```
# plot the data using a shading with a transparency term
# see the add.alpha() function for this
plot(torn, add = T, pch = 1, col = "#FB6A4A4C", cex = 0.4)
plot(us_states, add = T)
```

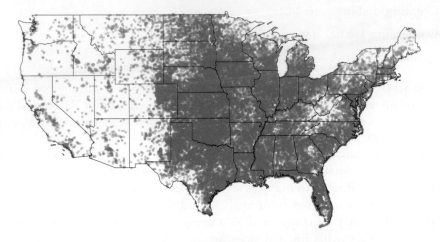

Figure 5.1 The tornado data

Remember that you can examine the attributes of a variable using the summary() function. So, for example, to see the projection and attributes of torn, enter:

```
summary(torn)
```

Now, consider the situation where the aim was to analyse the incidence of tornados in a particular area: we do not want to analyse *all* of the tornado data but only those records that describe events in our study area – the area we are interested in. The code below selects a group of US states, in this case Texas, New Mexico, Oklahoma and Arkansas – note the use of the OR logical operator '|' to make the selection – and then plots the tornado data over that.''

```
index <- us_states$STATE_NAME == "Texas" |
    us_states$STATE_NAME == "New Mexico" |
    us_states$STATE_NAME == "Oklahoma" |
    us_states$STATE_NAME == "Arkansas"
AoI <- us_states[index,]
```

This can be plotted using the usual commands as in the code below. You can see that the plot extent is defined by the spatial extent of area of interest (called AoI) and that all of the tornados within that extent are displayed.

```
plot(AoI)
plot(torn, add = T, pch = 1, col = "#FB6A4A4C")
```

However, it is possible to select *only* those records from the tornado data that are within the area we are interested in using a spatial intersection (sometimes referred to as a clip operation in GIS software such as ArcGIS). The gIntersection function allows us to do this as shown in the code below. The results are mapped in Figure 5.2:

```
AoI.torn <- gIntersection(AoI, torn)
par(mar=c(0,0,0,0))
plot(AoI)
plot(AoI.torn, add = T, pch = 1, col = "#FB6A4A4C")
```

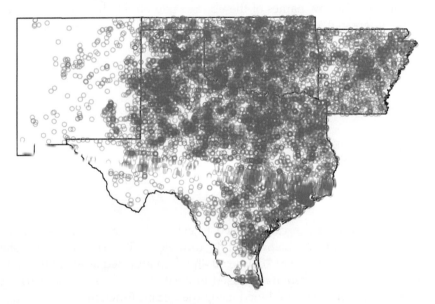

Figure 5.2 The tornado data in the defined area of interest

The gIntersection operation creates a SpatialPoints dataset of the locations of the tornados within the area of interest. However, if you examine the data created by the intersection, you will notice that it has lost its attributes: it has no data.frame and if you examine the first few rows of the AoI.torn object, by entering head(AoI.torn) at the R prompt, it returns only a list of coordinates.

To preserve the data attributes, the gIntersection command needs to be modified so that the results include the data attributes and not just their locations. This is done by including a parameter in the call to gIntersection to include object IDs. This takes slightly longer to run, but the variable that is created as a result of the operation contains references to the data frames of both the input spatial objects:

```
AoI.torn <- gIntersection(AoI, torn, byid = TRUE)
```

You can examine the attributes of the `AoI.torn` data by entering:

```
head(data.frame(AoI.torn))
head(rownames(data.frame(AoI.torn)))
tail(rownames(data.frame(AoI.torn)))
```

You will notice that the intersection object, `AoI.torn` has `rownames` that indicate the origins of each tornado point: they are a composite of the row names of both inputs. In this case the row names of the `us_states` object are from 1 to 50. The ones we are interested in can be extracted using the `index` variable created above:

```
rownames(data.frame(us_states[index,]))

## [1] "37" "40" "41" "46"

us_states$STATE_NAME[index]

## [1] Oklahoma  Texas  New Mexico Arkansas
## 51 Levels: Alabama Alaska Arizona Arkansas ... Wyoming
```

The `rownames` of `AoI.torn` can be used to extract the data from `us_states` and/or `torn`. In the examples below, first the tornado attributes and then the state in which the tornado occurred are extracted and then attached as attributes to the intersected data. These operations are used to create two `data.frame` variables `df1` and `df2` which are then combined using the `cbind` function.

To extract the tornado attributes from the `torn` data frame the `strsplit` function can be used to separate the `rownames` of the intersected data into references that relate to the intersection inputs. Note that another method for *splitting strings* is given in the box below using the `gsub` function. Then `as.numeric` is used to coerce the character vectors to numbers which are then used as an index to extract the data from the `torn` data frame:

```
# assign rownames to tmp and split the data by spaces " "
tmp <- rownames(data.frame(AoI.torn))
tmp <- strsplit(tmp, " ")
# assign the first and second parts of the split
```

```
torn.id <- (sapply(tmp, "[[", 2))
state.id <- (sapply(tmp, "[[", 1))
# use torn.id to subset the torn data and assign to df1
torn.id <- as.numeric(torn.id)
df1 <- data.frame(torn[torn.id,])
```

The state.id and torn.id can be used to link to each input data frame. At the end of these operations the variable df1 contains the information from the torn data.frame for each of the data points in the area of interest.

The strsplit function above is a convenient way for extracting the required information from character variables or *strings*. Another useful function is gsub, as in the code below. Notice the use of the space in the replace.val variable when it is defined using sprintf: "%s" to replace the unwanted text in the rownames of the AoI.torn character vector (in this case references to the US state data). In the code below, the elements of the variable tmp are reassigned or overwritten by the output of each iteration of the loop:

```
# set up some variables
state.list <- rownames(data.frame(us_states[index,]))
tmp <- rownames(data.frame(AoI.torn))
# loop through these, removing the state.list variable
for (i in 1: length(state.list)) {
    replace.val <- sprintf("%s ", state.list[i])
    tmp <- gsub(replace.val, " ", tmp)
}
# again use torn.id to subset the torn data and assign to df1
torn.id <- as.numeric(tmp)
df1 <- data.frame(torn[torn.id,])
```

To extract the state names for each tornado, the state.id can be used to create a second temporary variable df2. The two temporary data variables, df1 and df2, are joined together using cbind and assigned to a variable called df, the final data frame:

```
df2 <- us_states$STATE_NAME[as.numeric(state.id)]
df <- cbind(df2, df1)
names(df)[1] <- "State"
```

Now the SpatialPointsDataFrame function can be used to convert the inter-sected spatial data (AoI.torn) into a format with attributes in the data frame, df, which can in turn be written to a shapefile for use in other applications:

```
AoI.torn <- SpatialPointsDataFrame(AoI.torn, data = df)
# write out as a shapefile if you wish
# writePointsShape(AoI.torn, "AoItorn.shp")
```

In the above example, the state names were attached to the output of the intersec-tion. It is possible to extract and attach other attributes as well. The procedure below matches the state name from the intersection to the data held in us_states and then attaches this to the data frame of the intersection object, which can of course be converted to a SpatialPointsDataFrame variable. In effect the code attaches the data about the states to each tornado location:

```
# match df2 defined above to us_states$STATE_NAME
index2 <- match(df2, us_states$STATE_NAME)
# use this to select from the data frame of us_states
df3 <- data.frame(us_states)[index2,]
# bind together and rename the attribute
df3 <- cbind(df2, df1, df3)
names(df3)[1] <- "State"
# create spatial data
AoI.torn2 <- SpatialPointsDataFrame(AoI.torn, data = df3)
```

You should examine the help for gIntersection to see how it works and should note that it will operate on any pair of spatial objects provided they are projected using the same datum (in this case WGS84). In order to perform spatial operations you may need to re-project your data to the same datum using spTransform as described in Chapter 3.

5.3 BUFFERS

In many situations, we are interested in events or features that occur near to our area of interest as well as those within it. Environmental events such as tornados, for example, do not stop at state lines or other administrative boundaries. Similarly, if we were studying crime locations or spatial access to facilities such as shops or health services, we would want to know about locations near to the study area border. Buffer operations provide a convenient way of doing this, and buffers can be created in R using the gBuffer function.

Continuing with the example above, we might be interested in extracting the tornados occurring in Texas and those within 25 km of the state border. Thus the objective is to create a 25 km buffer around the state of Texas and to use that to select from the tornado dataset. The `gBuffer` function in the `rgeos` package allows us to do that, and requires that a distance for the buffer is specified in terms of the units used in the projection. However, in order to do this, a different projection is required as distances are difficult to determine directly from projections in degrees (essentially the relationship between planar distance measures such as metres and kilometres to degrees varies with latitude). And `gBuffer` will return an error message if you try to buffer a non-projected spatial dataset. Therefore, the code below uses the projected US data, `us_states2` and the resultant buffer is shown in Figure 5.3:

```
# select an Area of Interest and apply a buffer
AoI <- us_states2[us_states2$STATE_NAME == "Texas",]
AoI.buf <- gBuffer(AoI, width = 25000)
# map the buffer and the original area
par(mar=c(0,0,0,0))
plot(AoI.buf)
plot(AoI, add = T, border = "blue")
```

Figure 5.3 Texas with a 25 km buffer

The buffered object, shown in Figure 5.3 or objects can be used as input to `gIntersection` as above to expand the data that are extracted from the spatial overlay. You should also examine the impact on the output of other parameters in the `gBuffer` function that control how line segments are created, the geometry of the buffer, join styles, etc. Also, you should note that any sp object can be used as an input to the gBuffer function: try applying it to the breach dataset that is put into working memory when the newhaven data are loaded.

There are number of options for defining how the buffer is created. If you enter the code below, using IDs, then buffers are created around each of the counties within the georgia2 dataset:

```
data(georgia)
# apply a buffer to each object
buf.t <- gBuffer(georgia2, width = 5000, byid = T,
    id = georgia2$Name)
# now plot the data
plot(buf.t)
plot(georgia2, add = T, border = "blue")
```

The IDs of the resulting buffer dataset relate to each of the input features, which in the above code has been specified to be the county names. This can be checked by examining how the buffer object has been named using names(buf.t). If you are not convinced that the indexing has been preserved then you can compare the output with a familiar subset, Appling County:

```
plot(buf.t[1,])
plot(georgia2[1,], add = T, col = "blue")
```

5.4 MERGING SPATIAL FEATURES

In the first intersection example above, four US states were selected and used to define the area of interest over which the tornado data were extracted. An attribute describing in which state each tornado occurred was added to the data frame of the intersected object. In other instances we may wish to consider the area as a single object and to merge the features within it. This can be done using the gUnaryUnion function in the rgeos package which was used in Chapter 3 to create an outline of the state of Georgia from its constituent counties. In the code below the US states are merged into a single object and the plotted over the original data as shown in Figure 5.4:

```
AoI.merge <- gUnaryUnion(us_states)
# now plot
par(mar=c(0,0,0,0))
plot(us_states, border = "darkgreen", lty = 3)
plot(AoI.merge, add = T, lwd = 1.5)
```

The gUnaryUnion function is one a set of union functions, the rest of which are described in the rgeos help section. It takes a variable of class SpatialPolygons

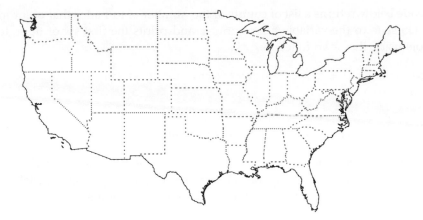

Figure 5.4 The outline of the merged US states created by `gUnaryUnion`, with the original state outlines in green

or `SpatialPolygonsDataFrame` with sub-geometries which it merges or, in set-theoretical terms, unions together. Once the merged objects have been created they can be used as inputs into the intersection and buffering procedures above in order to *select* data for analysis, as well as the analysis operations described below. The merged objects can also be used in a cartographic context to provide a border to the study area being considered.

5.5 POINT-IN POLYGON AND AREA CALCULATIONS

5.5.1 Point-in-Polygon

It is often useful to count the number of points in a `SpatialPoints` dataset that fall inside each zone in a polygon dataset. This can be done using the `poly.counts` function in the `GISTools` package, which extends the `gContains` function in the `rgeos` package.

Remember that you can examine how a function works by entering it into the console without the brackets:

```
poly.counts

## function (pts, polys)
## colSums(gContains(polys, pts, byid = TRUE))
## <environment: namespace:GISTools>
```

The code below returns a list of counts of the number of tornados that occur inside each US state to the variable `torn.count` and prints the first six of these to the console using the head function:

```
torn.count <- poly.counts(torn, us_states)
head(torn.count)

##    1     2    3      4      5     6
##   79   341   87   1121   1445   549
```

The numbers along the top are the 'names' of the elements in the variable `tmp`, which in this case are the polygon ID numbers of the `us_states` variable. The values below are the counts of the points in the corresponding polygons. You can check this by entering:

```
names(torn.count)
```

5.5.2 Area Calculations

Another useful `GISTools` function is `poly.areas` which returns the area (in squared map units) of each polygon, using the `gArea` function in `rgeos`. To check the projection, and therefore the map units, of an `sp` class object (i.e. including `SpatialPolygons`, `SpatialPoints`, etc.), use the `proj4string` function:

```
proj4string(us_states2)
```

This declares the projection to be in metres. To see the areas in square metres of each US state, enter:

```
poly.areas(us_states2)
```

These are not particularly useful and more realistic measures are to report areas in hectares or square kilometres:

```
# hectares
poly.areas(us_states2) / (100 * 100)
# square kilometres
poly.areas(us_states2) / (1000 * 1000)
```

Self-Test Question 1. Your task is to create the code to produce maps of the densities of breaches of the peace in New Haven in *breaches per square mile*. For the analysis you will need to use the `breach` point data and the census `blocks` in the `newhaven` dataset using the `poly.counts` and `poly.areas` functions. The maps should be produced using the `choropleth` function. Remember that the New Haven data are included in the `GISTools` package:

```
library(GISTools)
data(newhaven)
```

As with all the self-test questions in this book, worked answers are provided at the end of the chapter.

You should note that the New Haven is projected in feet. Thus to report the breaches of the peace per square mile you will need to apply the `ft2miles` function to the results of the `poly.area` calculation, and as areas are in squared units, you will need to apply it twice:

```
ft2miles(ft2miles(poly.areas(blocks)))
```

5.5.3 Point and Areas Analysis Exercise

An important advantage of using R to handle spatial data is that it is very easy to incorporate your data into statistical analysis and graphics routines. For example, in the New Haven `blocks` data frame, there is a variable called P_OWNEROCC which states the percentage of owner-occupied housing in each census block. It may be of interest to see how this relates to the breach of the of peace densities calculated in Self-Test Question 1. A useful statistic is the correlation coefficient generated by the `cor` function which causes the correlation to be printed out:

```
data(newhaven)
densities= poly.counts(breach,blocks) /
     ft2miles(ft2miles(poly.areas(blocks)))
cor(blocks$P_OWNEROCC,densities)

## [1] -0.2030
```

In this case the two variables have a correlation of around –0.2, a weak negative relationship, suggesting that in general, places with a higher proportion of owner-occupied homes tend to see fewer breaches of peace. It is also possible to plot the relationship between the quantities – close the plot window if it is still open before running this code:

```
plot(blocks$P_OWNEROCC,densities)
```

A more detailed approach might be to model the number of breaches of peace. Typically, these are relatively rare, and a Poisson distribution might be an appropriate model. A possible model might then be:

```
breaches ~ Poisson(AREA * exp(a + b * blocks$P_OWNEROCC))
```

where AREA is the area of a block, P_OWNEROCC is the percentage of owner-occupiers in the block, and a and b are coefficients to be estimated, a being the intercept term. The AREA variable plays the role of an *offset* – a variable that always has a coefficient of 1. The idea here is that even if breaches of peace were uniformly distributed, the number of incidents in a given census block would be proportional to the AREA of that block. In fact, we can rewrite the model such that the offset term is the log of the area:

```
breaches ~ Poisson(exp(a + b * blocks$P_OWNEROCC+log(AREA)))
```

Seeing the model written this way makes it clear that the offset term has a coefficient that must always be equal to 1. The model can be fitted in R using the following code:

```
# load and attach the data
data(newhaven)
attach(data.frame(blocks))
# calculate the breaches of the peace in each block
n.breaches = poly.counts(breach,blocks)
area = ft2miles(ft2miles(poly.areas(blocks)))
# fit the model
model1=glm(n.breaches~P_OWNEROCC,offset=log(area),family=
    poisson)
# detach the data
detach(data.frame(blocks))
```

The first two lines compute the counts, storing them in n.breaches and the areas, storing them in area. The next line fits the Poisson model. glm stands for 'generalized linear model', and extends the standard lm routine to fit models such as Poisson regression. As a reminder, further information about linear models and the R modelling language was provided in one of the information boxes in Chapter 3 and an example of its use was given. The family=poisson option specifies that a Poisson model is to be fitted here. The offset option specifies the offset term, and the first argument specifies the actual model to be fitted. The model fitting results are stored in the variable model1. Having created the model in this way, entering

```
model1
```

returns a brief summary of the fitted model. In particular, it can be seen that the estimated coefficients are a = 3.02 and b = –0.0310. A more detailed view can be obtained using:

```
summary(model1)
```

Now, among other things, the standard errors and Wald statistics for a and b are shown. The Wald Z statistics are similar to *t statistics* in ordinary least squares regression, and may be tested against the normal distribution. The results below summarise the information, showing that both a and b are significant – and that therefore there is a statistically significant relationship between owner-occupation and breach of peace incidents:

	Estimate	Std. error	Wald's Z	P-value
Intercept	3.02	0.11	27.4	<0.01
Owner Occ. %	−0.031	0.00364	−8.5	<0.01

It also possible to extract diagnostic information from fitted models. For example, the rstandard function extracts the standardised residuals from a model. Whereas residuals are the difference between the observed value (i.e. in the data) and the value when estimated using the model, standardised residuals are rescaled to have a variance of 1. If the model being fitted is correct, then these residuals should be independent, have a mean of 0, a variance of 1 and an approximately normal distribution. One useful diagnostic is to map these values. The code below first computes them, and stores them in a variable called s.resids:

```
s.resids = rstandard(model1)
```

Now, to plot the map it will be more useful to specify a shading scheme directly using the shading command:

```
resid.shades = shading(c(-2,2),c("red","grey","blue"))
```

This specifies that the map will have three class intervals: below −2, between −2 and 2, and above 2. These are useful intervals given that the residuals should be normally distributed, and these values are the approximate two-tailed 5% points of this distribution. Residuals within these points will be shaded grey, large negative residuals will be red, and large positive ones will be blue:

```
par(mar=c(0,0,0,0))
choropleth(blocks,s.resids,resid.shades)
# reset the plot margins
par(mar=c(5,4,4,2))
```

From Figure 5.5 it can be seen that in fact there is notably more variation than one might expect (there are 21 blocks shaded blue or red, about 16% of the total, when around 5% would appear based on the model's assumptions), and also that the shaded blocks seem to cluster together. This last observation casts doubt on

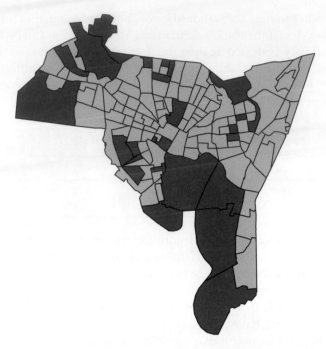

Figure 5.5 The distribution of the `model1` residuals, describing the relationship between breaches of the peace and owner-occupancy

the assumption of independence, suggesting instead that some degree of spatial correlation is present. One possible reason for this is that further variables may need to be added to the model, to explain this extra variability and spatial clustering amongst the residuals.

It is possible to extend this analysis by considering P_VACANT, the percentage of vacant properties in each census block, as well as P_OWNEROCC. This is done by extending `model1` and entering:

```
attach(data.frame(blocks))
n.breaches = poly.counts(breach,blocks)
area = ft2miles(ft2miles(poly.areas(blocks)))
model2=glm(n.breaches~P_OWNEROCC+P_VACANT,
    offset=log(area),family=poisson)
s.resids.2 = rstandard(model2)
detach(data.frame(blocks))
```

This sets up a new model, with a further term for the percentage of vacant housing in each block, and stores it in `model2`. Entering `summary(model2)` shows that the new predictor variable is significantly related to breaches of peace, with a positive relationship. Finally, it is possible to map the standardised residuals for the new model reusing the shading scheme defined above:

```
s.resids.2 = rstandard(model2)
par(mar=c(0,0,0,0))
choropleth(blocks,s.resids.2,resid.shades)
# reset the plot margins
par (mar=c(5,4,4,2))
```

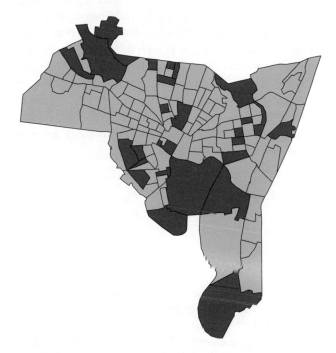

Figure 5.6 The distribution of the model2 residuals, describing the relationship between breaches of the peace with owner-occupancy and vacant properties

This time, Figure 5.6 shows that there are fewer red and blue shaded census blocks – although perhaps still more than we might expect, and there is still some evidence of spatial clustering. Adding the extra variable has improved things to some extent, but perhaps there is more investigative research to be done. A more comprehensive treatment of spatial analysis of spatial data attributes is given in Chapter 7.

5.6 CREATING DISTANCE ATTRIBUTES

Distance is fundamental to spatial analysis. For example, we may wish to analyse the number of locations (health facilities, schools, etc.) within a certain distance of the features we are considering. In the exercise below, distance measures are used to evaluate differences in accessibility for different social groups. These approaches form the basis of supply and demand modelling and provide inputs into location–allocation models.

Distance could be approximated using a series of buffers created at specific distance intervals around our features (whether point or polygons). These could be used to determine the number of features or locations that are within different distance ranges, as specified by the buffers using the `poly.counts` function above. However, the `gDistance` function calculates the Cartesian minimum (straight line) distance between two spatial datasets of class `sp`. In the code below, this function is used to determine the distances between the `places` variable (which are simply place holder locations for the names of districts New Haven but could be any kind of facility or *supply* feature), and the centroids of the census blocks in New Haven, in this case acting as *demand* locations. The `gDistance` function returns a to–from matrix of the distances between each pair of supply and demand points. In the first few lines of code, the projections of the two variables are set to be the same, before `gCentroid` is used to extract the geometric centroids of the census block areas and the distance between `places` and `centroids` are calculated:

```
data(newhaven)
proj4string(places) <- CRS(proj4string(blocks))
centroids. <- gCentroid(blocks, byid = T, id =
    rownames(blocks))
distances <- ft2miles(gDistance(places, centroids.,
    byid = T))
```

You can examine the result in relation to the inputs to `gDistance,` and you will see that the `distances` variable is a matrix of distances (in miles) from each of the 129 census block centroids to each of the nine locations described in the `places` variable. It is possible to use the census block polygons in the above `gDistance` calculation, but the distances returned will be to the nearest point of the census area. Using the census area centroid provides a more representative measure of the average distance experienced by people living in that area.

The `gWithinDistance` function tests whether each to–from distance pair is less than a specified threshold. It returns a matrix of `TRUE` and `FALSE` describing whether the distances between the elements of the two `sp` dataset elements are less than or equal to the specified distance or not. In the example below the distance specified is 1.2 miles.

```
distances <- gWithinDistance(places, blocks,
    byid = T, dist = miles2ft(1.2))
```

You should note that the `gDistance` and `gWithinDistance` functions work with whatever distance units are specified in the projections of the spatial features.

This means the inputs need to have the same units. Also remember that the newhaven data are projected in feet, hence the use of the `miles2ft` and `ft2miles` functions.

5.6.1 Distance Analysis/Accessibility Exercise

The use of distance measures in conjunction with census data is particularly useful for analysing access to the supply of some facility or service for different social groups. The code below replicates the analysis developed by Comber et al. (2008), examining access to green spaces. In this exercise a hypothetical example is used: we wish to examine the equity of access to the locations recorded in the `places` variable (supply) for different ethnic groups as recorded in the `blocks` dataset (demand), on the basis that we expect everyone to be within 1 mile of a facility. We will use the census data to approximate the number of people with and without access of less than 1 mile to the set of hypothetical facilities.

First, the distances variable is recalculated in case it was overwritten in the `gWithinDistance` example above. Then the minimum distance to a supply facility is determined for each census area using the `apply` function. Finally a logical statement is used to generate a `TRUE` or `FALSE` statement for each block:

```
distances <- ft2miles(gDistance(places, centroids., byid = T))
min.dist <- as.vector(apply(distances,1, min))
access <- min.dist < 1
# and this can be mapped
# plot(blocks, col = access)
```

The populations of each ethnic group in each census block can be extracted from the `blocks` dataset:

```
# extract the ethnicity data from the blocks variable
ethnicity <- as.matrix(data.frame(blocks[,14:18])/100)
ethnicity <- apply(ethnicity, 2, function(x) (x *
    blocks$POP1990))
ethnicity <- matrix(as.integer(ethnicity), ncol = 5)
colnames(ethnicity) <- c("White", "Black",
    "Native American", "Asian", "Other")
```

And then a crosstabulation is used to bring together the access data and the populations:

```
# use xtabs to generate a crosstabulation
mat.access.tab = xtabs(ethnicity~access)
# then transpose the data
```

```
data.set = as.data.frame(mat.access.tab)
#set the column names
colnames(data.set) = c("Access","Ethnicity", "Freq")
```

You should examine the data.set variable. This summarises all of the factors being considered: access, ethnicity and the counts associated with all factor combinations. If we make an assumption that there is an interaction between ethnicity and access, then this can be tested for using a generalised regression model with a Poisson distribution using the glm function:

```
modelethnic = glm(Freq~Access*Ethnicity,
    data=data.set,family=poisson)
# the full model can be printed to the console
# summary(modelethnic)
```

The model coefficient estimates show that there is significantly less access for some groups than would be expected under a model of equal access when compared to the largest ethnic group White, which was listed first in the data.set variable, and significantly greater access for the ethnic group Other. Examine the model coefficient estimates, paying particular attention to the AccessTRUE: coefficients:

```
summary(modelethnic)$coef
```

Then assign these to the a variable:

```
mod.coefs = summary(modelethnic)$coef
```

By subtracting 1 from the coefficients and converting them to percentages, it is possible to attach some likelihoods to the access for different groups when compared the ethnic group White. Again, you should examine the terms in the model outputs prefixed by AccessTRUE:, as below:

```
tab <- 100*(exp(mod.coefs[,1]) - 1)
tab <- tab[7:10]
names(tab) <- colnames(ethnicity)[2:5]
tab

##      Black Native American      Asian       Other
##     -35.08           -11.73     -29.83      256.26
```

The results in tab tell us that some ethnic groups have significantly less access to the hypothetical supply facilities when compared to the White ethnic group (as recorded in the census): the ethnic group Black have 35% less, Native Americans 12% less, (although this is not significant), Asians 30% less and Other 256% more access than the White ethnic group.

It is possible to visualise the variations in access for different groups using a mosaic plot. Mosaic plots show the counts (i.e. population) as well as the residuals associated with the interaction between groups and their access, the full details of which were given in Chapter 3.

```
mosaicplot(t(mat.access.tab),xlab='',ylab='Access to Supply',
      main="Mosaic Plot of Access",shade=TRUE,las=3,cex=0.8)
```

Self-Test Question 2. In working through the exercise above you have developed a number of statistical techniques. In answering this self-test question you will explore the impact of using census data summarised over different areal units in your analysis. Specifically, you will develop and compare the results of two statistical models using different census areas in the newhaven datasets: blocks and tracts. You will analyse the relationship between residential property occupation and burglaries. You will need to work through the code below before the tasks associated with this questions are posited. To see the relationship between the census tracts and the census blocks, enter:

```
plot(blocks,border='red')
plot(tracts,lwd=2,add=TRUE)
```

You can see that the census blocks are nested within the tracts.

The analysis described below develops a statistical model to describe the relationship between residential property occupation and burglary using two of the New Haven crime variables related to residential burglaries. These are both point objects, called burgres.f and burgres.n. The first of these, burgres.f, is a list of burglaries where entry was forced into the property, and burgres.n is a list of burglaries where entry was not forced, suggesting that the property was left insecure, perhaps by leaving a door or window open. The burglaries data cover the six-month period between 1 August 2007 and 31 January 2008.

The questions you will consider are:

- Do both kinds of residential burglary occur in the same places – that is, if a place is a high-risk area for non-forced entry, does it imply that it is also a high-risk area for forced entry?

- How does this relationship vary over different census units?

To investigate these, you should use a bivariate regression model that attempts to predict the density of forced burglaries from the density of non-forced ones. The indicators needed for this are the rates of burglary given the number of properties at risk. You should use the variable OCCUPIED, present in both the census blocks data frame and the the census tracts data frame, to estimate the number of properties at risk. If we were to compute rates per 1000 households, this would be: 1000*(number of burglaries in block)/OCCUPIED and since this is over a six-month period, doubling this quantity gives the number of burglaries per 1000 households per year. However, entering:

```
blocks$OCCUPIED
```

shows that some blocks have no occupied housing, so the above rate cannot be defined. To overcome this problem you should select the subset of the blocks with more than zero occupied dwellings. For polygon spatial objects, each individual polygon can be treated like a row in a data frame for the purposes of subset selection. Thus, to select only the blocks where the variable OCCUPIED is greater than zero, enter:

```
blocks2 = blocks[blocks$OCCUPIED > 0,]
```

We can now compute the burglary rates for forced and non-forced entries by first counting the burglaries in each block in blocks2 using the poly.counts function, dividing these numbers by the OCCUPIED counts and then multiplying by 2000 to get yearly rates per 1000 households. However, before we do this, you should remember that you need the OCCUPIED attribute from blocks2 and not blocks. Attach the blocks2 data and then calculate the two rate variables:

```
attach(data.frame(blocks2))
forced.rate = 2000*poly.counts(burgres.f,blocks2)/OCCUPIED
notforced.rate = 2000*poly.counts(burgres.n,blocks2)/
    OCCUPIED
detach(data.frame(blocks2))
```

You should have two rates stored in forced.rate and notforced.rate. A first attempt at modelling the relationship between the two rates could be via simple bivariate regression, ignoring any spatial dependencies in the error term. This is done using the lm function, which creates a simple regression model, model1:

```
model1 = lm(forced.rate~notforced.rate)
```

To examine the regression coefficients, enter:

```
summary(model1)
coef(model1)
```

The key things to note here are that the forced rate is related to the not-forced rate by the formula:

```
expected(forced rate) = a + b * (not forced rate)
```

where a is the `intercept` term and b is the slope or coefficient for the predictor variable. If the coefficient for the not-forced rate is statistically different from zero, indicated in the summary of the model, then there is evidence that the two rates are related. One possible explanation is that if burglars are active in an area, they will only use force to enter dwellings when it is necessary, making use of an insecure window or door if they spot the opportunity. Thus in areas where burglars are active, both kinds of burglary could potentially occur. However, in areas where they are less active it is less likely for either kind burglary to occur.

Having outlined the approach, your specific tasks in this question are:

1. To determine the coefficients a and b in the formula above for two different analyses using the `blocks` and `tracts` datasets.

2. To comment on the difference between the analyses using different areal units.

5.7 COMBINING SPATIAL DATASETS AND THEIR ATTRIBUTES

The point-in-polygon calculation using `poly.counts` generates counts of the points falling in each polygon. A common situation in spatial analysis is the need to combine (overlay) different polygon features that describe the spatial distribution of different variables, attributes or processes that are of interest. The problem is that the data may have different underlying area geographies. In fact, it is commonly the case that different agencies, institutions and government departments use different geographical areas, and even where they do not, geographical areas frequently change over time. In these situations, we can use the `gIntersection` function to identify the area of intersection between the datasets. With some manipulation it is possible to determine the proportions of the objects in dataset X that fall into each of polygon of dataset Y. This section uses a worked example to illustrate how this can be done in R.

In the subsequent self-test question you will develop a function to do this. As with all spatial operations on `sp` datasets, the input data need to have the same projections. You can examine their `proj4string` attributes to check and if need be use the `spTransform` function to put the data into the same projection.

A zone dataset will be created with the aim of calculating the number of houses in each zone. These will be extracted from the New Haven `tracts` data which includes the variable `HSE_UNITS`, describing the number of residential properties in each census tract. The zones are hypothetical, but could perhaps be zones used by the emergency services for planning purposes and resource allocation.

First, you should create the zones, number them with an ID and plot these on a map with the tracts data. This is easily done by defining a grid and then converting this to a SpatialPolygonsDataFrame object. Enter:

```
data(newhaven)
# define sample grid in polygons
    bb <- bbox(tracts)
grd <- GridTopology(cellcentre.offset=
    c(bb[1,1]-200,bb[2,1]-200),
    cellsize=c(10000,10000), cells.dim = c(5,5))
int.layer <- SpatialPolygonsDataFrame(
    as.SpatialPolygons.GridTopology(grd),
    data = data.frame(c(1:25)), match.ID = FALSE)
names(int.layer) <- "ID"
```

Projections can be checked using proj4string(int.layer) and proj4 string(tracts). These have the same projections, in this case NA, and so they can be intersected:

```
int.res <- gIntersection(int.layer, tracts, byid = T)
```

You can examine the intersected data, the original data and the zones in the same plot window, as in Figure 5.7.

```
# set some plot parameters
par(mfrow = c(1,2))
par(mar=c(0,0,0,0))
# plot and label the zones
plot(int.layer, lty = 2)
Lat <- as.vector(coordinates(int.layer)[,2])
Lon <- as.vector(coordinates(int.layer)[,1])
Names <- as.character(data.frame(int.layer)[,1])
# plot the tracts
plot(tracts, add = T, border = "red", lwd =2)
pl <- pointLabel(Lon, Lat, Names, offset = 0, cex =.7)
# set the plot extent
plot(int.layer, border = "white")
# plot the intersection
plot(int.res, col=blues9, add = T)
```

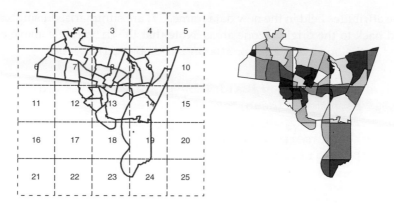

Figure 5.7 The zones and census tracts data before and after intersection

As in the `gIntersection` operation described in earlier sections, you can examine the result of the intersection:

```
names(int.res)
```

You will see that the names of the intersected objects are composites of the inputs. These can be used to link to the attributes held in the data frame of each input to the intersection, and then to create attributes for the intersection output data, in this case `int.res` and the original zone data `int.layer`.

First, the composite object names have to be split:

```
tmp <- strsplit(names(int.res), " ")
tracts.id <- (sapply(tmp, "[[", 2))
intlayer.id <- (sapply(tmp, "[[", 1))
```

Then, the proportions of the original tract areas need to be extracted – these will be used to proportionally allocate the counts of houses to the zones.

```
# generate area and proportions
int.areas <- gArea(int.res, byid = T)
tract.areas <- gArea(tracts, byid = T)
# match this to the new layer
index <- match(tracts.id, row.names(tracts))
tract.areas <- tract.areas[index]
tract.prop <- zapsmall(int.areas/tract.areas, 3)
# and create data frame for the new layer
df <- data.frame(intlayer.id, tract.prop)
houses <- zapsmall(tracts$HSE_UNITS[index] * tract.prop, 1)
df <- data.frame(df, houses, int.areas)
```

Finally, the attributes held in the new data frame, df, are summarised using xtabs and linked back to the original zone areas. Note that the df variable above could be attached to the SpatialPolygonsDataFrame object, int.res.

```
int.layer.houses <- xtabs(df$houses~df$intlayer.id)
index <- as.numeric(gsub("g", "", names(int.layer.houses)))
# create temporary variable
tmp <- vector("numeric", length = dim(data.frame(int.layer))[1])
tmp[index] <- int.layer.houses
i.houses <- tmp
```

Now the outputs can be attached to the original zone dataset:

```
int.layer <- SpatialPolygonsDataFrame(int.layer,
    data = data.frame(data.frame(int.layer),
    i.houses), match.ID = FALSE)
```

The results can be plotted as Figure 5.8 and checked against the original inputs in Figure 5.7:

```
# set the plot parameters and the shading variable
par(mar=c(0,0,0,0))
shades = auto.shading(int.layer$i.houses,
    n = 6, cols = brewer.pal(6, "Greens"))
# map the data
choropleth(int.layer, int.layer$i.houses, shades)
plot(tracts, add = T)
choro.legend(530000, 159115, bg = "white", shades,
    title = "No. of houses", under = "")
# reset the plot margins
par (mar=c(5,4,4,2))
```

Self-Test Question 3. Your task is to write a function that will return an intersected dataset, with an attribute of counts of some variable (houses, population, etc.) as held in another spatial polygon data frame. You should base your function on the code used in the illustrated example above. You should compile it such that the function returns the portion of the count attribute covered by each zone. For example, it should be able to intersect the int.layer data with the blocks data and return a SpatialPolygonsDataFrame dataset with an attribute of the number of people, as described in the POP1990 variable of blocks, covered by each zone. You should remember that spatial functions such as gIntersect require their inputs to have the same projection. The int.layer defined above and the tracts data have no projections. You may find it useful to align the projections

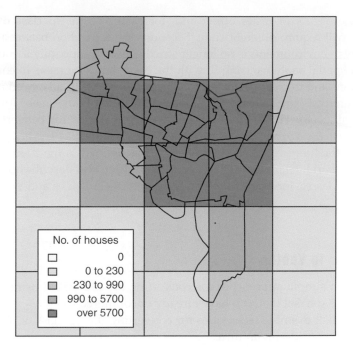

Figure 5.8 The zones shaded by the number of households after intersection with the census tracts

of the int.layer defined above and the blocks data in the following way using the rgdal package:

```
install.packages("rgdal", dep = T)
library(rgdal)
ct <- proj4string(blocks)
proj4string(int.layer) <- CRS(ct)
blocks <- spTransform(blocks, CRS(proj4string(int.layer)))
```

5.8 CONVERTING BETWEEN RASTER AND VECTOR

Very often we would like to move or convert our data between vector and raster environments. In fact the very persistence of these dichotomous data structures, with separate raster and vector functions and analyses in many commercial GIS software programs, is one of the long-standing legacies in GIS.

This section briefly describes methods for converting data between raster and vector structures. There are three reasons for this brief treatment. Firstly, many packages define their own data structures. For example, the functions in the PBSmapping package require a PolySet object to be passed to them. This means that conversion between one class of raster object and, for example, the sp class of Spatial Polygons will require different code. Secondly, the separation between raster and vector analysis environments is no longer strictly needed, especially if you are developing your spatial analyses using R, with the easy ability for users to compile their own functions and to create their own analysis tools. Thirdly, advanced raster mapping and analysis are extensively covered in other books (see, for example, Bivand et al. 2008). The sections below describe methods for converting the sp class of objects (SpatialPoints, SpatialLines and SpatialPolygons, etc.) to and from the RasterLayer class of objects as defined in the raster package, created by Robert J. Hijmans and Jacob van Etten. They also describe how to convert between sp classes, for example to and from SpatialPixels and SpatialGrid objects.

5.8.1 Raster to Vector

In this section simple approaches for converting are illustrated using datasets in the tornados dataset that you have already encountered.

First, we shall examine techniques for converting the sp class of objects to the raster class, considering in turn:

- points (SpatialPoints and SpatialPointsDataFrame)

- lines (SpatialLines and SpatialLinesDataFrame)

- areas (SpatialPolygons and SpatialPolygonsDataFrame)

You will need to load the data and the packages – you may need to install the raster package using the install.packages function if this is the first time that you have used it.

Converting points to raster

```
library(GISTools)
library(raster)
data(tornados)
# Points
r = raster(nrow = 180, ncols = 360, ext = extent(us_states2))
t2 <- as(torn2, "SpatialPoints")
r <- rasterize(t2, r, fun=sum)
```

The resultant raster has cells describing different tornado densities that can be mapped as in Figure 5.9:

```
# set the plot extent by specifying the plot colour 'white'
plot(r, col = "white")
plot(us_states2, add = T, border = "grey")
plot(r, add = T)
```

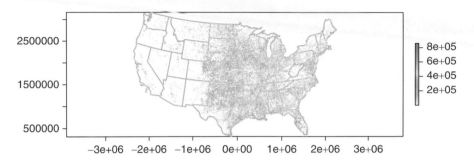

Figure 5.9 Converting points to raster format

Converting lines to raster

For illustrative purposes the code below creates a `SpatialLinesDataFrame` object of the outline of the polygons:

```
# Lines
us_outline <- as(us_states2 , "SpatialLinesDataFrame")
r <- raster(nrows = 180 , ncols = 360, ext = extent(us_states2))
r <- rasterize(us_outline , r, "STATE_FIPS")
```

This takes a bit longer to run, but again the results can be mapped and this time the shading describes the STATE_FIPS attribute – a numerical code for each US state (see Figure 5.10):

```
plot(r)
```

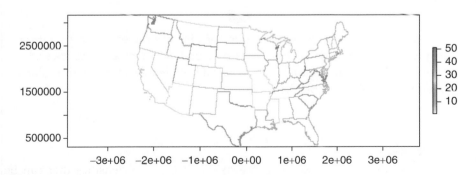

Figure 5.10 Converting lines to raster format

Converting polygons or areas to raster

Finally, polygons can easily be converted to a `RasterLayer` object using tools in the `raster` package and plotted as in Figure 5.11. You will note that in this case the 1997 population for each state is used to generate raster cell or pixel values.

```
# Polygons
r <- raster(nrow = 180 , ncols = 360, ext = extent(us_states2))
r <- rasterize(us_states2, r, "POP1997")

## Found 49 region(s) and 95 polygon(s)

plot(r)
```

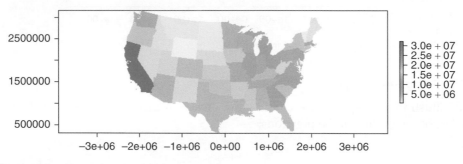

Figure 5.11 Converting polygons to raster format

It is instructive to examine the outputs of these processes. Enter:

```
r
```

This summarises the characteristics of the `raster` object, including the resolution, dimensions and extent.

It is possible to specify particular dimensions for the raster grid cells, rather than just dividing the dataset's extent by `ncol` and `nrow` in the `raster` function. The code below is a bit convoluted but cleanly allocates the values to raster grid cells of a specified size:

```
# specify a cell size in the projection units
d <- 50000
dim.x <- d
dim.y <- d
```

```
bb <- bbox(us_states2)
# work out the number of cells needed
cells.x <- (bb[1,2]-bb[1,1]) / dim.x
cells.y <- (bb[2,2]-bb[2,1]) / dim.y
round.vals <- function(x){
    if(as.integer(x) < x) {
        x <- as.integer(x) + 1
    } else {x <- as.integer(x)
            }}
# the cells cover the data completely
cells.x <- round.vals(cells.x)
cells.y <- round.vals(cells.y)
# specify the raster extent
ext <- extent(c(bb[1,1], bb[1,1]+(cells.x*d),
    bb[2,1],bb[2,1]+(cells.y*d)))
# now run the raster conversion
r <- raster(ncol = cells.x,nrow =cells.y)
extent(r) <- ext
r <- rasterize(us_states2, r, "POP1997")
# and examine the results
r
plot(r)
```

5.8.2 Converting to sp Classes

You may have noticed that the sp package also has two data classes that are able to represent raster data, or data are located on a regular grid. These are SpatialPixelsDataFrame and SpatialGridDataFrame. It is possible to convert the raster class objects using the as function. The example below converts the raster layer to SpatialPixelsDataFrame and to SpatialGridDataFrame objects.

First create a spatially coarse raster layer of US states similar to the above:

```
r <- raster(nrow = 60, ncols = 120, ext = extent(us_states2))
r <- rasterize(us_states2, r, "STATE_FIPS")

## Found 49 region(s) and 95 polygon(s)
```

Then the as function can be used to coerce this to SpatialPixelsDataFrame and SpatialGridDataFrame objects, which can also be mapped using the image or plot commands in the usual way, as in Figure 5.12:

```
g <- as(r, 'SpatialGridDataFrame')
p <- as(r, 'SpatialPixelsDataFrame')
# not run
# image(g, col = topo.colors(51))
# points(p, cex = 0.5)
par(mar=c(0,0,0,0))
plot(p, cex = 0.5, pch = 1, col = p$layer)
```

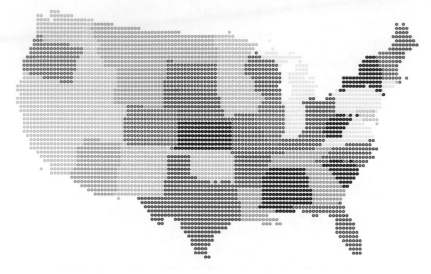

Figure 5.12 Plotting the `SpatialGrid` and `SpatialPoint` objects

You can also examine the data values held in the `data.frame` by entering:

```
head(data.frame(g))
head(data.frame(p))
```

The data can also be manipulated to select certain features, in this case selecting the states with populations greater than 10 million people. The code below assigns NA values to the data points that fail this test and plots the data as an `image` and as points (Figure 5.13):

```
# set up and create the raster
r <- raster(nrow = 60 , ncols = 120, ext = extent(us_states2))
r <- rasterize(us_states2 , r, "POP1997")

## Found 49 region(s) and 95 polygon(s)

r2 <- r
```

```
# subset the data
r2[r < 10000000] <- NA
g <- as(r2, 'SpatialGridDataFrame')
p <- as(r2, 'SpatialPixelsDataFrame')
# not run
# image(g, bg = "grey90")
par(mar=c(0,0,0,0))
plot(p, cex = 0.5, pch = 1)
```

Figure 5.13 Selecting data in SpatialGrid and SpatialPoint objects

5.8.3 Vector to Raster

The raster package contains a number of functions for converting from vector to raster formats. These include rasterToPolygons which converts to a SpatialPolygonsDataFrame object, and rasterToPoints which converts to a matrix object. Both are illustrated in the code below and the results shown in Figure 5.14. Notice how the original raster imposes a grid structure on the polygons that are created.

```
# load the data and convert to raster
data(newhaven)
# set up the raster, r
r <- raster(nrow = 60 , ncols = 60, ext = extent(tracts))
# convert polygons to raster
r <- rasterize(tracts , r, "VACANT")

## Found 29 region(s) and 30 polygon(s)

poly1 <- rasterToPolygons(r, dissolve = T)
```

```
# convert to points
points1 <- rasterToPoints(r)
# plot the points, rasterized polygons & orginal polygons
par(mar=c(0,0,0,0))
plot(points1, col = "grey", axes = FALSE, xaxt='n',
    ann=FALSE)
plot(poly1, lwd = 1.5, add = T)
plot(tracts, border = "red", add = T)
# reset the plot margins
par(mar=c(5,4,4,2))
```

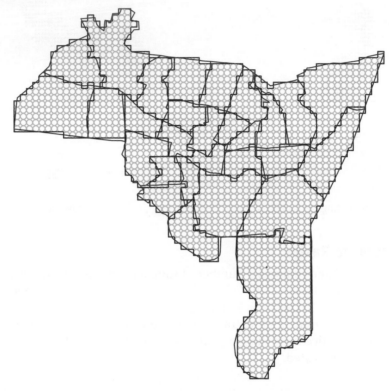

Figure 5.14 Converting from rasters to polygons and points, with the original polygon data in red

5.9 INTRODUCTION TO RASTER ANALYSIS

This section provides the briefest of overviews of how raster data may be manipulated and overlayed in a R in a similar way to a standard GUI GIS such as QGIS. This section will introduce the `raster` package, the reclassification of raster data as a precursor to some basic methods for performing what is sometimes referred to as *map algebra*, using a *raster calculator* or *raster overlay*. As a reminder, many packages include user guides in the form of a PDF document describing the package. This is listed at the top of the package index page. The `raster` package includes example code for the creation of raster data and different types of multi-layered raster composites. These will not be covered in this section. Rather, the coded examples illustrate some basic methods for manipulating and analysing raster layers in a similar way to what is often referred to as 'multi-criteria evaluation' or 'multi-criteria analysis'.

Raster analysis requires that the different data have a number of characteristics in common: typically they should cover the same spatial extent, the same spatial resolution (grid or cell size), and as with data for any spatial analysis, they should have the same projection or coordinate system. The data layers used in the example code in this section all have these properties. When you come to develop your own analyses, you may have to perform some manipulation of the data prior to analysis to ensure that your data also have these properties.

5.9.1 Raster Data Preparation

The Meuse data in the `sp` package will be used to illustrate the functions below. You could read in your raster data using the `readGDAL` function in the `rgdal` package, which provides an excellent engine for reading most commonly used raster formats. You can inspect the properties and attributes of the Meuse data by examining the associated help files `?meuse.grid`.

```
library(GISTools)
library(raster)
library(sp)
# load the meuse.grid data
data(meuse.grid)
# create a SpatialPixelsDataFrame object
coordinates(meuse.grid) <- ~x+y
meuse.grid <- as(meuse.grid, "SpatialPixelsDataFrame")
# create 3 raster layers
r1 <- raster(meuse.grid, layer - 3) #dist
r2 <- raster(meuse.grid, layer = 4) #soil
r3 <- raster(meuse.grid, layer = 5) #ffreq
```

The code above loads the `meuse.grid` data, converts it to a `SpatialPixels DataFrame` format and then creates three separate raster layers in the `raster` format. These three layers will form the basis of the analyses in this section. You could visually inspect their attributes by using some simple `image` commands:

```
image(r1, asp = 1)
image(r2, asp = 1)
image(r3, asp = 1)
```

5.9.2 Raster Reclassification

Raster analyses frequently employ simple numerical and mathematical operations. In essence they allow you to add, multiply, subtract, etc. raster data layers, and these operations are performed on a cell by cell basis. So for an addition this might be in the form:

```
Raster_Result <- Raster.Layer.1 + Raster.Layer.2
```

Remembering that raster data are numerical, if the `Raster.Layer.1` and `Raster.Layer.2` data both contained the values 1, 2 and 3, it would be difficult to know the origin, for example, of a value of 3 in the `Raster_Result` output. The r2 and r3 layers created above both contain values in the range 1–3 describing soil types and flooding frequency, respectively (as described in the help for the `meuse.grid` data). Therefore we may wish to reclassify them in some way to understand the results of any overlay operation.

It is possible to reclassify raster data in a number of ways.

First, the raster data values can be manipulated using simple mathematical operations. These produce raster outputs describing the mathematical combination of the input raster layers. The code below multiplies one of the layers by 10. This means that the result combining both raster data layers using the add (+) function contains a fixed set of values – in this case 9 – which are tractable to the combinations of inputs used. A value of 32 would indicate values of 3 in r3 (a flooding frequency of one in 50 years) and 2 in r2 (a soil type of 'Rd90C/VII', whatever that is). The results of this simple overlay are shown in Figure 5.15 and in the table of values printed. Note the use of the `spplot` function in the code below.

```
Raster_Result <- r2 + (r3 * 10)

table(as.vector(Raster_Result$values))

##

##   11   12  13   21   22   23   31   32   33

## 535 242   2 736 450 149 394 392 203

spplot(Raster_Result, col.regions=brewer.pal(9, "Spectral"),
    cuts=8)
```

A second approach to reclassifying raster data is to employ logical operations on the data layers prior to combining them. These return TRUE or FALSE for each raster grid cell, depending on whether it satisfies the logical condition. The resultant layers can then be combined in mathematical operations as above. For example,

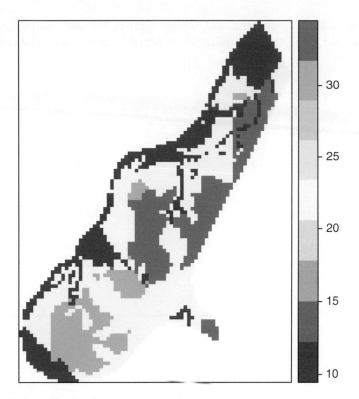

Figure 5.15   The result of a simple raster overlay

consider the analysis that wanted to identify the locations in the Meuse data that
satisfied the following conditions:

- Are greater than half of the rescaled distance away from the Meuse
  river;

- Have a soil class of 1, i.e. calcareous weakly developed meadow soils,
  light sandy clay;

- Have a flooding frequency class of 3, i.e. once in a 50-year period.

The following logical operations can be used to do this:

```
r1a <- r1 > 0.5
r2a <- r2 >= 2
r3a <- r3 < 3
```

These can then be combined using specific mathematical operations, depending on
the analysis. For example, a simple suitability Multi-Criteria Evaluation, where all

the conditions have to be true and where a crisp, Boolean output is required, would be coded using the multiplication function as below with the result shown in Figure 5.16:

```
Raster_Result <- r1a * r2a * r3a
table(as.vector(Raster_Result$values))

##
##    0    1
## 2924  179

plot(Raster_Result, legend = F, asp = 1)
# add a legend
legend(x='bottomright', legend = c("Suitable", "Not
    Suitable"), fill = (terrain.colors(n = 2)), bty = "n")
```

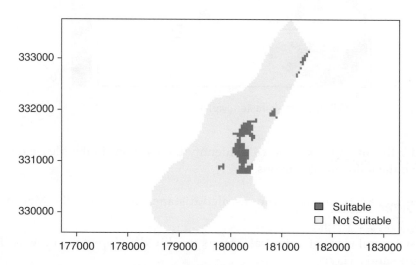

Figure 5.16 A raster overlay using a combinatorial AND

This is equivalent to a combinatorial AND operation, also known as an intersection. Alternatively the analysis may be interested in identifying where any of the conditions are true, a combinatorial OR operation, also known as a union, with a different result as shown in Figure 5.17:

```
Raster_Result <- r1a + r2a + r3a
table(as.vector(Raster_Result$values))
```

```
##
##      0      1      2      3
##    386   1526   1012    179
```

```
# plot the result and add a legend
image(Raster_Result, col = heat.colors(3), asp = 1)
legend(x='bottomright',
    legend = c("1 Condition", "2 Conditions",
    "3 Conditions"),
    fill = (heat.colors(n = 3)), bty = "n")
```

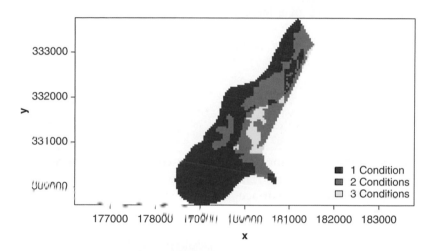

Figure 5.17   A raster overlay using a combinatorial OR

5.9.3 Other Raster Calculations

The above examples illustrated code to reclassify raster layers and then combined them using simple mathematical operations. You should note that it is possible to apply any kind of mathematical function to a raster layer. For example:

```
Raster_Result <- sin(r3) + sqrt(r1)
Raster_Result <- ((r1 * 1000 ) / log(r3) ) * r2
image(Raster_Result)
```

A number of other operations are possible using different functions included in the raster package. They are not given a full treatment here but are introduced such that the interested reader can explore them in more detail.

The calc function performs a computation over a single raster layer, in a similar manner to the mathematical operations in the preceding text. The advantage of the `calc` function is that it should be faster when computing more complex operations over large raster datasets.

```
my.func <- function(x) {log(x)}
Raster_Result <- calc(r3, my.func)
# this is equivalent to
Raster_Result <- calc(r3, log)
```

The `overlay` function provides an alternative to the mathematical operations illustrated in the reclassification examples above for combining multiple raster layers. The advantage of the `overlay` function, again, is that it is more efficient for performing computations over large `raster` objects.

```
Raster_Result <- overlay(r2,r3,
    fun = function(x, y) {return(x + (y * 10))} )
# alternatively using a stack
my.stack <- stack(r2, r3)
Raster_Result <- overlay(my.stack, fun = function(x, y)
    (x + (y * 10)) )
```

There are a number of distance functions for computing distances to specific features. The `distanceFromPoints` calculates the distance between a set of points to all cells in a raster surface and produces a distance or cost surface as in Figure 5.18.

```
# load meuse and convert to points
data(meuse)
coordinates(meuse) <- ~x+y
# select a point layer
soil.1 <- meuse[meuse$soil == 1,]
# create an empty raster layer
# this is based on the extent of meuse
r <- raster(meuse.grid)
dist <- distanceFromPoints(r, soil.1)
plot(dist)
plot(soil.1, add = T)
```

You are encouraged to explore the `raster` package (and indeed the `sp` package) in more detail if you are specifically interested in raster based analyses. There are a number of other distance functions, functions for computing over neighbourhoods (focal functions), accessing raster cell values and assessing spatial configurations of raster layers.

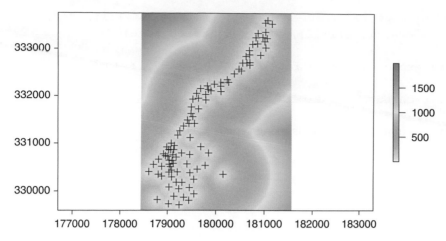

Figure 5.18   A raster analysis of distance to points

ANSWERS TO SELF-TEST QUESTIONS

Q1. Here is the code to maps the densities of breaches of the peace in New Haven in breaches per square mile:

```
densities = poly.counts(breach,blocks)  /
    ft2miles(ft2miles(poly.areas(blocks)))
density.shades <- auto.shading(densities,
    cols=brewer.pal(5, "Oranges"), cutter=rangeCuts)
choropleth(blocks,densities,shading=density.shades)
choro.legend(533000,161000,density.shades)
title("Incidents per Sq. Mile")
```

Note that much of the concentration of incidents occurs in a small number of places.
Q2. First, calculate the coefficients for the analysis using census blocks:

```
# Analysis with blocks
blocks2 = blocks[blocks$OCCUPIED > 0,]
attach(data.frame(blocks2))
forced.rate = 2000*poly.counts(burgres.f,blocks2)/OCCUPIED
notforced.rate = 2000*poly.counts(burgres.n,blocks2)/
    OCCUPIED
model1 = lm(forced.rate~notforced.rate)
coef(model1)

##     (Intercept)  notforced.rate
##           5.467           0.379
```

```
cat("expected(forced rate)= ",coef(model1)[1], "+",
    coef(model1)[2], "* (not forced rate) ")

## expected(forced rate)= 5.467 + 0.379 * (not forced rate)

detach(data.frame(blocks2))
```

Now, calculate the coeffcients using census `tracts`:

```
# Analysis with tracts
tracts2 = tracts[tracts$OCCUPIED > 0,]
# align the projections
ct <- proj4string(burgres.f)
proj4string(tracts2) <- CRS(ct)
# now do the analysis
attach(data.frame(tracts2))
forced.rate = 2000*poly.counts(burgres.f,tracts2)/OCCUPIED
notforced.rate = 2000*poly.counts(burgres.n,tracts2)/OCCUPIED
model2 = lm(forced.rate~notforced.rate)
coef(model2)

##   (Intercept) notforced.rate
##       5.2435         0.4133

cat("expected(forced rate) = ",coef(model2)[1], "+",
    coef(model2)[2], "* (not forced rate) ")
## expected(forced rate) =  5.243 + 0.4133 * (not forced
rate)

detach(data.frame(tracts2))
```

These two analyses show that, in this case, there are only small differences between the coefficients arising from analyses using different areal units.

```
cat("expected(forced rate) = ",coef(model1)[1], "+",
    coef(model1)[2], "* (not forced rate) ")

## expected(forced rate) = 5.467 + 0.379 * (not forced rate)

cat("expected(forced rate) = ",coef(model2)[1], "+",
    coef(model2)[2], "* (not forced rate)")

## expected(forced rate) = 5.243 + 0.4133 * (not forced rate)
```

This analysis tests what is referred to as the modifiable areal unit problem, first identified in the 1930s, and extensively researched by Stan Openshaw in the 1970s and beyond – see Openshaw (1984) for a comprehensive review. Variability in analyses can arise when data are summarised over different spatial units, and the importance of the modifiable areal unit problem cannot be overstated as a critical consideration in spatial analysis.

Q3. The simplest way to write the function required would be simply to use the code in the preceding text and to wrap it in a function:

```
int.poly.counts <- function(int.layer, tracts,
    tracts.var, var.name) {
  int.res <- gIntersection(int.layer, tracts, byid = T)
  # split the intersection references
  tmp <- strsplit(names(int.res), " ")
  tracts.id <- (sapply(tmp, "[[", 2))
  intlayer.id <- (sapply(tmp, "[[", 1))
  # calculate areas
  int.areas <- gArea(int.res, byid = T)
  tract.areas <- gArea(tracts, byid = T)
  # match this to the new layer
  index <- match(tracts.id, row.names(tracts))
  tract.areas <- tract.areas[index]
  tract.prop <- zapsmall(int.areas/tract.areas, 3)
  # and create data frame for the new layer
  df <- data.frame(intlayer.id, tract.prop)
  houses <- zapsmall(tracts.var[index] * tract.prop, 1)
  df <- data.frame(df, houses, int.areas)
  # Finally, link back to the original areas
  int.layer.houses <- xtabs(df$houses~df$intlayer.id)
  index <- as.numeric(gsub("g", "", names(int.layer.houses)))
  # create temporary variable
  tmp <- vector("numeric", length = dim(data.frame(int.layer))[1])
  tmp[index] <- int.layer.houses
  i.houses <- tmp
  # create output data
  int.layer2 <- SpatialPolygonsDataFrame(int.layer,
    data = data.frame(data.frame(int.layer), i.houses),
    match.ID = FALSE)
  names(int.layer2) <- c("ID", var.name)
  return(int.layer2)
}
```

And this could be used to evaluate the inputs as in the worked example:

```
int.layer2 <- int.poly.counts(int.layer,
    tracts,tracts$HSE_UNITS, "i.house" )
```

However, the code is not very transparent and better names could be used for the various intermediate internal variables that are created to make the function more understandable to someone else or you at a later date.

```
int.poly.counts <- function(int.layer1, int.layer2,
    int.layer2.var, var.name) {
  int.res <- gIntersection(int.layer1, int.layer2, byid = T)
  tmp <- strsplit(names(int.res), " ")
  int.layer2.id <- (sapply(tmp, "[[", 2))
  intlayer.id <- (sapply(tmp, "[[", 1))
  int.areas <- gArea(int.res, byid = T)
  tract.areas <- gArea(int.layer2, byid = T)
  index <- match(int.layer2.id, row.names(int.layer2))
  tract.areas <- tract.areas[index]
  tract.prop <- zapsmall(int.areas/tract.areas, 3)
  df <- data.frame(intlayer.id, tract.prop)
  var <- zapsmall(int.layer2.var[index] * tract.prop, 1)
  df <- data.frame(df, var, int.areas)
  int.layer1.var <- xtabs(df$var~df$intlayer.id)
  index <- as.numeric(gsub("g", " ", names(int.layer1.var)))
  tmp <- vector("numeric", length = dim(data.frame(int.layer1))[1])
  tmp[index] <- int.layer1.var
  i.var <- tmp
  int.layer.out <- SpatialPolygonsDataFrame(int.layer1,
    data = data.frame(data.frame(int.layer1), i.var),
    match.ID = FALSE)
  names(int.layer.out) <- c("ID", var.name)
  return(int.layer.out)}
```

This can then be tentatively applied to other data, after making sure that it has a similar projected (i.e. consistent with distance and area calculations) coordinate system. A full implementation of this function and the results of applying it to int.layer and blocks, after they have had their spatial reference systems aligned, is described below and shown in Figure 5.19.

```
# Set up the packages and data
```

```
library(GISTools)
library(rgdal)
data(newhaven)
# define the intersection layer just to make sure
bb <- bbox(tracts)
grd <- GridTopology(cellcentre.offset=
    c(bb[1,1]-200,bb[2,1]-200),
    cellsize=c(10000,10000), cells.dim = c(5,5))
int.layer <- SpatialPolygonsDataFrame(
    as.SpatialPolygons.GridTopology(grd),
    data = data.frame(c(1:25)), match.ID = FALSE)
names(int.layer) <- "ID"

# now run with some data
# match prj4strings
ct <- proj4string(blocks)
proj4string(int.layer) <- CRS(ct)
int.layer <- spTransform(int.layer,
    CRS(proj4string(blocks)))
# now run the function
int.result <- int.poly.counts(int.layer, blocks,
    blocks$POP1990, "i.pop" )
# set plot parameters
par(mar=c(0,0,0,0))

# map the results
shades = auto.shading(int.result$i.pop,n = 5,
    cols = brewer.pal(5, "OrRd"))
choropleth(int.result, int.result$i.pop, shades)
plot(blocks, add = T, lty = 2, lwd = 1.5)
choro.legend(530000, 159115, bg = "white", shades,
    title = "Count", under = " ")
```

You can check the assigned populations in relation to Figures 5.7 and 5.19.

```
matrix(data.frame(int.result)[,2], nrow = 5, ncol = 5,
    byrow = T)
```

```
##          [,1]   [,2]    [,3]   [,4]  [,5]
## [1,]     154   5682    556      0   236
## [2,]    1962  20354  41712  17125  3088
## [3,]       0   3476  20603  10494     0
## [4,]       0      0    587   4054     0
## [5,]       0      0    208    261     0
```

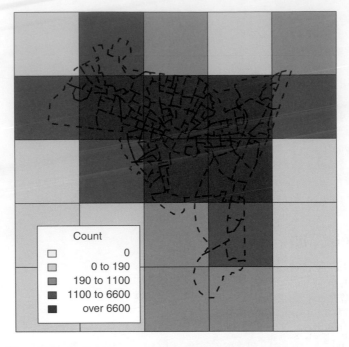

Figure 5.19 The zones shaded by population after intersection with the census blocks

REFERENCES

Bivand, R.S., Pebesma, E.J. and Gómez-Rubio, V. (2008) *Applied Spatial Data Analysis with R.* New York: Springer.

Comber, A.J., Brunsdon, C. and Green, E. (2008) Using a GIS-based network analysis to determine urban greenspace accessibility for different ethnic and religious groups. *Landscape and Urban Planning*, 86: 103–114.

Openshaw S. (1984) The modifiable areal unit problem, CATMOG 38, *Geo Abstracts*, Norwich. http://qmrg.org.uk/files/2008/11/38-maup-openshaw. pdf

6

POINT PATTERN ANALYSIS USING R

6.1 INTRODUCTION

In this and the next chapter, some key ideas of spatial statistics will be outlined, together with examples of statistical analysis based on these ideas, via R. The two main areas of spatial statistics that are covered are those relating to *point patterns* (this chapter) and *spatially referenced attributes* (next chapter). One of the characteristics of R, as open source software, is that R packages are contributed from a variety of authors, each using their own individual styles of programming. In particular, for point pattern analysis the `spatstat` package is often used, whilst for spatially referenced attributed, `spdep` is favoured. One the one hand `spdep` handles spatial data in the same way as `sp`, `maptools` and `GISTools`, while on the other hand `spatstat` does not. Also, for certain specific tasks, other packages may be called upon, whose mode of working differs from either of those packages. Whilst this may seem a daunting prospect, the aim of these two chapters is to introduce the key ideas of spatial statistics, as well as providing guidance in the choice of packages, and help in converting data formats. Fortunately, although some packages use different data formats, conversion is generally straightforward, and examples will appear throughout the chapters, whenever necessary.

6.2 WHAT IS SPECIAL ABOUT SPATIAL?

In one sense, the motivations for statistical analysis of spatial data are the same as those for non-spatial data:

- To explore and visualise the data;
- To create and calibrate models of the process generating the data;
- To test hypotheses related to the processes generating the data.

However, a number of these requirements are strongly influenced by the nature of spatial data. The study of mapping and cartography may be regarded as an entire subject area within the discipline of information visualisation, which focuses exclusively on geographical information.

In addition, the kinds of hypotheses one might associate with spatial data are quite distinctive – for example, focusing on the detection and location of spatial clusters of events, or on whether two kinds of event (say, two different types of crime) have the same spatial distribution. Similarly, models that are appropriate for spatial data are distinctive, in that they often have to allow for spatial autocorrelation in their random component – for example, a regression model generally include a random error term, but if the data are spatially referenced, one might expect nearby errors to be correlated. This differs from a 'standard' regression model where each error term is considered to apply independently, regardless of location. In the remainder of this section, point patterns (one of two key types of spatial data considered in this book) will be considered. Firstly, these will be described.

6.2.1 Point Patterns

Point patterns are collections of geographical points assumed to have been generated by a random process. In this case, the focus of inference and modelling is on model(s) of the random processes, and their comparison. Typically, a point dataset consists of a set of observed (x, y) coordinates, say $\{(x_1, y_1), (x_2, y_2), \ldots, (x_n, y_n)\}$, where n is the number of observations. As an alternative notation, each point could be denoted by a vector $\mathbf{x}_i$, where $\mathbf{x}_i = (x_i, y_i)$. Using the data formats used in sp, maptools and so on, these data could be represented as SpatialPoints or SpatialPointsDataFrame objects. Since these data are seen as random, many models are concerned with the probability densities of the random points, $v(\mathbf{x}_i)$.

Another area of interest is the *interrelation* between the points. One way of thinking about this is to consider the probability density of one point $\mathbf{x}_i$ conditional on the remaining points $\{\mathbf{x}_1, \ldots, \mathbf{x}_{i-1}, \mathbf{x}_{i+1}, \ldots, \mathbf{x}_n\}$. In some situations $\mathbf{x}_i$ is independent of the other points. However, for other processes this is not the case. For example, if $\mathbf{x}_i$ is the location of the reported address for a contagious disease, then it is more likely to occur near one of the points in the dataset (due to the nature of contagion), and therefore not independent of the values of $\{\mathbf{x}_1, \ldots, \mathbf{x}_{i-1}, \mathbf{x}_{i+1}, \ldots, \mathbf{x}_n\}$.

Also important is the idea of a *marked process*. Here, random sets of points drawn from a number of different populations are superimposed (for example, household burglaries using force and household burglaries not using force) and the relationship between the different sets is considered. The term 'marked' is used here as the dataset can be viewed as a set of points where each point is tagged (or marked) with its parent population. Using the data formats used by sp, a marked process could be represented as a spatial points data frame – although the spatstat package uses a different format.

6.3 TECHNIQUES FOR POINT PATTERNS USING R

Having outlined the two main data types that will be considered, and the kinds of model that may be applied, in this section more specific techniques will be discussed, with examples of how they may be carried out using R. In this section, we will focus on random point patterns.

6.3.1 Kernel Density Estimates

The simplest way to consider random two-dimensional point patterns is to assume that each random location x_i is drawn independently from an unknown distribution with probability density function $f(x_i)$. This function maps a location (represented as a two-dimensional vector) onto a probability density. If we think of locations in space as a very fine pixel grid, and assume a value of probability density is assigned to each pixel, then summing the pixels making up an arbitrary region on the map gives the probability that an event occurs in that area. It is generally more practical to assume an *unknown f*, rather than, say, a Gaussian distribution, since geographical patterns often take on fairly arbitrary shapes – for example, when applying the technique to patterns of public disorder, areas of raised risk will occur in a number of locations around a city, rather than a simplistic radial 'bell curve' centred on the city's mid-point.

A common technique used to estimate $f(x_i)$ is the *kernel density estimate* or KDE (Silverman, 1986). KDEs operate by averaging a series of small 'bumps' (probability distributions in two dimensions, in fact) centred on each observed point. This is illustrated in Figure 6.1. In algebraic terms, the approximation to $f(x)$, for an arbitrary location $x = (x, y)$, is given by

$$\hat{f}(x) = \hat{f}(x, y) = \frac{1}{n h_x h_y} \sum_i k\left(\frac{x - x_i}{h_x}, \frac{y - y_i}{h_y} \right) \tag{6.1}$$

Each of the 'bumps' (central panel in Figure 6.1) map on to the kernel function $k\left(\frac{x - x_i}{h_x}, \frac{y - y_i}{h_y} \right)$ in equation (6.1) and the entire equation describes the 'bump averaging' process, leading to the estimate of probability density on the right-hand panel. Note that there are also parameters h_x and h_y (frequently referred to as the *bandwidths*) in the x and y directions; their dimension is length, and they represent the radii of the bumps in each direction. Varying h_x and h_y alters the shape of the estimated probability density surface – in brief, low values of h_x and h_y lead to very 'spiky' distribution estimates, and very high values, possibly larger than the span of the x_i locations, tend to 'flatten' the estimate so it appears to resemble the k-function itself; effectively this gives a superposition of nearly identical k-functions with relatively small perturbations in their centre points.

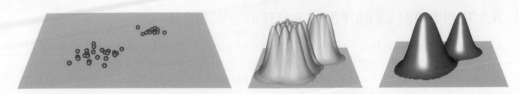

Figure 6.1 Kernel density estimation: initial points (left); bump centred on each point (centre); average of bumps giving estimate of probability density (right)

This effect of varying h_x and h_y is shown in Figure 6.2. Typically h_x and h_y take similar values. If one of these values is very different in magnitude than the other, kernels elongated in either the x or y direction result. Although this may be useful when there are strong directional effects, we will focus on the situation where values are similar for the examples discussed here. To illustrate the results of varying the bandwidths, the same set of points used in Figure 6.1 is used to provide KDEs with three different values of h_x and h_y – on the left, they both take a very low value, giving a large number of peaks; in the centre, there are two peaks; and on the right, only one.

An obvious problem is that of choosing appropriate h_x and h_y given a dataset $\{x_i\}$. There are a number of formulae to provide 'automatic' choices, as well as some more sophisticated algorithms. Here, a simple rule is used, as proposed by Bowman and Azzalini (1997) and Scott 1992:

$$h_x = \sigma_x \left(\frac{2}{3n} \right)^{\frac{1}{6}} \tag{6.2}$$

where σ_x is the standard deviation of the x_i. A similar formula exists for h_y, replacing σ_x with σ_y the standard deviation of the y_i The central KDE in Figure 6.2 is based on choosing h_x and h_y using this method.

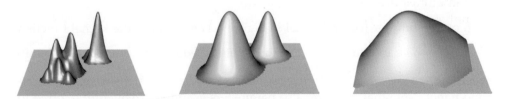

Figure 6.2 Kernel density estimation bandwidths: h_x and h_y too low (left); h_x and h_y appropriate (centre); h_x and h_y too high (right)

6.3.2 Kernel Density Estimation Using R

There are a number of packages in R that provide code for computing KDEs. Here, the `GISTools` library introduced earlier in this book will be used. The steps used to produce a KDE map here are as follows:

1. *Compute the KDE.* The function to carry out kernel density estimation is kde.points. This estimates the value of the density over a grid of points, and returns the result as a grid object. Here it takes two arguments – the set of points to use, and another geographical object, whose bounding box will be used to set the extent of the grid object to be created. A further optional argument allows the bandwidths to be specified. If it is omitted (as here) bandwidths are supplied via the formula in equation (6.2). Here, the breaches of the peace (public disturbances) dataset for New Haven, Connecticut, first introduced in Chapter 3, is used as an example – recall that this is provided in the GISTools package – here loaded using data(newhaven).

2. *Plot the KDE.* Here the KDEs will be mapped as filled contour lines, rather than represented as three-dimensional objects as in Figures 6.1 and 6.2. In this way it is easier to add other geographical entities. The level.plot command plots the resultant grid from the KDE – although this will be seen as a rectangular grid extending beyond the New Haven study area.

3. *Clip the plot to the study area.* To clip the grid with the boundaries of the study area some further software tools are used. poly.outer provides a new SpatialPolygons object, effectively consisting of a rectangle with a hole having the shape of the second argument – a SpatialPolygons or SpatialPolygonsDataFrame object. The first argument is any kind of spatial object (in this case a spatial polygon data frame of census tracts in New Haven), and is used to determine the boundary of the rectangle. The polygon thus produced acts as a kind of 'mask', overwriting the parts of the grid that lie outside of the polygon. Finally, the extend argument expands this rectangular mask by the specified number of units in each direction – sometimes the default rectangle (which fits over the first argument polygon exactly) needs to be extended to cover other features of the map. The add.masking function then draws this object onto the map. Finally, in case some of the boundaries of the study area tracts may have been overwritten (this sometimes happens as the boundaries of the polygonal hole may coincide exactly with those of the study area), the tracts are redrawn.

The code block to perform these operations is given below, and the resultant KDE map is shown in Figure 6.3.

```
# R Kernel Density
require(GISTools)
data(newhaven)
```

```
# Compute Density
breach.dens <- kde.points(breach,lims=tracts)
# Create a level plot
level.plot(breach.dens)
# Use 'masking' to clip around blocks
masker <- poly.outer(breach.dens,tracts,extend=100)
add.masking(masker)
# Add the tracts again
plot(tracts,add=TRUE)
```

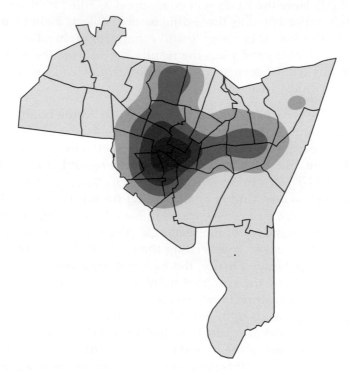

Figure 6.3 KDE map for breaches of the peace

Self-Test Question 1. As a further exercise, try adding a scale, and a layer of roads to this map. The help for map.scale is useful here, and an example is given in the help for the newhaven dataset.

6.4 FURTHER USES OF KERNEL DENSITY ESTIMATION

As well as estimating the probability density function $f(x, y)$, kernel density estimation also provides a helpful visual tool for displaying point data. Although plotting point data directly can show all of the information in a small dataset, if the dataset is larger it is hard to discriminate between relative densities of points: essentially, when points are very closely packed, the map symbols begin to overprint and exact numbers are hard to determine; this is illustrated in Figure 6.4. On the left is a plot of locations. The points plotted are drawn from a two-dimensional Gaussian distribution, and their relative density increases towards the centre. However, except for a penumbral region, the intensity of the dot pattern appears to have roughly fixed density. As the KDE estimates relative density, this problem is addressed – as may be seen in the KDE plot in Figure 6.4 (right).

Figure 6.4 The overplotting problem: point plot (left) and KDE plot (right)

KDE is also useful for comparative purposes. In the New Haven dataset there are also data relating to burglaries from residential properties. These are divided into two classes, burglaries that involve forced entry and burglaries that do not. It may be of interest to compare the spatial distributions of the two groups. In the `newhaven` dataset, `burgres.f` is a `SpatialPoints` object with points for the occurrence of forced entry residential burglaries, and `burgres.n` is a `SpatialPoints` object with points for non-forced entries. Based on the recommendation to compare patterns in data using small multiples of graphical panels (Tufte, 1990), KDE maps for forced and non-forced burglaries may be shown side by side. This is achieved using the following block of R code, which essentially reuses the previous block, but substitutes the `SpatialPoints` object used in the KDE computations, and repeats the operation for two maps side by side. The result is seen in Figure 6.5. Although there are some similarities in the two patterns – likely due to the underlying pattern of housing – it may be seen that for the non-forced entries there is a more prominent peak in the east, whilst for forced entries the stronger peak is to the west.

```
# R Kernel Density comparison
require(GISTools)
data(newhaven)
# Set up parameters to create two plots side by side,
# with 2 line margin at the top, no margin to bottom, left
# or right
par(mfrow=c(1,2),mar=c(0,0,2,0))
# Compute density for forced entry burglaries and
create plot
brf.dens <- kde.points(burgres.f,lims=tracts)
level.plot(brf.dens)
# Use 'masking' as before
masker <- poly.outer(brf.dens,tracts,extend=100)
add.masking(masker)
plot(tracts,add=TRUE)
# Add a title
title("Forced Burglaries")

# Compute density for non-forced entry burglaries and
create plot
brn.dens <- kde.points(burgres.n,lims=tracts)
level.plot(brn.dens)
# Use 'masking' as before
masker <- poly.outer(brn.dens,tracts,extend=100)
add.masking(masker)
plot(tracts,add=TRUE)
# Add a title
title("Non-Forced Burglaries")
# reset par(mfrow)
par(mfrow=c(1,1))
```

6.4.1 Hexagonal Binning Using R

An alternative visualisation tool for geographical point datasets with larger numbers of points is *hexagonal binning*. In this approach, a regular lattice of small hexagonal cells is overlaid on the point pattern, and the number of points in each cell is counted.

Forced Burglaries　　　　**Non–Forced Burglaries**

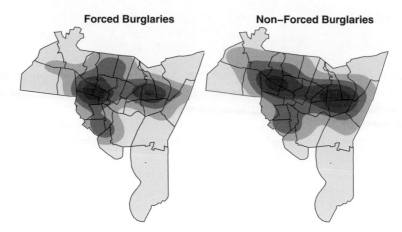

Figure 6.5　KDE maps to compare forced and non-forced burglary patterns

The cells are then shaded according to the counts. This method also overcomes the overplotting problem. However, hexagonal binning is not directly available in GISTools, and it is necessary to use another package. One possibility is the fMultivar package. This provides a routine for hexagonal binning called hexBinning, which takes a two-column matrix of coordinates and provides an object representing the hexagonal grid and the counts of points in each hexagonal cell. Note that this function does not work directly with sp-type spatial data objects. This is mainly because it is designed to apply hexagonal binning to any kind of data (for example, scatter plot points where the x and y variables are not geographical coordinates). However, it is perfectly acceptable to subject geographical points to this kind of analysis.

First, make sure that the fMultivar package is installed in R. If not, enter

```
install.packages("fMultivar", depend = TRUE)
```

Then use the hexBinning function.

```
# Load the package with hex binning
require(fMultivar)
# Create the hexagonal bins
hbins <-hexBinning(coordinates(breach))
```

The object hbins contains the binning information. In particular, it contains the centroid of each hexagonal bin, and the count of points in each bin:

```
head(hbins$x)
## [1] 542284 549289 550906 548212 561144 547673
head(hbins$y)
## [1] 163291 165273 165933 166594 166594 167254
```

```
head(hbins$z)
```

```
## [1] 1 1 1 1 1 1
```

Note that z refers to the count in each bin. Also, bins with zero counts are not recorded, so 1 is the smallest value of z that can appear. To draw these on the map, the full polygonal coordinates associated with each centroid need to be entered – the variables u and v contain the relative offsets for hexagons, so that when the centroids are added to these variables, the polygons for specific polygons are created:

```
# Hex binning code block
# Set up the hexagons to plot, as polygons
u <- c(1, 0, -1, -1, 0, 1)
u <- u * min(diff(unique(sort(hbins$x))))
v <- c(1,2,1,-1,-2,-1)
v <- v * min(diff(unique(sort(hbins$y))))/3
```

Next, the background map (US Census blocks in New Haven) are drawn. Finally, the hexagons are added, here using a loop in R, so that each hexagon centre is visited in turn, and the appropriate polygon is created and shaded according to the count of points in that polygon. In this case it can be seen that there is a maximum of nine points in any polygon:

```
max(hbins$z)
```

```
## [1] 9
```

Thus, a palette of nine shades is created (via the function brewer.pal from the RColorBrewer package) is created. Note that nine is the maximum number of shades allowed for the palette used here – so if the highest value of z had exceeded 9, it would have been necessary to scale this down. Also note that at the time of writing there is no 'pre-built' function to draw hexagonal bin plots over maps, hence this code builds up this functionality from basic tools such as polygon drawing. The code to do this follows, giving the map in Figure 6.6.

```
# Draw a map with blocks
plot(blocks)

# Obtain a shading scheme
shades <-brewer.pal(9,"Greens")

# Draw each polygon, with an appropriate shade
for (i in 1:length(hbins$x)) {
```

```
polygon(u + hbins$x[i], v + hbins$y[i],
    col = shades[hbins$z[i]],
    border = NA)}

# Re-draw the blocks
plot(blocks,add=TRUE)
```

Figure 6.6 Hexagonal binning of breach of the peace events

As an alternative graphical representation, it is also possible to draw hexagons whose area is proportional to the point count. This is done by creating a variable `scaler` with which to multiply the relative polygon coordinates (this relates to the *square root* of the count in each polygon, since it is *areas* of the hexagons that should reflect the counts). This is all achieved via a modification of the previous code, listed below. The graphical output is shown in Figure 6.7.

```
# Draw a map with blocks
plot(blocks)
```

```
# Obtain a shading scheme
scaler <- sqrt(hbins$z/9)

# Draw each polygon, with an appropriate shade
for (i in 1:length(hbins$x)) {
  polygon(u*scaler[i] + hbins$x[i], v*scaler[i]
        + hbins$y[i],
    col = 'indianred',
    border = NA)}

# Re-draw the blocks
plot(blocks,add=TRUE)
```

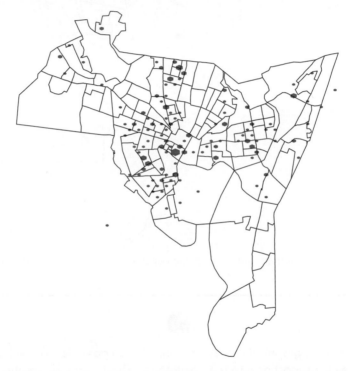

Figure 6.7 Hexagonal binning of breach of the peace events – proportional symbolism

6.5 SECOND-ORDER ANALYSIS OF POINT PATTERNS

In this section, an alternative approach to point patterns will be considered. Whereas KDEs assume that the spatial distributions for a set of points are independent but have a varying intensity, the second-order methods considered in this section assume that *marginal* distributions of points have a fixed intensity, but that the *joint* distribution of all points is such that individual distributions of points are not independent.[1] This process describes situations in which the occurrences of events are related in some way; for example, if a disease is contagious, the reporting of an incidence in one place might well be accompanied by other reports nearby. The *K*-function (Ripley, 1981) is a very useful tool for describing processes of this kind. The *K*-function is a function of distance, defined by

$$K(d) = \lambda^{-1} E(N_d) \tag{6.3}$$

where N_d is the number of events $\mathbf{x}_i$ within a distance d of a randomly chosen event from all recorded events $\{\mathbf{x}_1,...,\mathbf{x}_n\}$, and λ is the intensity of the process, measured in events per unit area. Consider the situation where the distributions of $\mathbf{x}_i$ are independent, and the marginal densities are uniform – often termed a Poisson process, or *complete spatial randomness* (CSR). In this situation one would expect the number of events within a distance d of a randomly chosen event to be the intensity λ multiplied by area of a circle of radius d, so that

$$K_{CSR}(d) = \pi d^2 \tag{6.4}$$

The situation in equation (6.4) can be thought of as a benchmark to assess the clustering of other processes. For a given distance d, the function value $K_{CSR}(d)$ gives an indication of the expected number of events found around a randomly chosen event, under the assumption of a uniform density with each observation being distributed independently of the others. Thus for a process having a *K*-function $K(d)$, if $K(d) > K_{CSR}(d)$ this suggests that there is an excess of nearby points – or, to put it another way, there is clustering at the spatial scale associated with the distance d. Similarly, if $K(d) < K_{CSR}(d)$ this suggests spatial dispersion at this scale – the presence of one point suggests other points are *less* likely to appear nearby than for a Poisson process.

The consideration of spatial scale is important (many processes exhibit spatial clustering at some scales, and dispersion at others), so that the quantity $K(d) - K_{CSR}(d)$ may change sign with different values of d. For example, the process illustrated in Figure 6.8 shows clustering at low values of d – for small distances (such as d_2 in the figure) there is an excess of points near to other points compared to CSR, but for intermediate distances (such as d_1 in the figure) there is an undercount of points.

When working with a sample of data points $\{\mathbf{x}_i\}$, the *K*-function for the underlying distribution will not usually be known. In this case, an estimate must be

---

1 A further stage in complication would be the situation where individual distributions are not independent, but also the marginal distributions vary in intensity; however, this will not be considered here.

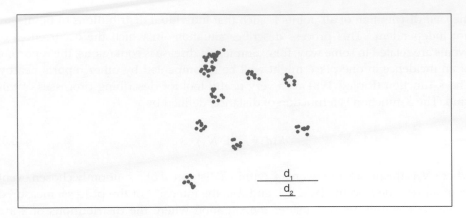

Figure 6.8 A spatial process with clustering and dispersion

made using the sample. If d_{ij} is the distance between $\mathbf{x}_i$ and $\mathbf{x}_j$ then an estimate of $K(d)$ is given by

$$\widehat{K}(d) = \widehat{\lambda}^{-1} \sum_i \sum_{j \neq i} \frac{I(d_{ij} < d)}{n(n-1)} \tag{6.5}$$

where $\widehat{\lambda}$ is an estimate of the intensity – given by

$$\widehat{\lambda} = \frac{n}{|A|} \tag{6.6}$$

with $|A|$ being the area of a study region defined by a polygon A. Also $I(.)$ is an indicator function taking the value 1 if the logical expression in the brackets is true, and 0 otherwise. To consider whether this sample comes from a clustered or dispersed process, it is helpful to compare $\widehat{K}(d)$ to $K_{CSR}(d)$.

Statistical inference is important here. Even if the dataset had been generated by a CSR process, an estimate of the K-function would be subject to sampling variation, and could not be expected to match $K_{CSR}(d)$ perfectly. Thus, it is necessary to test whether the sampled $\widehat{K}(d)$ is sufficiently unusual with respect to the distribution of $\widehat{K}$ estimates one might expect to see under CSR to provide evidence that the generating process for the sample is *not* CSR. The idea is illustrated in Figure 6.9. Here, 100 K-function estimates (based on equation (6.5)) from random CSR samples of 100 points (the same number of points as in Figure 6.8) are are superimposed, together with the estimate from the point set shown in Figure 6.8. From this it can be seen that the estimate from the clustered sample is quite different from the range of estimates expected from CSR.

Another aspect of sampling inference for K-functions is the dependency of $\widehat{K}(d)$ on the shape of the study area. The theoretical form $K_{CSR}(d) = \lambda \pi d^2$ is based on assumption of points occurring in an infinite two-dimensional plane. The fact that

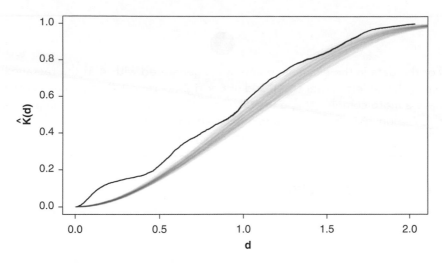

Figure 6.9 Sample K-functions under CSR

a 'real-world' sample will be taken from a finite study area (denoted here by A) will lead to further deviation of sample-based estimates of $\hat{K}(d)$ from the theoretical form. This can also be seen in Figure 6.9 – although for the lower values of d the CSR estimated K-function curves resemble the quadratic shape expected, the curves 'flatten out' for higher values of d. This is due to the fact that for larger values of d, points will only be observed in the intersection of a circle of radius d around a random x_i and the study area A. This will result in fewer points being observed than the theoretical K-function would predict. This effect continues, and when d is sufficiently large any circle centred on one of the points will encompass the entirety of A. At this point, any further increase in d will result in no change in the number of points contained in the circle – this provides an explanation of the flattening-out effect seen in the figure.

Above, the idea is to consider a CSR process constrained to the study area. However another viewpoint is that the study area defines a subset of all points generated on the full two-dimensional plane. To estimate the K-function for the full-plane process some allowance for edge effects on the study area needs to be made. Ripley (1976) proposed the following modification to equation (6.5):

$$\hat{K}(d) = \hat{\lambda}^{-1} \sum_i \sum_{j \neq i} \frac{2I(d_{ij} < d)}{n(n-1)w_{ij}} \tag{6.7}$$

where w_{ij} is the area of intersection between a circle centred at x_i, passing through x_j and the study area A. Inference about the estimated K-function can then be carried out using the approach used above, but with $\hat{K}(d)$ based on equation (6.7).

For the data in the example, points were generated with *A* as the rectangle having lower left corner (-1, -1) and upper right corner (1, 1). In practice *A* may have a more complex shape (a polygon outline of a county, for example; for this reason, assessing the sampling variability of the *K*-function under sampling must often be achieved via simulation, as seen in Figure 6.9.

6.5.1 Using the *K*-function in R

In R, a useful package for computing estimated *K*-functions (as well as other spatial statistical procedures) is spatstat. This is capable of carrying out the kind of simulation illustrated earlier in this section.

The *K*-function estimation as defined above may be estimated in the spatstat package using the Kest function. Here the locations of bramble canes (Hutchings, 1979; Diggle, 1983) are analysed, having been obtained as a dataset supplied with spatstat via the data(bramblecanes) command. They are plotted in Figure 6.10. Different symbols represent different ages of canes – although initially we will just consider the point pattern for *all* canes.

```
# K-function code block
# Load the spatstat package
require (spatstat)
#Obtain the bramble cane data
data (bramblecanes)
plot (bramblecanes)
```

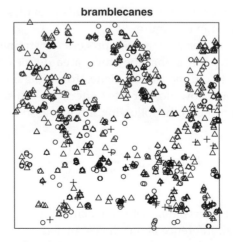

Figure 6.10 Bramble cane locations

Next the `Kest` function is used to obtain an estimate for the K-function of the spatial process underlying the distribution of the bramble canes. The `correction='border'` argument requests that an edge-corrected estimate (as in equation (6.7)) be used.

```
kf <- Kest(bramblecanes,correction='border')
# Plot it
plot(kf)
```

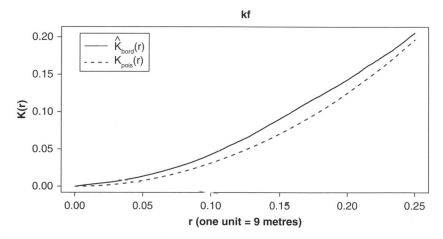

Figure 6.11   Ripley's K-function plot

The result of plotting the K-function, as shown in Figure 6.11, compares the estimated function (labelled $\hat{K}$bord) to the theoretical function under CSR (labelled $\hat{K}$pois). It may be seen that the data appear to be clustered (generally the empirical K-function is greater than that for CSR, suggesting that more points occur close together than would be expected under CSR). However, this perhaps needs a more rigorous investigation, allowing for sampling variation via simulation as set out above.

This simulation approach is sometimes referred to as *envelope* analysis, the envelope being the highest and lowest values of $\hat{K}(d)$ for a value of d. Thus the function for this is called `envelope`. This takes a `ppp` object and a further function as an argument. The function here is `Kest` – there are other functions also used to describe spatial distributions which will be discussed later, which `envelop` can use, but for now we focus on `Kest`. The envelope object may also be plotted – as shown in the following code which results in Figure 6.12:

```
# Code block to produce k-function with envelope
# Envelope function
```

```
kf.env <- envelope(bramblecanes,Kest,correction="border")
# Plot it
plot(kf.env)
```

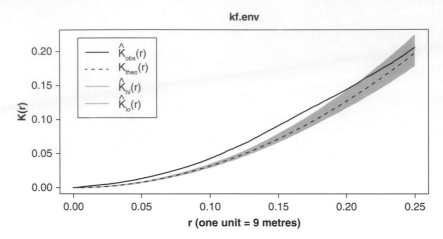

Figure 6.12 *K*-function with envelope

From this it can be seen that the estimated *K*-function for the sample takes on a higher value than the envelope of simulated *K*-functions for CSR until *d* becomes quite large, suggesting strong evidence that the locations of bramble canes do indeed exhibit clustering. However, it can reasonably be argued that comparing an estimated $\hat{K}(d)$ and an envelope of randomly sampled estimates under CSR is not a formal significance test. In particular, since the sample curve is compared to the envelope for several *d* values, multiple significance testing problems may occur. These are well explained by Bland and Altman (1995) – in short, when carrying out *several* tests, the chance of obtaining a false positive result in *any* test is raised. If the intention is to evaluate a null hypothesis of CSR, then a single number measuring departure of $\hat{K}(d)$ from $K_{CSR}(d)$, rather than the *K*-function may be more appropriate – so that a single test can be applied. One such number is the *maximum absolute deviation* (MAD: Ripley, 1977, 1981). This is the absolute value of the largest discrepancy between the two functions:

$$\text{MAD} = max_d \left| \hat{K}(d) - K_{CSR}(d) \right| \tag{6.8}$$

In R, we enter:

```
mad.test(bramblecanes,Kest)

## Generating 99 simulations of CSR ...
## 1,  2,  3,  4,  5,  6,  7,  8,  9, 10, 11, 12, 13, 14, 15,
## 16, 17, 18, 19, 20, 21, 22, 23, 24, 25, 26, 27, 28, 29, 30,
```

```
## 31, 32, 33, 34, 35, 36, 37, 38, 39, 40, 41, 42, 43, 44, 45,
## 46, 47, 48, 49, 50, 51, 52, 53, 54, 55, 56, 57, 58, 59, 60,
## 61, 62, 63, 64, 65, 66, 67, 68, 69, 70, 71, 72, 73, 74, 75,
## 76, 77, 78, 79, 80, 81, 82, 83, 84, 85, 86, 87, 88, 89, 90,
## 91, 92, 93, 94, 95, 96, 97, 98, 99.
##
## Done.
##
## Maximum absolute deviation test of CSR
## Monte Carlo test based on 99 simulations
## Summary function: K(r)
## Reference function: sample mean
## Interval of distance values: [0, 0.25] units (one unit = 9
## metres)
##
## data: bramblecanes
## mad = 0.016, rank = 1, p-value = 0.01
```

In this case it can be seen that the null hypotheses of CSR can be rejected at the 1% level. An alternative test is advocated by Loosmore and Ford (2006) where the test statistic is

$$u_i = \sum_{d_k = d_{min}}^{d_{max}} \left[\hat{K}_i(d_k) - \bar{K}_i(d_k) \right]^2 \delta_k \tag{6.9}$$

in which $\bar{K}_i(t_k)$ is the average value of $\hat{K}(d)$ over the simulations, the d_k are a sequence of sample distances ranging from d_{min} to d_{max} and $\delta_k = d_{k+1} - d_k$. Essentially this attempts to measure the sum of the squared distance between the functions, rather than the maximum distance. This is implemented by spatstat via the dclf.test function, which works similarly to mad.test.

```
dclf.test(bramblecanes,Kest)
```

```
## Generating 99 simulations of CSR ...
## 1, 2, 3, 4, 5, 6, 7, 8, 9, 10, 11, 12, 13, 14, 15,
## 16, 17, 18, 19, 20, 21, 22, 23, 24, 25, 26, 27, 28, 29, 30,
## 31, 32, 33, 34, 35, 36, 37, 38, 39, 40, 41, 42, 43, 44, 45,
## 46, 47, 48, 49, 50, 51, 52, 53, 54, 55, 56, 57, 58, 59, 60,
## 61, 62, 63, 64, 65, 66, 67, 68, 69, 70, 71, 72, 73, 74, 75,
## 76, 77, 78, 79, 80, 81, 82, 83, 84, 85, 86, 87, 88, 89, 90,
## 91, 92, 93, 94, 95, 96, 97, 98, 99.
##
## Done.
```

```
##
## Diggle-Cressie-Loosmore-Ford test of CSR
## Monte Carlo test based on 99 simulations
## Summary function: K(r)
## Reference function: sample mean
## Interval of distance values: [0, 0.25] units (one unit = 9
## metres)
##
## data: bramblecanes
## u = 0, rank = 1, p-value = 0.01
```

Again, results suggest rejecting the null hypothesis of CSR – see the reported *p*-value.

6.5.2 The *L*-function

An alternative to the *K*-function for identifying clustering in spatial processes is the *L*-function. This is defined in terms of the *K*-function:

$$L(d) = \sqrt{\frac{K(d)}{\pi}} \tag{6.10}$$

Although just a simple transformation of the *K*-function, its utility lies in the fact that under CSR, $L(d) = d$; that is, the *L*-function is linear, having a slope of 1 and passing through the origin. Visually identifying this in a plot of estimated *L*-functions is generally easier than identifying a quadratic function, and therefore *L*-function estimates are arguably a better visual tool. The Lest function provides a sample estimate of the *L*-function (by applying the transform in equation (6.10) to $\hat{K}(d)$) which can be used in place of Kest. As an example, recall that the envelope function could take alternatives to *K*-functions to create the envelope plot: in the following code, an envelope plot using *L*-functions for the bramble cane data is created (see Figure 6.13):

```
# Code block to produce k-function with envelope
# Envelope function
lf.env <- envelope(bramblecanes,Lest,correction="border")
# Plot it
plot(lf.env)
```

Similarly, it is possible to apply MAD tests or Lossmore and Ford tests using *L* instead of *K*. Again mad.test and dclf.test allow an alternative to *K*-functions to be specified. Indeed, Besag (1977) recommends using *L*-functions in place of *K*-functions in this kind of test. As an example, the following code applies the MAD test to the bramble cane data using the *L*-function.

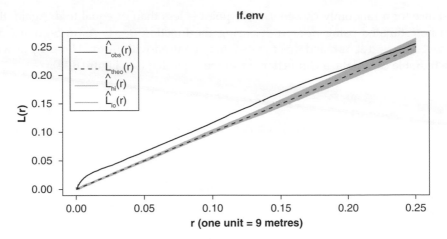

Figure 6.13 *L*-function with envelope

```
mad.test(bramblecanes,Lest)

## Generating 99 simulations of CSR ...
## 1, 2, 3, 4, 5, 6, 7, 8, 9, 10, 11, 12, 13, 14, 15,
## 16, 17, 18, 19, 20, 21, 22, 23, 24, 25, 26, 27, 28, 29, 30,
## 31, 32, 33, 34, 35, 36, 37, 38, 39, 40, 41, 42, 43, 44, 45,
## 46, 47, 48, 49, 50, 51, 52, 53, 54, 55, 56, 57, 58, 59, 60,
## 61, 62, 63, 64, 65, 66, 67, 68, 69, 70, 71, 72, 73, 74, 75,
## 76, 77, 78, 79, 80, 81, 82, 83, 84, 85, 86, 87, 88, 89, 90,
## 91, 92, 93, 94, 95, 96, 97, 98, 99.
##
## Done.
##
## Maximum absolute deviation test of CSR
## Monte Carlo test based on 99 simulations
## Summary function: L(r)
## Reference function: sample mean
## Interval of distance values: [0, 0.25] units (one unit = 9
## metres)
##
## data: bramblecanes
## mad = 0.0175, rank = 1, p-value = 0.01
```

6.5.3 The *G*-function

Yet another function used to describe the clustering in point patterns is the *G*-function. This is the cumulative distribution of the nearest neighbour distance for a randomly selected x_i. Thus, given a distance d, $G(d)$ is the probability that the nearest neighbour distance for a randomly chosen sample point is less than or equal to d. Again, this can be estimated using `spatstat`, using the function `Gest`. As in Section 6.5.2, `envelope`, `mad.test` and `dclf.test` may be used with `Gest`. Here, again with the bramble cane data, a G-function envelope is plotted (see Figure 6.14):

```
# Code block to produce G-function with envelope
# Envelope function
gf.env <- envelope(bramblecanes,Gest,correction="border")
# Plot it
plot(gf.env)
```

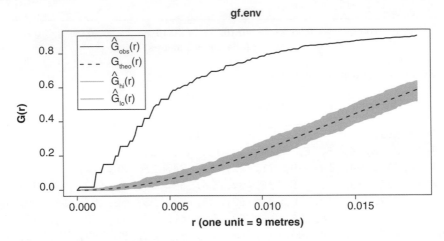

Figure 6.14 *G*-function with envelope

the estimate of the G-function for the sample is based on the empirical proportion of nearest neighbour distances less than d, for several values of d. In this case the envelope is the range of estimates for given d values, for samples generated under CSR. Theoretically, the expected G-function for CSR is

$$G(d) = 1 - \exp(-\lambda \pi d) \tag{6.11}$$

This is also plotted in Figure 6.14, as G_{theo}.

One complication is that `spatstat` stores spatial information in a different way than `sp`, `GISTools` and related packages, as noted earlier. This is not a major hurdle, but it does mean that objects of types such as `SpatialPointsDataFrame` must be converted to `spatstat`'s ppp format. This is a compendium format containing both a set of points and a polygon describing the study area *A*, and can be created from a `SpatialPoints` or `SpatialPointsDataFrame` object combined with a `SpatialPolygons` or `SpatialPolygonsDataFrame` object. This is achieved via the `as` and `as.ppt` functions from the `maptools` package.

```
require (maptools)
require (spatstat)

# Bramblecanes is a data set in ppp format from
spatstat
data (bramblecanes)

# Convert the data to SpatialPoints, and plot them
bc.spformat <- as (bramblecanes,"SpatialPoints")
plot (bc.spformat)

# It is also possible to extract the study polygon
# referred to as a window in spatstat terminology
# Here it is just a rectangle...

bc.win <- as (bramblecanes$win,"SpatialPolygons" )
plot (bc.win,add=TRUE)
```

It is also possible to convert objects in the other direction, via the as.ppp function. This takes two arguments, the coordinates of the SpatialPoints or SpatialPointsDataFrame object (extracted using the coordinates function), and an owin object created from a SpatialPolygons or SpatialPolygonsDataFrame via as.win. owin objects are single polygons used by spatstat to denote study areas, and are a component of ppp objects. In the following example, the burgres.n point dataset from GISTools is converted to ppp format and a *G*-function is computed and plotted.

```
# convert burgres. n to a ppp object
br.n.ppp <- as.ppp (coordinates (burgres.n),
  W=as.owin ((gUnaryUnion (blocks))))
br.n.gf <- Gest (br.n.ppp)
plot (br.n.gf)
```

6.6 LOOKING AT MARKED POINT PATTERNS

A further advancement of the analysis of patterns of points of a single type is the consideration of *marked* point patterns. Here, several kinds of points are considered in a dataset, instead of only a single kind. For example, in the newhaven dataset, there are point data for several kinds of crime. The term 'marked' is used, as each point is thought of as being tagged (or marked) with a specific type. As with the analysis of single kinds of points (or 'unmarked' points), the points are still treated as two-dimensional random quantities. It is also possible to apply tests and analyses to each individual kind of point – for example, testing each mark type against a null hypothesis of CSR, or computing the K-function for that mark type. However, it is also possible to examine the relationships between the point patterns of different mark types. For example, it may be of interest to determine whether forced-entry residential burglaries occur closer to non-forced-entry burglaries than one might expect if the two sets of patterns occurred independently.

One method of investigating this kind of relationship is the *cross-K-function* between marks of type i and j. This is defined as

$$K_{ij}(d) = \lambda_j^{-1} E(N_{dij}) \tag{6.12}$$

where N_{dij} is the number of events $\mathbf{x}_k$ of type j within a distance d of a randomly chosen event from all recorded events $\{\mathbf{x}_1,...,\mathbf{x}_n\}$ of type i, and λ_j is the intensity of the process marked j – measured in events per unit area (Lotwick and Silverman, 1982). If the process for points with mark j is CSR, then $K_{ij}(d) = \lambda_j \pi d^2$. A similar simulation-based approach to that set out for K, L and G in earlier sections may be used to investigate $K_{ij}(d)$ and compare it to a hypothesised sample estimate of $K_{ij}(d)$ under CSR.

The empirical estimate of $K_{ij}(d)$ is obtained in a similar way to that in equation (6.5):

$$\hat{K}_{ij}(d) = \hat{\lambda}_j^{-1} \sum_k \sum_l \frac{I(d_{kl} < d)}{n_i n_j} \tag{6.13}$$

where k indexes all of the i-marked points and l indexes all of the j-marked processes, and n_i and n_j are the respective numbers of points marked i and j. A correction (of the form in equation (6.7)) may also be applied. There is also a cross-L-function, $L_{ij}(d)$, which relates to the cross-K-function in the same way that the standard K-function relates to the standard L-function.

6.6.1 Cross-L-function Analysis in R

There is a function in spatstat, called Kcross, to compute cross-K-functions, and a corresponding function called Lcross for cross-L-functions. These take a ppp object and values for i and j as the key arguments. Since i and j refer to mark types, it is also necessary to identify the marks for each point in a ppp object. This can be done via the marks function. For example, for the bramblecanes object, the points are marked in relation to the age of the cane (see Hutchings, 1979) with three levels of age (labelled as 0, 1 and 2 in increasing order). Note that the marks are factors. These may be listed by enteing:

```
marks(bramblecanes)
```

```
##   [1] 0 0 0 0 0 0 0 0 0 0 0 0 0 0 0 0 0 0 0 0 0 0 0 0 0 0 0 0 0 0 0 0 0 0 0
##  [36] 0 0 0 0 0 0 0 0 0 0 0 0 0 0 0 0 0 0 0 0 0 0 0 0 0 0 0 0 0 0 0 0 0 0 0
##  [71] 0 0 0 0 0 0 0 0 0 0 0 0 0 0 0 0 0 0 0 0 0 0 0 0 0 0 0 0 0 0 0 0 0 0 0
## [106] 0 0 0 0 0 0 0 0 0 0 0 0 0 0 0 0 0 0 0 0 0 0 0 0 0 0 0 0 0 0 0 0 0 0 0
## [141] 0 0 0 0 0 0 0 0 0 0 0 0 0 0 0 0 0 0 0 0 0 0 0 0 0 0 0 0 0 0 0 0 0 0 0
## [176] 0 0 0 0 0 0 0 0 0 0 0 0 0 0 0 0 0 0 0 0 0 0 0 0 0 0 0 0 0 0 0 0 0 0 0
## [211] 0 0 0 0 0 0 0 0 0 0 0 0 0 0 0 0 0 0 0 0 0 0 0 0 0 0 0 0 0 0 0 0 0 0 0
## [246] 0 0 0 0 0 0 0 0 0 0 0 0 0 0 0 0 0 0 0 0 0 0 0 0 0 0 0 0 0 0 0 0 0 0 0
## [281] 0 0 0 0 0 0 0 0 0 0 0 0 0 0 0 0 0 0 0 0 0 0 0 0 0 0 0 0 0 0 0 0 0 0 0
## [316] 0 0 0 0 0 0 0 0 0 0 0 0 0 0 0 0 0 0 0 0 0 0 0 0 0 0 0 0 0 0 0 0 0 0 0
## [351] 0 0 0 0 0 0 0 0 1 1 1 1 1 1 1 1 1 1 1 1 1 1 1 1 1 1 1 1 1 1 1 1 1 1 1
## [386] 1 1 1 1 1 1 1 1 1 1 1 1 1 1 1 1 1 1 1 1 1 1 1 1 1 1 1 1 1 1 1 1 1 1 1
## [421] 1 1 1 1 1 1 1 1 1 1 1 1 1 1 1 1 1 1 1 1 1 1 1 1 1 1 1 1 1 1 1 1 1 1 1
## [456] 1 1 1 1 1 1 1 1 1 1 1 1 1 1 1 1 1 1 1 1 1 1 1 1 1 1 1 1 1 1 1 1 1 1 1
## [491] 1 1 1 1 1 1 1 1 1 1 1 1 1 1 1 1 1 1 1 1 1 1 1 1 1 1 1 1 1 1 1 1 1 1 1
## [526] 1 1 1 1 1 1 1 1 1 1 1 1 1 1 1 1 1 1 1 1 1 1 1 1 1 1 1 1 1 1 1 1 1 1 1
## [561] 1 1 1 1 1 1 1 1 1 1 1 1 1 1 1 1 1 1 1 1 1 1 1 1 1 1 1 1 1 1 1 1 1 1 1
## [596] 1 1 1 1 1 1 1 1 1 1 1 1 1 1 1 1 1 1 1 1 1 1 1 1 1 1 1 1 1 1 1 1 1 1 1
## [631] 1 1 1 1 1 1 1 1 1 1 1 1 1 1 1 1 1 1 1 1 1 1 1 1 1 1 1 1 1 1 1 1 1 1 1
## [666] 1 1 1 1 1 1 1 1 1 1 1 1 1 1 1 1 1 1 1 1 1 1 1 1 1 1 1 1 1 1 1 1 1 1 1
## [701] 1 1 1 1 1 1 1 1 1 1 1 1 1 1 1 1 1 1 1 1 1 1 1 1 1 1 1 1 1 1 1 1 1 1 1
## [736] 1 1 1 1 1 1 1 1 1 2 2 2 2 2 2 2 2 2 2 2 2 2 2 2 2 2 2 2 2 2 2 2 2 2 2
## [771] 2 2 2 2 2 2 2 2 2 2 2 2 2 2 2 2 2 2 2 2 2 2 2 2 2 2 2 2 2 2 2 2 2 2 2
## [806] 2 2 2 2 2 2 2 2 2 2 2 2 2 2 2 2
## Levels: 0 1 2
```

It is also possible to assign values to marks of a ppp object using the expression

```
marks(x) <-    . . .
```

where . . . is any valid R expression creating a factor variable with the same length of number elements as there are points in the ppp object x. This is useful if converting a SpatialPointsDataFrame into a ppp representing a marked process.

As an example here, we compute and plot the cross-L function for levels 0 and 1 of the bramblecanes object (the resultant plot is shown in Figure 6.15):

```
ck.bramble <-Lcross(bramblecanes,i=0,j=1,correction=
                    'border')
plot(ck.bramble)
```

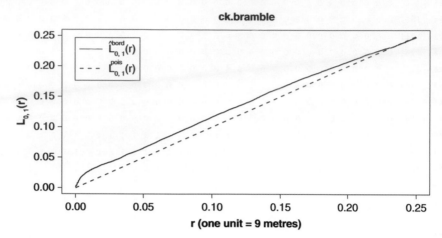

Figure 6.15 Cross-L-function for levels 0 and 1 of the bramble cane data

The `envelope` function may also be used (see Figure 6.16):

```
ckenv.bramble <- envelope(bramblecanes,Lcross,i=0,j=1,
correction='border')
plot(ckenv.bramble)
```

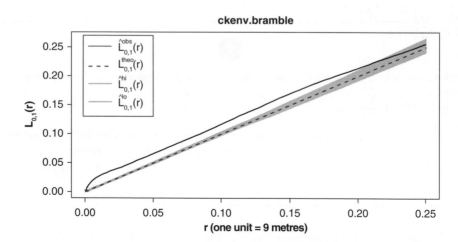

Figure 6.16 Cross-L-function envelope for levels 0 and 1 of the bramble cane data

Thus, it would seem that there is a tendency for more young (level 1) bramble canes to occur close to very young (level 0) canes. This can be formally tested, as both `mad.test` and `dclf.test` can be used with `Kcross` and `Lcross`. Here the use of `Lcross` with `dclf.test` is demonstrated:

```
dclf.test(bramblecanes,Lcross,i=0,j=1,correction='border')

## Generating 99 simulations of CSR ...
## 1, 2, 3, 4, 5, 6, 7, 8, 9, 10, 11, 12, 13, 14, 15,
## 16, 17, 18, 19, 20, 21, 22, 23, 24, 25, 26, 27, 28, 29, 30,
## 31, 32, 33, 34, 35, 36, 37, 38, 39, 40, 41, 42, 43, 44, 45,
## 46, 47, 48, 49, 50, 51, 52, 53, 54, 55, 56, 57, 58, 59, 60,
## 61, 62, 63, 64, 65, 66, 67, 68, 69, 70, 71, 72, 73, 74, 75,
## 76, 77, 78, 79, 80, 81, 82, 83, 84, 85, 86, 87, 88, 89, 90,
## 91, 92, 93, 94, 95, 96, 97, 98, 99.
##
## Done.
##
## Diggle-Cressie-Loosmore-Ford test of CSR
## Monte Carlo test based on 99 simulations
## Summary function: L["0", "1"](r)
## Reference function: sample mean
## Interval of distance values: [0, 0.25] units (one unit = 9
## metres)
##
## data: bramblecanes
## u = 0, rank = 1, p-value = 0.01
```

6.7 INTERPOLATION OF POINT PATTERNS WITH CONTINUOUS ATTRIBUTES

The previous section can be thought of as outlining methods for analysing point patterns with *categorical*-level attributes. An alternative issue is the analysis of point patterns in which the points have continuous (or measurement scale) attributes, such as height above sea level, soil conductivity or house price. A typical problem here is *interpolation*: given a sample of measurements – say $\{z_1, ..., z_n\}$ at locations $\{x_1, ..., x_n\}$ – the goal is to estimate the value of z at some new point x. Possible methods for doing this can be based on fairly simple algorithms, or on more sophisticated spatial statistical models. Here, three key measures will be covered:

1. Nearest neighbour interpolation

2. Inverse distance weighting

3. Kriging

6.7.1 Nearest Neighbour Interpolation

The first of these, *nearest neighbour interpolation*, is the simplest conceptually, and can be stated as below:

- Find i such that $|x_i - x|$ is minimised
- The estimate of z is z_i.

In other words, to estimate z at **x**, use the value of z_i at the closest observation point to **x**. Since the set of closest points to x_i for each i form the set of Thiessen (Voronoi) polygons for the set of points, an obvious way to represent the estimates is as a set of Thiessen (Voronoi) polygons corresponding to the x_i points, with respective attributes of z_i. In rgeos there is no direct function to create Voronoi polygons, but Carson Farmer[2] has made some code available to do this, providing a function called voronoipolygons. This has been slightly modified by the authors, and is listed below. Note that the modified version of the code takes the points from a spatial points data frame as the basis for the Voronoi polygons on a spatial polygons data frame, and carries across the attributes of the points to become attributes of the corresponding Voronoi polygons. Thus, in effect, if the z value of interest is an attribute in the input spatial points data frame then the nearest neighbour interpolation is implicitly carried out when using this function.

The function makes use of Voronoi computation tools carried out in another package called deldir – however, this package does not make use of Spatial* object types, and therefore this function provides a 'front end' to allow its integration with the geographical information handling tools in rgeos, sp and maptools. Do not be too concerned if you find the code difficult to interpret – at this stage it is sufficient to understand that it serves to provide a spatial data manipulation function that is otherwise not available.

```
#
# Original code from Carson Farmer
# http://www.carsonfarmer.com/2009/09/voronoi-polygons-
with-r/
# Subject to minor stylistic modifications
#
require(deldir)
require(sp)
voronoipolygons = function(layer) {
  crds <- layer@coords
  z <- deldir(crds[,1], crds[,2])
  w <- tile.list(z)
  polys <- vector(mode='list', length=length(w))
```

---

2 See http://www.carsonfarmer.com/2009/09/voronoi-polygons-with-r/

```
for (i in seq(along=polys)) {
  pcrds <- cbind(w[[i]]$x, w[[i]]$y)
  pcrds <- rbind(pcrds, pcrds[1,])
  polys[[i]] <- Polygons(list(Polygon(pcrds)),
                          ID=as.character(i))
}
SP <- SpatialPolygons(polys)
voronoi <- SpatialPolygonsDataFrame(SP,
    data=data.frame(x=crds[,1],
    y=crds[,2],
    layer@data,
    row.names=sapply(slot(SP, 'polygons'),
       function(x) slot(x, 'ID')))))
return(voronoi)
}
```

A look at the data

Having defined this function, the next stage is to use it on a test dataset. One such dataset is provided in the gstat package. This package provides tools for a number of approaches to spatial interpolation – including the other two listed in this chapter. Of interest here is a data frame called fulmar. Details of the dataset may be obtained by entering ?fulmar once the package gstat has been loaded. The data are based on airborne counts of the sea bird *Fulmaris glacialis* during August and September of 1998 and 1999, over the Dutch part of the North Sea. The counts are taken along transects corresponding to flight paths of the observation aircraft, and are transformed to densities by dividing counts by the area of observation, 0.5 km^2.

In this and the following sections you will analyse the data described above. Firstly, however, this data should be read in to R, and converted into a Spatial* object. The first thing you will need to do is enter the code to define the function voronoipolygons as listed above. The next few lines of code will read in the data (stored in the data frame fulmar) and then convert them into a spatial points data frame. Note that the fulmar sighting density is stored in column fulmar in the data frame fulmar – the location is specified in columns x and y. The point object is next converted into a Voronoi spatial polygons data frame to provide nearest neighbour interpolations. Having created both the point and Voronoi polygon objects, the code below then plots these (see Figure 6.17):

```
library(gstat)
library(maptools)
data(fulmar)
fulmar.spdf <- SpatialPointsDataFrame(cbind(fulmar$x,
                                            fulmar$y),
                                      fulmar)
```

```
fulmar.spdf <- fulmar.spdf[fulmar.spdf$year==1999,]
fulmar.voro <- voronoipolygons(fulmar.spdf)
par(mfrow=c(1,2),mar=c(0.1,0.1,0.1,0.1))
plot(fulmar.spdf,pch=16)
plot(fulmar.voro)

# reset par(mfrow)
par(mfrow=c(1,1))
```

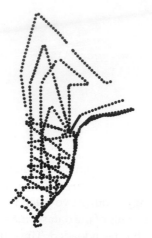 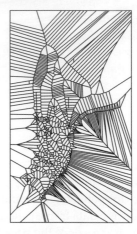

Figure 6.17 Fulmar sighting transects: (left) points; (right) Voronoi diagram

The paths of the transects become clear when the data are plotted. For the most part they are linear, although one path follows the Netherlands coast. Towards the southwest, north–south oriented paths are crossed by other zig-zag paths providing a fairly comprehensive coverage. Further north, coverage is sparser. In terms of the Voronoi diagrams, one notable artefact is that the areas of the polygons vary with the density of the points (when the points are internal) – and that edge points have polygons of infinite area (here trimmed to an enclosing rectangle). These are typical features of Voronoi polygons, but they can give rather strange characteristics to spatial interpolation. To see this, a choropleth map of the nearest neighbour densities is created. In this case, the Brewer palette `Purples` is used (higher intensity implies greater density) with break points at densities of 5, 15, 25 and 35 birds/km^2. The `par` statement controls some of the parameters used to create the plot. The `mfrow` parameter tells R to create multiple plots within the window. The plots can be thought of as a matrix, and `c(1,2)` specifies a matrix of one row and two columns – in other words, a pair of plots. The `mar` parameter specifies the margin between the drawing area in the plot and the whole area allocated. The four quantities are – in order – the bottom, left, top and right side margins in centimetres. Here these are made quite small, to allow more area to depict the map. Note that the margin area is used to add axes and titles in conventional graphs, but when working with maps with no axes, this space is not needed.

Again, some of the rather strange characteristics of the Voronoi polygon representation are apparent. In particular, the very large polygons on the edges visually dominate the interpolations somewhat, and the irregular shapes of the polygons lead to a fairly confusing visualisation. Although this approach is sometimes used as a 'quick and dirty' estimation tool (possibly as inputs to numerical models or indicators), the visual approach here does demonstrate some of the stranger characteristics of the approach. While it is possible to detect an increased density towards the north-east of the study area, it is harder to identify any subtler patterns due to the distorting effect of the variety of polygon shapes and sizes. Arguably the most problematic aspect of this approach is that the interpolated surfaces are discontinuous, and in particular that the discontinuities are an artefact of the locations of the samples. For this reason, methods such as the two others covered here are preferred. The following code results in Figure 6.18:

```
library(gstat)
library(GISTools)
sh <-shading(breaks=c(5,15,25,35),
   cols=brewer.pal(5,'Purples'))
par(mar=c(0.1,0.1,0.1,0.1))
choropleth(fulmar.voro,fulmar.voro$fulmar,shading=sh,border=NA)
plot(fulmar.voro,border='lightgray',add=TRUE,lwd=0.5)
choro.legend(px='topright',sh=sh)
```

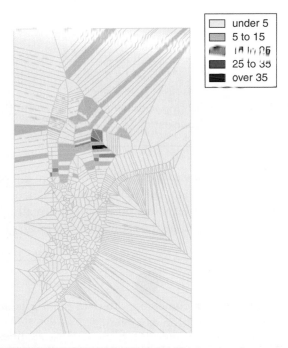

Figure 6.18 Nearest neighbour estimate of fulmar density

6.7.2 Inverse Distance Weighting

In the *inverse distance weighting* (IDW) approach to interpolation, to estimate the value of z at location $\mathbf{x}$ a weighted mean of nearby observations is taken, rather than relying on a single nearest neighbour. To accommodate the idea that observations of z at points closer to $\mathbf{x}$ should be given more importance in the interpolation, greater weight is given to these points – in particular, if w_i is the weight given to z_i, then the estimate of z at location $\mathbf{x}$ is

$$\hat{z}(\mathbf{x}) = \frac{\sum_i w_i z_i}{\sum_i w_i} \tag{6.14}$$

where

$$w_i = |\mathbf{x} - \mathbf{x}_i|^{-\alpha} \tag{6.15}$$

and $\alpha \geq 0$. Typically $\alpha = 1$ or $\alpha = 2$, giving an inverse or inverse square relationship.

There are some interesting relationships between IDW and other methods. If $\alpha = 0$ then $w_i = 1$ for all i, and z is just the mean of all the z_i regardless of location. Also, note that the ratio of w_i to w_k, where k is the index of the closest observation to $\mathbf{x}$, is

$$\left.\begin{array}{ll} \left(\dfrac{|\mathbf{x} - \mathbf{x}_k|}{|\mathbf{x} - \mathbf{x}_i|}\right)^{\alpha} & \text{if } i \neq k \\ 1 & \text{if } i = k \end{array}\right\} \tag{6.16}$$

and so if $\alpha \to \infty$ then the weighting is dominated by w_k – and the estimate of z tends to the nearest neighbour estimate.

If the value of $\mathbf{x}$ coincides with one of the $\mathbf{x}_i$ values then there is a problem with the weighting, as w_i is infinite. However, the IDW estimate is then defined to be the value of z_i. If a number (say, k) of distinct observations are all taken at the same location, so that $\mathbf{x}_{i1} = \mathbf{x}_{i2} = \ldots = \mathbf{x}_{ik}$, then the estimate is the mean of $z_{i1}, z_{i2}, \ldots, z_{ik}$.

The definition of IDW when $\mathbf{x}$ coincides with data point $\mathbf{x}_i$ is understood by noting that the IDW can be written as

---

$$\hat{z}(x) = \frac{\Sigma_i d_i^{-\alpha} z_i}{\Sigma_i d_i^{-\alpha}} \, , \text{ where } d_i = |x - x_i| \tag{6.17}$$

and if the numerator and denominator are multiplied by d_i^{α} then

$$\hat{z}(x) = \frac{z_i + d_i \, \Sigma_{k \neq i} \, d_k^{-\alpha} z_k}{1 + d_i \, \Sigma_{k \neq i} \, d_k^{-\alpha}} \tag{6.18}$$

and in the limiting case where $d_i \rightarrow 0$ this expression is just z_i as in the definition above. Also note that in the case where there are coincident locations, so that $d_{i_1} = d_{i_2} = \cdots = d_{i_k} = d$, say then by multiplying denominator and numerator by d we have

$$\hat{z}(x) = \frac{z_{i_1} + z_{i_2} + \ldots + z_{i_k} + d\Sigma_{k \notin \{i_1, \, i_2, \ldots, \, i_k\}} \, d_k^{-\alpha} z_k}{k + d\Sigma_{k \notin \{i_1, \, i_2, \ldots, \, i_k\}} \, d_k^{-\alpha}} \tag{6.19}$$

and again, as $d \rightarrow 0$ the limit is the mean of $z_{i_1}, z_{i_2}, \ldots, z_{i_k}$.

Computing IDW with the gstat package

There are a number of ways to compute IDW interpolation. Here, the gstat package will be considered. This package is also useful for kriging, the third approach to spatial interpolation covered here (Section 6.8). Thus knowledge of this package is helpful for both methods. Here, the package is demonstrated using the fulmar data used earlier. The following code carries out the IDW interpolation, and plots the interpolated surface. Firstly, you will need a set of sample points at which the IDW estimates are computed. The function spsample in the package maptools creates a sample grid.

Given a spatial polygons data frame and a number of points, if the argument type='regular' is provided, it will generate a spatial points data frame with a regular grid of points covering the polygon. The density of the grid such that the number of grid points is as close as possible to the number provided.[3] Here a grid with around 6000 points is created. Since the previous object fulmar.voro has a rectangular footprint, this causes the creation of a rectangular grid.

After this, the IDW estimate is created, using the idw function. This requires the model to be specified (here the formula fulmar~1 implies that we are performing a simple interpolation) – the x_i locations are in fulmar.spdf and the points at

---

3 It is not always possible to find a grid with *exactly* the right number of points

which estimates are made are supplied in s.grid. The parameter idp (interpolation distance parameter) is just the value of α in the IDW – here set to 1.

```
library(maptools)  # Required package
library(GISTools)  # Required package
library(gstat)  # Set up the gstat package
# Define a sample grid then use it as a set of points
# to estimate fulmar density via IDW, with alpha=1
s.grid <- spsample(fulmar.voro,type='regular',n=6000)
idw.est <- gstat::idw(fulmar~1,fulmar.spdf,
   newdata=s.grid,idp=1.0)
```

You may wonder why the idw function is referred to as gstat::idw. This is because an earlier package you loaded (spatstat) also has a function called idw. The notation here tells R you want to use the function in gstat. If you do not have spatstat loaded this notation is not needed - simply idw will do. However, if you are still in the same session where spatstat was used, it is difficult to guarantee which version of the function would be called. Using gstat::idw removes the ambiguity.

The object idw.est is a SpatialPointsDataFrame containing the IDW estimates at each of the sample points (actually a rectangular grid) in a variable called var1. pred. The next few lines extract the unique *x* and *y* locations in the grid, and format var1.pred into a matrix, predmat.

```
# Extract the distinct x and y coordinates of the grid
# Extract the predicted values and form into a matrix
# of gridded values
ux <- unique(coordinates(idw.est)[,1])
uy <- unique(coordinates(idw.est)[,2])
predmat <- matrix(idw.est$var1.pred,length(ux),length(uy))
```

Having created this, an alternative interpolation with $\alpha = 2$ is created using the same approach. The 'raw' IDW is stored in idw.est2 and then stored in the matrix predmat2:

```
idw.est2 <- gstat::idw(fulmar~1,fulmar.spdf,
                  newdata=s.grid,idp=2.0)
predmat2 <- matrix(idw.est2$var1.pred,length(ux),length(uy))
```

Finally, both of these interpolations are mapped via the `filled.contour` function. Note that this function *adds* contours to an existing plot. Drawing the `fulmar.voro` object with colours and borders set to NA is admittedly a hack, but a useful way of creating a blank plot window with the correct extent, that the filled contour plot may be added to. Finally, although the `.filled.contour` uses a different way of specifying shading and break levels, the method from `GISTools` is used to create legends. The following code produces Figure 6.19:

```
# Draw the map. The first plot command draws nothing,

par(mar=c(0.1,0.1,0.1,0.1),mfrow=c(1,2))
plot(fulmar.voro,border=NA,col=NA)
.filled.contour(ux,uy,predmat,col=brewer.pal(5,'Purples'),
               levels=c(0,2,4,6,8,30))

# Draw the legend
sh <-shading(breaks=c(2,4,6,8),
             cols=brewer.pal(5,'Purples'))
choro.legend(px='topright',sh=sh,bg='white')

plot(fulmar.voro,border=NA,col=NA)
.filled.contour(ux,uy,predmat2,col=brewer.pal(5,'Purples'),
               levels=c(0,2,4,6,8,30))
choro.legend(px='topright',sh=sh,bg='white')
```

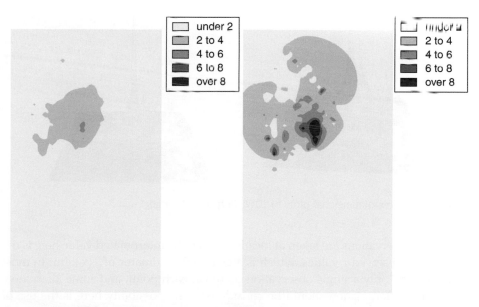

Figure 6.19 IDW Interpolation (LHS:$\alpha = 1$, RHS:$\alpha = 2$)

6.8 THE KRIGING APPROACH

Viewing the maps of fulmar density produced by the IDW approach, these appear to be more satisfactory than the nearest neighbour interpolation, at least in that they do consist of flat regions with a set of arbitrary linear discontinuities. However, one fact to note is that IDW interpolation always passes *exactly* through uniquely located measurement points. If the data are the result of very reliable measurement, and the underlying process is largely deterministic, this is fine. However, if the process is subject to random errors in measurement or sampling, or the underlying process is stochastic, there will be a degree of random variability in the observed z_i values – essentially z_i could be thought of as an expected 'true' value plus some random noise – so that $z_i = T(\mathbf{x}_i) + E_i$, where E_i is a random quantity with mean zero, and $T(\mathbf{x}_i)$ is a trend component. In these circumstances it is more useful to estimate the $T(\mathbf{x}_i)$ than z_i. Unfortunately, IDW interpolation does not do this. The problem here is that since this method passes through z_i it is interpolating the noise in the data as well as the trend. This is illustrated particularly well with perspective plots of the IDW interpolations. The spikes seen in the IDW surfaces for both $\alpha = 1$ and $\alpha = 2$ are a consequence of forcing the surface to go through random noise. The following R code will create these plots (see Figure 6.20):

```
par(mfrow=c(1,2),mar=c(0,0,2,0))
persp(predmat,box=FALSE)
persp(predmat2,box=FALSE)
```

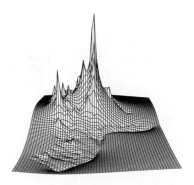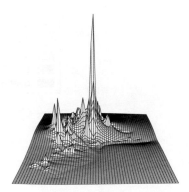

Figure 6.20   Three-dimensional plots of IDW: (left) $\alpha = 1$; (right) $\alpha = 2$

If multiple observations are taken at location $\mathbf{x}_i$ then the interpolated value here is the mean of the observed z values, which is a creditable estimator of $T(\mathbf{x}_i)$, but in most circumstances, only a single observation occurs at each point, and some alternative approach to interpolation should be considered. One possibility here is the use of *kriging* (Matheron, 1963). The theory behind this approach is relatively complex (see, for example, Cressie (1993)), but a brief outline will be given. For another practical overview of the method, see Brunsdon (2009).

6.8.1 A Brief Introduction to Kriging

In kriging, the observed quantity z_i is modelled to be the outcome of a random process:

$$z_i = f(\mathbf{x}_i) + \upsilon(\mathbf{x}_i) + \varepsilon_i \tag{6.20}$$

where $f(\mathbf{x}_i)$ is a deterministic trend function, $\upsilon(\mathbf{x}_i)$ is a random function and ε_i is a random error of observation. The deterministic trend function is typical of the sorts of function often encountered in regression models – for example, a planar or quadratic function of $\mathbf{x}$ – or often just a constant mean value function. ε_i is a random variate, associated with the measurement or sampling error at the point $\mathbf{x}_i$. ε_i is assumed to have a Gaussian distribution with mean zero and variance σ^2. This is sometimes called the 'nugget' effect – kriging was initially applied in the area of mining and used to estimate mineral concentration. However, although this was modelled as a continuous quantity, in reality minerals such as gold occur in small nuggets – and exploratory mining samples taken at certain locations would be subject to highly localised variability, depending on whether or not a nugget was discovered. This effect may well be apparent in the fulmar sighting data – an observatory flight at the right time and place may spot a flock of birds, whereas one with a marginally different flight path, or slightly earlier or later may miss this.

The final term is the random function $\upsilon(\mathbf{x})$. This is perhaps the most complex to explain. If you would like to gain some further insight into this concept, read the next section. If, however, you are happy to take the kriging approach on trust, you can skip this section.

6.8.2 Random Functions

Here, rather than a single random number, the entire function is random.

A simple example of a random function might be $f(x) = a + bx$, where a and b are random numbers (say, independent Gaussian with mean zero and variances σ_a^2, σ_b^2). Since these functions are straight lines, one can think of $\upsilon(x)$ as a straight line with a random slope and intercept. For any given value of x, one could ask what the expected value of $\upsilon(x)$ is, and also what its variance is.

It is possible to derive the mean value of $\upsilon(x)$ for any value of x by noting that

$$E(\upsilon(x)) = E(a) + E(b)x \tag{6.21}$$

and that since $E(a) = E(b) = 0$, $E(\upsilon(x)) = 0$. This implies that if a sample of several random straight lines were generated in this way, taking their average value would give something close to zero, regardless of x. However, although the average value of $v(x)$ may be close to zero, how might its variance change with x? Since a and b are independent,

$$\text{Var}(v(x)) = \sigma_a^2 + x^2\sigma_b^2 \qquad (6.22)$$

Thus, variance of the expected value of $v(x)$ increases with large absolute values of x.

Finally, suppose the function was evaluated at two values of x, say x_1 and x_2. Then some similar, but more complex, working shows that the correlation between $v(x_1)$ and $v(x_2)$ is

$$\frac{\sigma_a^2 + x_1 x_2 \sigma_b^2}{\sqrt{(\sigma_a^2 + x_1^2 \sigma_b^2)(\sigma_a^2 + x_2^2 \sigma_b^2)}} \qquad (6.23)$$

Table 6.1 Some semivariogram functions

Name	Functional form
Exponential	$\gamma(d) = a(1 - \exp(-d/b))$
Gaussian	$\gamma(d) = a(1 - \exp(-\frac{1}{2}d^2/b^2))$
Matérn	$\gamma(d) = a\left(1 - \left(2^{\kappa-1}\Gamma(\kappa)\right)^{-1}(d/b)^\kappa K_\kappa(d/b)\right)$
Spherical	$\gamma(d) = \begin{cases} a\left(\frac{3}{2}(d/b) - \frac{1}{2}(d/b)^3\right) & \text{if } d \le b \\ a & \text{otherwise} \end{cases}$

The idea here is that it is possible to define a correlation function that is related to the initial random function. It is possible, in some cases, to reverse this notion, and to define a random function in terms of the bivariate correlation function. This idea is central to kriging and geostatistics. In this case, however, a number of extensions to the above idea are applied:

- The function is defined for a vector $\mathbf{x}$ rather than a scalar x.

- Stationarity: The correlation function depends only on the distance between two vectors: say, $\rho(|\mathbf{x}_1 - \mathbf{x}_2|) = \rho(d)$ for some correlation function ρ.

- Typically the relationship is defined in terms of the *variogram*: $\gamma(d) = 2\sigma^2(1 - \rho(d))$.

- The function $v(\mathbf{x})$ is not specified directly, but deduced by 'working backwards' from $\gamma(d)$ and some observed data.

The last modification is really just convention – most practitioners of kriging specify the relationship between points in this way, rather than as a correlation or covariance. If the process is stationary, then

$$\gamma(d) = \frac{1}{2} \mathrm{E}\left[\left(v(\mathbf{x}_1) - v(\mathbf{x}_2) \right)^2 \right]$$

(6.24)

and this can be empirically estimated from data by taking average values of the squared difference of $v(\mathbf{x}_1)$ and $v(\mathbf{x}_2)$ where the distance between $\mathbf{x}_1$ and $\mathbf{x}_2$ falls into a specified band.

Not all functional forms are valid semivariograms – however, a number of functions that are valid are well known, such as those shown in Table 6.1.

In all of these functions, the degree of correlation between $v(\mathbf{x}_1)$ and $v(\mathbf{x}_2)$ is assumed to reduce as distance increases. a and b are parameters respectively controlling the scale of variance and the extent to which nearby observations are correlated. For the Matérn semivariogram, κ is an additional shape parameter, and $K_\kappa(\cdot)$ is a modified Bessel function of order κ. If K = 1/2 this is equivalent to an exponential semivariogram, and as $\kappa \to \infty$ it approaches a Gaussian semivariogram.

6.8.3 Estimating the Semivariogram

As suggested earlier, equation (6.24) can be used as a way of estimating the semivariogram. Essentially all pairwise point distances are grouped into bands, and the average squared difference between $v(\mathbf{x}_1)$ and $v(\mathbf{x}_2)$ is computed for each band. Then, for one of the semivariogram functions listed above (or possibly another), a semivariogram curve is fitted – this involves finding the values of a and b that best fit the banded average squared differences described above. Note that for the Matérn case, κ is sampled at a small number of values, rather than finding a precise optimal value.

Once this is done, although $v(\mathbf{x})$ has not been explicitly calibrated, an estimate of $\gamma(d)$ is now available. In the R package gstat the semivariogram estimation procedure is carried out with the variogram function. The boundaries argument specifies the distance bands to work with. Here it is used with the fulmar data, and the boundaries are in steps of 5 km up to 250 km. The result of this is stored in evgm. Following the calibration of the estimated semivariogram evgm, by grouped averaging as described above, a semivariogram curve is fitted – in this case a Matérn curve. The kind of curve to fit is specified in the vgm function. The parameters are, in order, an estimate of a, a specification of the kind of semivariogram (Mat is Matérn, Exp is exponential, Gau is Gaussian and Sph is spherical). The next two parameters are b and κ, respectively. Note that the values provided here are initial guesses – the `fit.variogram` function takes this specification and the `evgm` and calibrates the parameters to get a best-fit semivariogram. The result is then plotted using the `plot` function (see Figure 6.21).

```
evgm <-variogram(fulmar~1,fulmar.spdf,
                  boundaries=seq(0,250000,l=51))
fvgm <-fit.variogram(evgm,vgm(3,"Mat",100000,1))
plot(evgm,model=fvgm)
```

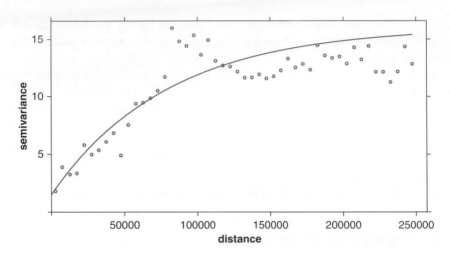

Figure 6.21 Kriging semivariogram

Once a semivariogram has been fitted it can be used to carry out the interpolation. The `fit.variogram` function estimates the 'nugget' variance discussed earlier, as well as the semivariogram parameters. Once this is done, it is possible to carry out the interpolation: essentially if a set of z_i values are available at locations x_i for $i = 1, ..., n$ and an estimate of $\gamma(d)$ is available, then $f(x)$ and $v(x)$ can be estimated for arbitrary x locations. Until this point, the estimation of the trend $f(x)$ has not been considered, but it is possible to estimate this (using more conventional regression approaches), or, if the trend is just a constant value μ, say, then the calibration of this value, and the estimation of $\mu + v(x)$ – essentially the interpolated value – can be carried out simultaneously using a technique termed *ordinary kriging* (see Wackernagel, 2003: 31, for example).

Operationally the interpolations are achieved by taking a weighted combination of the z_i values, $\Sigma_i w_i z_i$. In matrix form, if w_i is the weight applied to z_i, $\hat{\mu}$ is an estimate of μ, d_{ij} is the distance between x_i and x_j and d_i is the distance between sample location x_i and x, an arbitrary location at which it is desired to carry out the interpolation, then

$$\begin{bmatrix} w_1 \\ \vdots \\ w_n \\ 1 \end{bmatrix} = \begin{bmatrix} \gamma(d_{11}) & \cdots & \gamma(d_{1n}) & 1 \\ \vdots & \ddots & \vdots & \vdots \\ \gamma(d_{n1}) & \cdots & \gamma(d_{nn}) & 1 \\ 1 & \cdots & 1 & 0 \end{bmatrix}^{-1} \begin{bmatrix} \gamma(d_1) \\ \vdots \\ \gamma(d_n) \\ 1 \end{bmatrix}$$

(6.25)

However, users of `gstat` do not need to implement this, as it is made available via the `krige` function. This works in much the same way as the `idw` function, although the semivariogram model must also be supplied. This is carried out below, followed by a drawing of the fulmar density surface in the same way as before. An added bonus of kriging is that it is possible to obtain variances of the interpolated estimates as well as the estimate itself – these are derived from the statistical model – and stored in `var1.var`, alongside `var1.est`. They are useful, as they give an indication of the reliability of the estimates. Below, both the interpolated values and their variances are computed and shown in contour plots (Figure 6.22).

```
krig.est <-krige(fulmar~1,fulmar.spdf,newdata=s.grid,
                 model=fvgm)
predmat3 <-matrix(krig.est$var1.pred,length(ux),length(uy))
par(mar=c(0.1,0.1,0.1,0.1),mfrow=c(1,2))
plot(fulmar.voro,border=NA,col=NA)
filled.contour(ux,uy,pmax(predmat3,0),col=brewer.pal
               (5,'Purples'),
               levels=c(0,8,16,24,32,40))
sh <- shading(breaks=c(8,16,24,32),
              cols=brewer.pal(5,'Purples'))
choro.legend(px='topright',sh=sh,bg='white')
errmat3 <-matrix(krig.est$var1.var,length(ux),length(uy))
plot(fulmar.voro,border=NA,col=NA)
.filled.contour(ux,uy,errmat3,col=rev(brewer.pal
                (5,'Purples')),
                levels=c(0,3,6,9,12,15))
sh <- shading(breaks=c(3,6,9,12),
              cols=rev(brewer.pal(5,'Purples')))
choro.legend(px='topright',sh=sh,bg='white')
```

The plots show the interpolation and the variance. Note that on the variance map, levels are lowest (and hence reliability is highest) near to the transect flight paths – generally speaking, interpolations are at their most reliable when they are close to the observation locations.

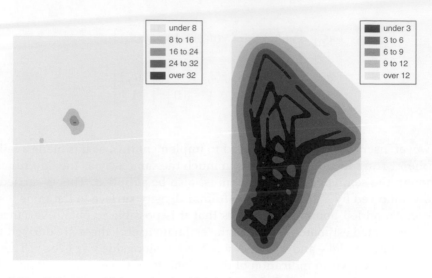

Figure 6.22   Estimates of fulmar density (right), and associated variance (left)

Finally, a perspective plot shows that although the interpolated surface is still fairly rough, some of the 'spikiness' of the IDW surface has been removed, as the surface is not forced to pass through all of the z_i (Figure 6.23).

```
persp(predmat3,box=FALSE)
```

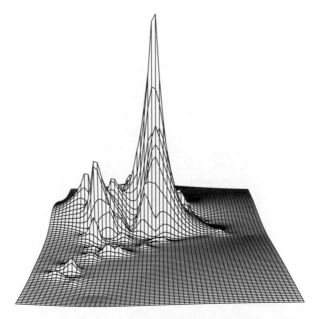

Figure 6.23   Three-dimensional plot of kriging-based interpolation

Self-Test Question 2. Try fitting an exponential variogram to the fulmar data, and creating the surface plot and maps. You may want to look at the help for fit. variogram to find out how to specify alternative variogram models.

6.9 CONCLUDING REMARKS

In this chapter, a number of techniques for analysing random patterns of two-dimensional points (with associated measurements in the case of interpolation), have been outlined. The key areas are first-order approaches (where the probability density function for the process is assumed to vary, and an attempt is made to estimate it) and second-order approaches (where the dependency between the spatial distributions of points is considered – this includes K-functions and related topics, as well as kriging). Although the chapter does not cover all possible aspects of this, it should provide an overview. As a further exercise, the reader may wish to investigate, for example, H-functions (Hansen et al., 1999) and their implementation in spatstat, or *universal kriging* (Wackernagel, 2003) where the deterministic trend function is assumed to be something more complex than a constant, as in ordinary kriging.

ANSWERS TO SELF-TEST QUESTIONS

U1. The suggested map (Figure 6.24) could be achieved with the following code:

```
# R Kernel density
require(GISTools)
data(newhaven)
# Compute Density
breach.dens <- kde.points(breach,lims=tracts)
# Create a level plot
level.plot(breach.dens)
# Use 'masking' to clip around blocks
masker <- poly.outer(breach.dens,tracts,extend=100)
add.masking(masker)
# Add the tracts again
plot(tracts,add=TRUE)
# Add the roads
plot(roads,col='grey',add=TRUE)
# Add the scale
map.scale(534750,152000,miles2ft(2),"Miles",4,0.5,
          sfcol='red')
```

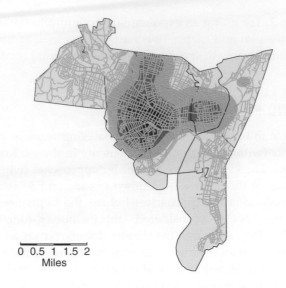

0 0.5 1 1.5 2
Miles

Figure 6.24   KDE map for breaches of the peace, with roads and map scale

Q2. The exponential variogram model is specified using the "Exp" argument in fit.variogram – the code to produce the variogram is given below, and the result is shown in Figure 6.25. Following this, the same procedures for producing a perspective plot or contour maps used in the above example may also be applied here.

```
evgm <- variogram(fulmar~1,fulmar.spdf,
                  boundaries=seq(0,250000,l=51))
fvgm <- fit.variogram(evgm,vgm(3,"Exp",100000,1))
plot(evgm,model=fvgm)
```

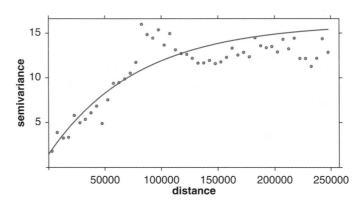

Figure 6.25   Kriging semivariogram (exponential model)

REFERENCES

Besag, J. (1977) Discussion of Dr. Ripley's paper. *Journal of the Royal Statistical Society, Series B*, 39: 193–195.

Bland, J.M. and Altman, D.G. (1995) Multiple significance tests: The Bonferroni method. *British Medical Journal*, 310: 170.

Bowman, A. and Azzalini, A. (1997) *Applied Smoothing Techniques for Data Analysis: The Kernel Approach with S-Plus Illustrations*. Oxford: Oxford University Press.

Brunsdon, C. (2009) Geostatistical analysis of lidar data. In G. Heritage and A. Large (eds), *Laser Scanning for the Environmental Sciences*. Chichester: Wiley-Blackwell.

Cressie, N. (1993) *Statistics for Spatial Data*. New York: John Wiley & Sons.

Diggle, P.J. (1983) *Statistical Analysis of Spatial Point Patterns*. London: Academic Press.

Hansen, M., Baddeley, A. and Gill, R. (1999) First contact distributions for spatial patterns: regularity and estimation. *Advances in Applied Probability*, 31: 15–33.

Hutchings, M. (1979) Standing crop and pattern in pure stands of *Mercurialis perennis and Rubus fruticosus* in mixed deciduous woodland. *Oikos*, 31: 351–357.

Loosmore, N.B. and Ford, E.D. (2006) Statistical inference using the *G* or *K* point pattern spatial statistics. *Ecology*, 87(8): 1925–1931.

Lotwick, H.W. and Silverman, B.W. (1982) Methods for analysing spatial processes of several types of points. *Journal of the Royal Statistical Society, Series B*, 44(3): 406–413.

Matheron, G. (1963) Principles of geostatistics. *Economic Geology*, 58: 1246–1266.

Ripley, B.D. (1976) The second order analysis of stationary point processes. *Journal of Applied Probability*, 13: 255–266.

Ripley, B.D. (1977) Modelling spatial patterns (with discussion). *Journal of the Royal Statistical Society, Series B*, 39: 172–212.

Ripley, B.D. (1981) *Spatial Statistics*. New York: John Wiley & Sons.

Scott, D. (1992) *Multivariate Density Estimation: Theory, Practice, and Visualization*. New York: John Wiley & Sons.

Silverman, B.W. (1986) *Density Estimation for Statistics and Data Analysis*. London: Chapman & Hall.

Tufte, E.R. (1990) *Envisioning Information*. Cheshire, CT: Graphics Press.

Wackernagel, H. (2003) *Multivariate Geostatistics*. Berlin: Springer.

7

SPATIAL ATTRIBUTE ANALYSIS WITH R

7.1 INTRODUCTION

Spatially referenced observations are a kind of data that is very similar to an ordinary dataset, for example a set of observations[1] $\{z_1, ..., z_n\}$. The only difference is that each observation is associated with some form of spatial reference – typically a point or a polygon. Unlike the processes modelled in point pattern analysis, the polygons or points are considered as fixed, non-random entities. Here, the observations $\{z_1, ..., z_n\}$ are the random quantities. In one kind of frequently used model, the probability distributions of the z_i depend on their spatial references, and some other parameters, which may need to be estimated from the data. For example, if each observation z_i is referenced by a spatial location (x_i, y_i) then it may be modelled by a normal distribution with variance σ_2 and mean $a + bx_i + cy_i$ – thus the distribution of z_i depends on the spatial location and the parameters a, b, c and σ. A model of this kind is useful for modelling broad geographical trends – for example, whether house prices to the east of a state in the US tend to be lower or higher than those to the west. This situation might be the case if the state is on the coast, and housing closer to the coast generally fetches a higher price.

An alternative approach is to model the correlation between observations z_i and z_j as dependent on their spatial references. For example, the variables $\{z_1, ..., z_n\}$ may have a multivariate normal distribution whose variance–covariance matrix (giving the covariances between each pair of z-variables) depends on the distances between points $\{(x_1, y_1), ..., (x_n, y_n)\}$. Alternatively, if the observations are associated with polygons rather than points (for example, this would be the case if the zs were unemployment rates for counties, with county boundaries expressed as polygons) then correlations or covariances could be a function of the *adjacency matrix* of the polygons: a 0–1 matrix indicating whether each polygon pair share any common boundary. This can be the case where processes can be thought of as random

---

1 Here we use z for the data values, as x and y are sometimes used to denote location.

(unlike the fixed pattern due to proximity to the coast in the last example) but still exhibiting spatial patterns – for example, the measurement of crop yields, where groups of nearby fields may exhibit similar values due to shared soil characteristics.

7.2 THE PENNSYLVANIA LUNG CANCER DATA

In this section, the dataset that will be used in the first set of examples will be introduced. This is a set of county-level lung cancer counts for 2002. The counts are stratified in ethnicity (with rather broad categories 'white' and 'other'), gender, and age ('under 40', '40 to 59', '60 to 69' and 'over 70'). In addition, a table of proportion of smokers per county is provided. Population data were obtained from the 2000 decennial census, lung cancer and smoking data were obtained from the Pennsylvania Department of Health website.[2] All of these data are provided by the SpatialEpi package – so it will be necessary to install the package and its dependencies before trying the code segments in this chapter. To do this from the command line in R, ensure your computer is connected to the internet, and that you have appropriate permissions, and then enter

```
install.packages('SpatialEpi',depend=TRUE)
```

In conjuction with GISTools, it is then possible to use this dataset – which is stored in an object called pennLC. This is a list with a number of components:

- geo A table of county IDs, with longitudes latitudes of the geographic centroid of each county

- data A table of county IDs, number of cases population subdivided by race, gender and age

- smoking A table of county IDs and proportion of smokers

- spatial.polygon A SpatialPolygons object giving the boundaries of each county in latitude and longitude (geographical coordinates)

Using the packages GISTools and rgdal, for example, standard methods may be used to produce a choropleth map of smoking uptake in Pennsylvania. In the code below (all making use of techniques from earlier chapters), the map of Pennsylvania is transformed from geographical coordinates to UTM projection[3] for zone 17. Note this has EPSG reference number[4] 3724, as is used in the spTransform function. Next a shading object is created from the lung cancer rates (rescaled to percentages and stored in smk). These are then used to create a

2 http://www.dsf.health.state.pa.us/

3 http://www.history.noaa.gov/stories_tales/geod1.html

4 http://www.epsg.org

choropleth map, and a legend, as seen in Figure 7.1. Note that this is produced on a notional window of 8 cm × 8 cm – you may have to resize the window or set `par(mar=c(0,0,0,0))` to ensure the legend is visible.

```
# Make sure the necessary packages have been loaded
require(SpatialEpi)
require(GISTools)
require(rgdal)

# Read in the Pennsylvania lung cancer data
data(pennLC)

# Extract the SpatialPolygon info
penn.state.latlong <- pennLC$spatial.polygon

# Convert to UTM zone 17N
penn.state.utm <- spTransform(penn.state.latlong,
                    CRS("+init=epsg:3724 +units=km"))

# Obtain the smoking rates
smk <- pennLC$smoking$smoking * 100

# Set up a shading object, draw choropleth and legend
shades <- auto.shading(smk,n=6,cols=brewer.pal(5,'Blues'))
choropleth(penn.state.utm,smk,shades)
choro.legend(538.5336,4394,shades,
title='Smoking Uptake (% of popn.)')
```

This produces a basic choropleth map of smoking rates in Pennsylvania. From this, it may be seen that these tend to show some degree of spatial clustering – counties having higher rates of uptake are generally near to other counties with higher rates of uptake, and similarly for lower rates of uptake. This is quite a common occurrence – and this kind of spatial clustering will be seen in the coming sections, for smoking rates, patterns in death rates, and in the classes used in the stratification of the population.

7.3 A VISUAL EXPLORATION OF AUTOCORRELATION

An important descriptive statistic for spatially referenced attribute data – and, in particular, measurement scale data – is spatial autocorrelation. In Figure 7.1 it was seen that counties in Pennsylvania tended to have similar smoking uptake rates to their neighbours. This is a way in which spatial attribute data are sometimes different from other data, and it suggests that models used for other data are not always appropriate. In particular, many statistical tests and models are based on the assumption that each observation in a set of measurements is distributed independently of the others – so

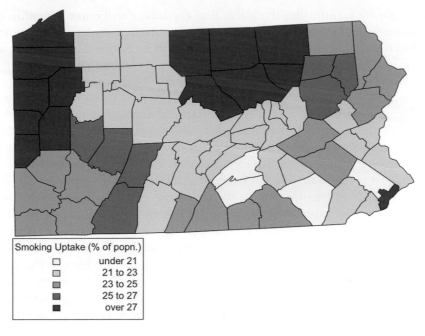

Figure 7.1 Pennsylvania smoking rates

that in a set of observations $\{z_1, ..., z_n\}$, each z_i is modelled as being drawn from, say, a Gaussian distribution, with probability density

$$\phi(z_i \mid \mu, \sigma) = \frac{1}{\sqrt{2\pi\sigma^2}} \exp\left[-\frac{(z_i - \mu)^2}{2\sigma^2}\right]$$

(7.1)

where μ and σ are respectively the population mean and standard deviation of the distribution of the data. However, the distribution itself is not a key issue here. More important is the assumption that for each z_i the distribution is independent of the other observations $\{z_1, ..., z_{i-1}, z_{i+1}, ..., z_n\}$, so that the joint distribution is

$$\Phi(\mathbf{z}) = \prod_{i=1}^{n} \phi(z_i \mid \mu, \sigma)$$

(7.2)

where $\mathbf{z}$ denotes the vector $(z_1, ..., z_n)^T$. The reason why this common assumption is important here is that it is frequently *untrue* for spatial data. Figure 7.1 suggests that it is unlikely that, say, two observations z_i and z_j are independent, if i and j index adjacent counties in Pennsylvania. It seems that a more realistic model would allow for some degree of correlation between nearby observations. Correlation of this kind is referred to as *spatial autocorrelation*. There are a number of ways in which spatial autocorrelation can be modelled, but in this section visual exploration will be considered.

We begin by scrutinising the claim that the image in Figure 7.1 really does demonstrate correlation. This can be done via significance testing in later sections, but here some useful visual approaches will be outlined. The first of these is to compare the pattern seen in the map to a set of random patterns, where the observed smoking rates are assigned randomly to counties. Here, six maps are drawn, one based on the actual data and the rest created using random permutations. These are drawn in a 3 × 2 rectangular grid arrangement. For the random part of this, the `sample` function is used. Given a single argument, which is a vector, this function returns a random permutation of that argument. If there is a second integer argument (n) which is less than the length of the first argument, it returns just *n* randomly chosen elements, drawn without replacement. Thus, the `sample(1:6,1)` expression in the following code block selects a number from 1 to 6, and the expression `sample(smk)` returns a random permutation of the smoking rates. Thus, there are two random elements in the code. Not only are five of the six maps are based on random permutations, but also the position in the figure of the actual data map is chosen at random. The idea of this second randomisation is that not even the coder will know which of the six maps represents the true data. If on inspection there is one clearly different pattern – and it appears obvious which of the maps this is, then there is strong visual evidence of autocorrelation.

```
# Set up the parameters - six plots in 3 rows by 2 cols
# set margins as smaller than usual to allow bigger maps
par(mfrow=c(3,2),mar=c(1,1,1,1)/2)

# Which one will be the real data?
real.data.i <- sample(1:6,1)

# Draw six plots.   Five will be random, one will be the
real data
for (i in 1:6) {
  if (i == real.data.i) {
    choropleth(penn.state.utm,smk,shades)}
  else {
    choropleth(penn.state.utm,sample(smk),shades)}
}
# reset par(mfrow)
par(mfrow=c(1,1))
```

Having drawn these maps (see Figure 7.2), an informal self-test is to reveal which map *is* the real data:

```
real.data.i
```

```
## [1] 4
```

Figure 7.2 Randomisation of smoking uptake ratos

Note that the results here will not be identical to those you obtain, due to the random nature of the process. One point it is worth making is that the 'random' maps do show some groups of similar neighbours – commonly this is the case: the human eye tends to settle on regularities in maps, giving a tendency to identify clusters, even when the data are generated by a process without spatial clustering. This is why procedures such as the previous one are necessary, to make visual cluster identification more robust. This approach is a variant on that due to Wickham et al. (2010).

7.3.1 Neighbours and Lagged Mean Plots

An alternative visual approach is to compare the value in each county with the average values of its neighbours. This can be achieved via the `lag.listw` function in the `spdep` library. This library provides a number of tools for handling data with spatial referencing, particularly data that are attributes of `SpatialPolygons` such as the Pennsylvania data here. A lagged mean plot can be generated if we have a list of which counties each county has as neighbours. Neighbours can be defined in several ways, but a common definition is that a pair of counties (or other polygons in different examples) who share some part of their boundaries are neighbours. If this is the *queen's case* definition, then even a pair of counties meeting at a single corner point are considered neighbours. The more restrictive *rook's case* requires that the common boundary must be a linear feature. This is illustrated in Figure 7.3.

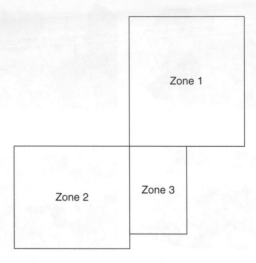

Figure 7.3 Rook's case and queen's case neighbours: zones 1 and 2 are neighbours only under queen's case; zone pairs 1,3 and 2,3 are neighbours under both cases.

Neighbour lists of either case can be extracted using the poly2nb function in spdep. These are stored in an nb object – basically a list of neighbouring polygons for each polygon.

```
require(spdep)
penn.state.nb <- poly2nb(penn.state.utm)
penn.state.nb

## Neighbour list object:
## Number of regions: 67
## Number of nonzero links: 346
## Percentage nonzero weights: 7.708
## Average number of links: 5.164
```

As seen in the block above, printing out an nb object lists various characterstics, such as the average number of neighbours each polygon has – in this case 5.164.

Note that in the default situation, queen's case neighbours are computed. To compute the rook's case, the optional argument queen=FALSE is added to poly2nb.

It is also possible to plot an nb object – this represents neighbours as a network (see Figure 7.4):

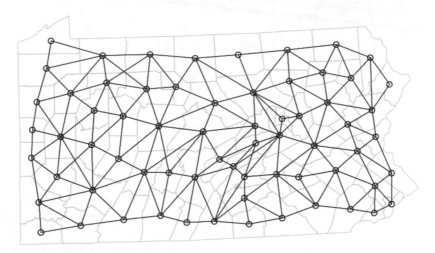

Figure 7.4 Depiction of neighbouring counties of Pennsylvania as a network (queen's case).

```
plot(penn.state.utm,border='lightgrey')
plot(penn.state.nb,coordinates(penn.state.utm),
add=TRUE,col='red')
```

Note that, to plot this network, node locations are also required. These are the second argument to the plot command for an nb object. Here, coordinates(penn.state.utm) provides the label points for the Pennsylvania counties, in UTM coordinates. Finally, the plots are also useful to compare the rook's case to the queen's case neighbourhoods (see Figure 7.5):

```
# Calculate the Rook's case neighbours
penn.state.nb2 <- poly2nb(penn.state.utm,queen=FALSE)
# Plot the counties in background
plot(penn.state.utm,border='lightgrey')
# Plot the Queen's case neighbourhoods info as a network
plot(penn.state.nb,coordinates(penn.state.utm),
add=TRUE,col='blue',lwd=2)
# Now overlay the Rook's case neighbours
plot(penn.state.nb2,coordinates(penn.state.utm),
add=TRUE,col='yellow')
```

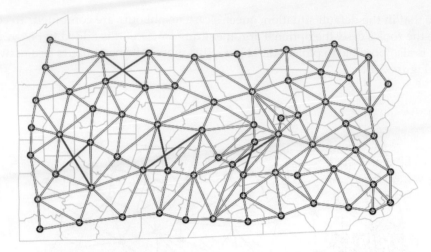

Figure 7.5 Comparison of neighbouring counties of Pennsylvania (rook's vs. queen's case).

Here the queen's case only neighbours are apparent (these are the blue links on the network) – there are eight of these. For now, we will work with rook's case neighbours. The next stage is to consider the *lagged mean plot* – as discussed above, this is a plot of the value of z_i for each polygon i against the mean of the z-values for the neighbours of polygon i. If δ_i is the set of indices of the neighbours of polygon i, and $|\delta_i|$ is the number of elements in this set, then this mean (denoted as $\tilde{z}_i$) is defined by

$$\tilde{z}_i = \sum_{j \in \delta_i} \frac{1}{|\delta_i|} z_i \qquad (7.3)$$

Thus, the lagged mean is a weighted combination of values of the neighbours. In this case, the weights are the same within each neighbour list, but in some cases they may differ (for example, if weighting were inversely related to distance between polygon centres). In spdep another kind of object – listw – is used to store a list of neighbours, together with their weights. A listw object can be created from an nb object using the nb2listw function in spdep:

```
# Convert the neighbour list to a listw object – use
Rook's case...
penn.state.lw <- nb2listw(penn.state.nb2)
penn.state.lw

## Characteristics of weights list object:
## Neighbour list object:
## Number of regions: 67
## Number of nonzero links: 330
## Percentage nonzero weights: 7.351
## Average number of links: 4.925
```

```
##
## Weights style: W
## Weights constants summary:
##      n    nn   S0      S1      S2
## W   67  4489   67   28.74   274.6
```

As a default, this function creates weights as given in equation (7.3) – this is the `'Weights style: W'` in the printout above. Other possible approaches to weights are possible – use `?nb2listw` if you wish to investigate this further. Having obtained a *listw* object, the function `lag.listw` computes a spatially lagged mean (i.e. a vector of $\tilde{z}_i$ values) – here, these are calculated, and then mapped (see Figure 7.6):

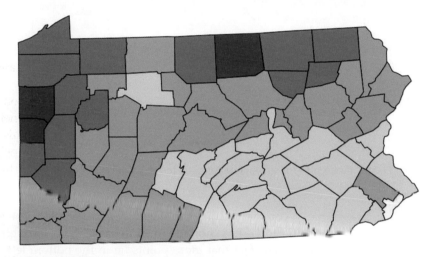

Figure 7.6 Lagged means of smoking uptake rates

```
smk.lagged.means <- lag listw(penn.state.lw,smk)
choropleth(penn.state.utm,smk.lagged.means,shades)
```

Finally, a lagged mean plot is produced – as described this is a scatter plot of z_i against $\tilde{z}_i$. Here the line $x = y$ is added to the plot as a point of reference. The idea is that when nearby polygons tend to have similar z_i values, there should be a linear trend in the plots. However, if each z_i is independent, then z_i will be uncorrelated to $\tilde{z}_i$ and the plots will show no pattern. Below, code is given to produce the plot shown in Figure 7.7:

```
plot(smk,smk.lagged.means,asp=1,xlim=range(smk),ylim=range
(smk))
abline(a=0,b=1)
abline(v=mean(smk),lty=2)
abline(h=mean(smk.lagged.means),lty=2)
```

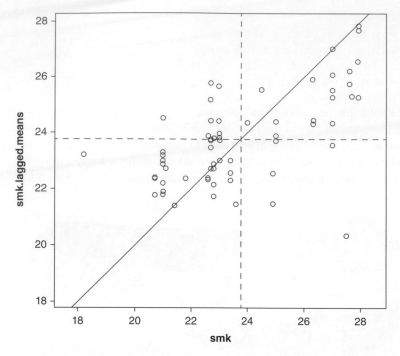

Figure 7.7 Lagged mean plot for smoking uptake – alternative method.

The `abline(a=0,b=1)` command adds the line $x = y$ to the plot. The two following `abline` commands add dotted horizontal and vertical lines through the mean values of the variables. The fact that more points lie in the bottom left and upper right quadrants created by the two lines suggests that there is some degree of positive association between z_i and $\tilde{z}_i$ – this means generally that when z_i is above average, so is $\tilde{z}_i$, and when one is below average, so is the other.

Note that this procedure is also termed a *Moran plot* or *Moran scatterplot* – see Anselin (1995, 1996). In fact there is a function that combines the above steps, and adds some functionality, called `moran.plot`. However, working through the steps is helpful in demonstrating the ways in which `spdep` handles neighbour-based data. Below, the `moran.plot` approach is demonstrated:

```
moran.plot(smk,penn.state.lw)
```

In addition to the code earlier, and as shown in Figure 7.8, this approach also identifies points with a high influence in providing a best-fit line to the plot – see, for example, Belsley et al. (1980) or Cook and Weisberg (1982).

Self-Test Question. One further modification of this approach is based on the observation that although the permutation approach does simulate no spatial

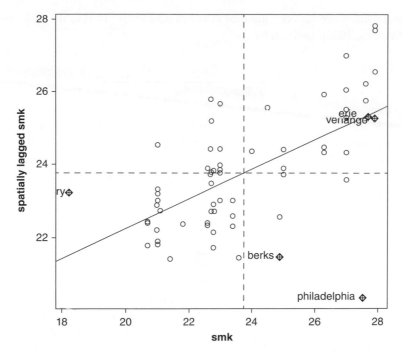

Figure 7.8 Lagged mean plot for smoking uptake – alternative method

influence on correlation, observations are in fact correlated – since the randomised data are a *permutation* of the actual data, the fact that z_i gets assigned one particular value implies that no other variables can take this value.[5] An alternative simulation would assign values to counties based on sampling *with* replacement. In this case we are no longer conditioning on the exact set of observed uptake rates, but on an empirical estimate of the cumulative distribution function of the data, assuming that observations are independent. Modify the above code to carry out this alternative approach. Hint: use the help facility to find the optional arguments to the sample function.

7.4 MORAN'S *I*: AN INDEX OF AUTOCORRELATION

In this section, the exploratory approaches of Section 7.3 will be taken a step further. As stated earlier, autocorrelation is the tendency of z_i values of nearby polygons to be related. Rather like the Pearson correlation coefficient, which measures the dependency between a pair of variables, there are also coefficients (or indices)

---

5 Unless there are repeated values in the data, but even then a similar argument applies.

to measure autocorrelation. One that is very commonly used is the *Moran's I coefficient* (Moran, 1950), defined by

$$I = \frac{n}{\Sigma_i \Sigma_j w_{ij}} \frac{\Sigma_i \Sigma_j w_{ij}(z_i - \bar{z})(z_j - \bar{z})}{\Sigma_i(z_i - \bar{z})^2} \qquad (7.4)$$

where w_{ij} is the (i, j)th element of a weights matrix $\mathbf{W}$, specifying the degree of dependency between polygons j and j. As before, this could be a neighbour indicator, so that $w_{ij} = 1$ if polygons i and j are neighbours and $w_{ij} = 0$ otherwise, or the rows of the matrix could be standardised to sum to 1, in which case $\mathbf{Wz}$ is the vector of lagged means $\tilde{z}_i$ as defined in Section 7.3.

You may have noticed that the matrix $\mathbf{W}$ contains the same information as the `listw` objects discussed earlier. This is certainly true, but the latter stores information in quite a different, and usually more compact, way. The `listw` object notes, for each polygon, a list of its neighbours and their associated weights. For the polygon's non-neighbours, nothing needs to be stored. On the other hand, the $\mathbf{W}$ matrix has $n \times n$ elements. Each row of $\mathbf{W}$ contains information for *all* n polygons – although for many of them, $w_{ij} = 0$. Computation using the matrix form in R is generally less efficient – for example, although $\mathbf{Wz}$ is the vector of spatially lagged means, computing it directly as W %*% z would result in several numbers being multiplied by zero, and these resultant zeros being added up. If there are a lot of polygons, and typically they have, say, four or five neighbours, then the matrix format would also have a much higher storage overhead – and much of this would be filled with zeros.

Given the computational advantages of `listw`, why consider matrices? There are two important reasons. First, when considering the algebraic properties of quantities like Moran's I, matrix expressions are easy to manipulate. Second, although it is mostly the case that the `listw` form is more compact, it does store two items of data for every neighbour – the index of the neighbouring polygon, and the associated weight. Thus, if neighbours were defined in a very permissive way, so that $\mathbf{W}$ had few zero elements, the storage overheads might exceed that for standard matrices. A matrix with no zeros requires n^2 items of information, but the `listw` form requires $2n^2$. In this situation, calculations would also take longer. This is also true when the result of a computation has few zeros even if the supplied input does, as is the case in matrix inversion, for example.

It is also worth noting that, if $\mathbf{W}$ is standardised so that its rows sum to 1, then $\Sigma_i\Sigma_j w_{ij} = n$. In this case, equation (7.4) simplifies to

$$I = \frac{\Sigma_i\Sigma_j w_{ij}q_iq_j}{\Sigma_i q_i^2} \tag{7.5}$$

where $q_i = z_i - \bar{z}$; that is, q_i is z_i recentred around the mean value of z. If the vector of q_is is written as $\mathbf{q}$ then equation (7.5) may be written in vector–matrix form as

$$I = \frac{\mathbf{q}^T\mathbf{W}\mathbf{q}}{\mathbf{q}^T\mathbf{q}} \tag{7.6}$$

It may be checked that if the q_is are plotted in a lagged mean plot – as in Figure 7.8 or 7.7, and a regression line is fitted, then I is the slope of this line. This helps to interpret the coefficient. Larger values of I suggest that there is a stronger relationship between nearby z_i values. Furthermore, I may be negative in some circumstances – suggesting that there can be a degree of inverse correlation between nearby z_i values, giving a checkerboard pattern on the map. For example, a company may choose to site a chain of stores to be spread evenly across the state, so that occurrence of a store in one county may imply that there is no store in a neighbouring county.

7.4.1 Moran's *I* in R

The package spdep provides functions to evaluate Moran's I for a given dataset and W matrix. As noted in the earlier information box, it is sometimes more effective to store the W matrix in listw form – and this is done for the computation of Moran's I here. The function used to compute Moran's I is called moran.test – and can be used as below:

```
moran.test(smk,penn.state.lw)

##
## Moran's I test under randomisation
##
## data:        smk
## weights: penn.state.lw
##
## Moran I statistic standard deviate = 5.418, p-value =
    3.022e-08
## alternative hypothesis: greater
## sample estimates:
## Moran I statistic      Expectation      Variance
##          0.404431         -0.015152      0.005998
```

The above code supplies more than the actual Moran's I estimate itself – but for now note that the value is about 0.404 for the Pennsylvania smoking uptake data.

This is fine, but one problem is deciding whether the above value of I is sufficiently high to suggest that an autocorrelated process model is a plausible alternative to an assumption that the smoking uptake rates are independent. There are two issues here:

1. Is this value of I a relatively large level on an absolute scale?

2. How likely is the observed I value, or a larger value, to be obversed if the rates *were* independent?

The first of these is a benchmarking problem. Like correlation, Moran's I is a dimensionless property – so that, for example, with a given set of polygons and associated **W** matrix, area-normalised rates of rainfall would have the same Moran's I regardless of whether rainfall was measured in millimetres or inches. However, while correlation is always restricted to lie within the range [−1, 1] – making, say a value of 0.8 reasonably easy to interpret – the range of Moran's I varies with the **W** matrix. This may be computed – see de Jong et al. (1984). For the **W** matrix here, I can range between −0.579 and 1.020. Thus on an absolute scale the reported value suggests a reasonable degree of spatial autocorrelation.

The maximum and minimum values of I are shown (in de Jong et al., 1984) to be the maximum and minimum values of the eigenvalues of $(\mathbf{W} + \mathbf{W}^T)/2$. If you do not know what an eigenvalue is, do not worry too much. However, if you would like to find out, it is generally discussed in introductory textbooks on linear algebra, such as Marcus and Minc (1988). An R function to find the maximum and minimum I values from a `listw` object is defined below. `listw2mat` converts a `listw` object to a matrix.

```
moran.range <- function(lw) {
  wmat <- listw2mat(lw)
  return(range(eigen((wmat + t(wmat))/2)$values))
}
moran.range(penn.state.lw)
## [1] -0.5786     1.0202
```

The second issue is essentially a classical statistical inference problem. Assuming a null hypothesis of no spatial autocorrelation, what is the probability of obtaining a sample Moran's I as extreme as (or more extreme than) the observed one? This probability is the p-value for the hypothesis of no spatial autocorrelation.

However, the null hypothesis statement 'no spatial autocorrelation' is quite broad, and two more specific hypotheses will be considered here. The first is the assumption that each z_i is drawn from an independent Gaussian distribution, with mean μ and variance σ_2. Under this assumption, it can be shown that I is approximately normally distributed with mean $E(I) = -1/(n-1)$. The variance of this distribution is quite complex – readers interested in seeing the formula could consult, for example, Fotheringham et al. (2000). If the variance is denoted $V_{norm}(I)$ then the test statistic is

$$\frac{I - E(I)}{V_{norm}(I)} \tag{7.7}$$

This will be approximately normally distributed with mean 0 and variance 1, so that p-values may be obtained by comparison with the standard normal distribution.

The other form of the test is a more formal working of the randomisation idea set out in Section 7.3. In this case, no assumption is made about the distribution of the z_i – but it is assumed that any permutation of the z_i against the polygons is equally likely. Thus, the null hypothesis is still one of 'no spatial pattern', but it is conditional on the observed data. Under this hypothesis, it is also possible to compute the mean and variance of I. As before, the expected value if I is $E(I) = -1/(n-1)$; the formula for the variance is different from that for the normality assumption, but also complex – again the formula is given in Fotheringham et al. (2000). If this variance is denoted by $V_{rand}(I)$ then the test statistic is

$$\frac{I - E(I)}{V_{rand}(I)}. \tag{7.8}$$

In this case, the distribution of the text statistic in expression (7.8) is also close to the normal distribution – and the quantity in this expression can also be compared to the normal distribution with mean 0 and variance 1 to obtain p-values. Both kinds of test are available in R via the `moran.test` function shown earlier. As noted earlier, as well as Moran's I statistic itself, this function prints out some further information. In particular, looking again at this output, it can be seen that the expectation, variance and test statistic for Moran's I statistic is output (the test statistic is labelled 'Moran I statistic standard deviate'), as well as the associated p-value. As a default, the output refers to the randomised hypotheses – that is, $V_{rand}(I)$ is used. Thus, looking at the output from `moran.test(smk,penn.state.lw)` again, it can be seen that there is strong evidence to reject the randomisation null hypothesis in favour of an alternative hypothesis of $I > 0$ for the smoking uptake rates.

The argument `randomisation` allows the normal distribution assumption, and hence $V_{norm(I)}$ to be used instead:

```
moran.test(smk,penn.state.lw,randomisation=FALSE)
```

##

```
## Moran's I test under normality
##
## data:        smk
## weights: penn.state.lw
##
## Moran I statistic standard deviate = 5.449, p-value =
    2.53e-08
## alternative hypothesis: greater
## sample estimates:
## Moran I statistic      Expectation      Variance
##            0.404431       -0.015152      0.005929
```

From this, it can be seen that there is also strong evidence to reject the null hypothesis of the z_i being independently normally distributed, again in favour of an alternative that $I > 0$.

7.4.2 A Simulation-Based Approach

The previous tests approximate the test statistic by a normal distribution with mean 0 and variance 1. However, this distribution is asymptotic – that is, as n increases, the actual distribution of the test statistic gets closer to the normal distribution. The rate at which this happens is affected by the arrangement of the polygons – essentially, in some cases, the value of n for which a normal approximation is reasonable is lower than for others (Cliff and Ord, 1973, 1981).

For this reason, it may be reasonable to employ a simulation-based approach here, instead of using a theoretical, but approximate approach. In this approach – which applies to the permutation-based hypothesis – a number of random permutations (say, 10,000) of the data are drawn, and assigned to polygons, using the `sample` function in R, as in Section 7.3. For each randomly drawn permutation, Moran's I is computed. This provides a simulated sample of draws of Moran's I from the randomisation null hypothesis. The true Moran's I is then computed from the data. If the null hypothesis is true, then the probability of drawing the observed data is the same as any other permutation of the z_i among the polygons. Thus, if m just the number if simulated Moran's I values exceeding the observed one, and M is the total number of simulations, then the probability of getting the observed Moran's I or a greater one is

$$p = \frac{m+1}{M+1} \tag{7.9}$$

This methodology is due to Hope (1968). The function `moran.mc` in `spdep` allows this to be computed:

```
moran.mc(smk,penn.state.lw,10000)

##
##    Monte-Carlo simulation of Moran's I
##
## data:     smk
## weights: penn.state.lw
## number of simulations + 1: 10001
##
## statistic = 0.4044, observed rank = 10001, p-value =
   9.999e-05
## alternative hypothesis: greater
```

Note that the third argument provides the number of simulations. Once again, there is evidence to reject the null hypothesis that any permutation of z_i is equally likely in favour of the alternative that $I > 0$.

7.5 SPATIAL AUTOREGRESSION

Moran's I, which has been discussed in the previous sections, can be thought of as a measure of spatial autocorrelation. However, up to this point no consideration has been given to a *model* of a spatially autocorrelated process. In this section, two spatial models will be considered – these are termed *spatial autoregressive* models. Essentially they regress the z_i value for any given polygon on values of z_j for neigh-bouring polygons. The two models that will be considered are the *simultaneous autoregressive* (SAR) and *conditional autoregressive* (CAR) models. In each one, the models can also be thought of as multivariate distributions for z, with the variance–covariance matrix being dependent on the W matrix considered earlier.

The SAR model may be specified as

$$z_i = \mu + \sum_{j=1}^{n} b_{ij}\left(z_j - \mu\right) + \varepsilon_i \tag{7.10}$$

where ε_i has a Gaussian distribution with mean 0 and variance σ_i^2 (often $\sigma_i^2 = \sigma^2$ for all i, so that the variance of ε_i is constant across zones), $E(z_i) = \mu$ and b_{ij} are constants, with $b_{ii} = 0$ and usually $b_{ij} = 0$ if polygon i is not adjacent to polygon j – thus, one possibility is that b_{ij} is λw_{ij}. Here, λ is a paramater specifying the degree of spatial dependence. When $\lambda = 0$ there is no dependence; when it is positive, positive autocorrelation exists; and when it is negative, negative correlation exists. μ is an overall level constant (as it is in a standard normal distribution model). If the rows of **W** are normalised to sum to 1, then the deviation from u for z_i is dependent on the deviation from μ for the z_j values for its neighbours.

The CAR model is specified by

$$z_i \mid \left\{ z_j : j \neq i \right\} \sim N\left(\mu + \sum_{j=1}^{n} c_{ij}\left(z_j - \mu \right), \tau_i^2 \right)$$ (7.11)

where, in addition to the above definitions, $N\ (.,.)$ denotes a normal distribution with the usual mean and variance parameters, τ_i^2 is the conditional variance of z_i given $\{z_j : j \neq i\}$ and c_{ij} are constants such that $c_{ii} = 0$ and, as with b_{ij} in the SAR model, typically $c_{ij} = 0$ if polygon i is not adjacent to polygon j. Again, a common model is to set $c_{ij} = \lambda w_{ij}$. μ and λ have similar interpretations to the SAR model. A detailed discussion in Cressie (1991) refers to the matrices $\mathbf{B} = [b_{ij}]$ and $\mathbf{C} = [c_{ij}]$ as 'spatial dependence' matrices. Note that this model can be expressed as a multivariate normal distribution in $\mathbf{z}$ as

$$\mathbf{z} \sim N(\mu \mathbf{1}, (\mathbf{I} - \mathbf{C})^{-1}\mathbf{T})$$ (7.12)

where $\mathbf{1}$ is a column vector of 1s (of size n) and $\mathbf{T}$ is a diagonal matrix composed of the τ_i – see Besag (1974), for example. Note that this suggests that the matrix $(\mathbf{I} - \mathbf{C})^{-1}\mathbf{T}$ must be symmetrical.[6] If the $\mathbf{W}$ matrix is row-normalised, and the $c_{ij} = \lambda w_{ij}$ model is used, then this implies that τ_i must be proportional to $\left[\sum_j c_{ij} \right]^{-1}$.

7.6 CALIBRATING SPATIAL REGRESSION MODELS IN R

The SAR model may be calibrated using the `spautolm` function from *spdep*. This uses the notation also used in the `lm` function – and related functions – to specify models. In the next section, the SAR and CAR models will be expanded to consider further predictor variables, rather than just neighbouring values of z_i. However, for now the basic model may be specified by using the notation for a linear model with just a constant term for the mean of the predicted variable – this is μ in equation (7.11) or (7.10). This is simply `Var.Name ~ 1`, with `Var.Name` replaced with the actual variable name of interest (for example, `smk` in the smoking rate examples used in previous sections). A further parameter, `family`, specifies whether an SAR or a CAR model is fitted. The function returns a regression model object – among other things, this allows the values of coefficients, fitted values and so on to be extracted. An example of use is as follows:

```
sar.res <- spautolm(smk~1,listw=penn.state.lw)
sar.res

##
## Call:
```

6 And also positive definite.

```
## spautolm(formula = smk ~ 1, listw = penn.state.lw)
##
## Coefficients:
## (Intercept)        lambda
##      23.7689       0.6179
##
## Log likelihood: -142.9
```

From this it can be seen that $\lambda = 0.618$ and $\mu = 23.769$, to 3 decimal places. While the estimate for μ is easily interpretable, deciding where the reported level of λ is of importance is harder. One possibility is to find the standard error of λ – this is reported as the `lambda.se` component of the spatial autoregression object:

```
sar.res$lambda.se
```

```
## [1] 0.113
```

An approximate 5% confidence interval can be found in the standard way – by finding a band given by the estimate of λ plus or minus twice the standard error:

```
sar.res$lambda + c(-2,2)*sar.res$lambda.se
```

```
## [1] 0.3919 0.8440
```

As before, this suggests that a null hypothesis of $\lambda = 0$ is highly unlikely.

It is also possible to calibrate CAR models in the same way, and similarly obtain an approximate confidence interval for λ. This is achieved - in our example - via the `family` parameter to `spautolm`:

```
car.res <- spautolm(smk~1,listw=penn.state.lw,
family='CAR')
car.res
```

However, at the time of writing, the help document for this function points out:

> the function does not (yet) prevent asymmetric spatial weights being used with 'CAR' family models. It appears that both numerical issues (convergence in particular) and uncertainties about the exact spatial weights matrix used make it difficult to reproduce ... results,

Experimentation with the above code suggests similar convergence issues occur here, hence attention will be focused on SAR model for the R examples.

7.6.1 Models with Predictors: A Bivariate Example

Both the CAR and SAR models can be modified to include predictor variables as well as incorporate autocorrelation effects. This is achieved by replacing a constant μ by an observation-specific μ_i for each z_i, where μ_i is some function of a predictor variable (say, P_i). If the relationship between μ_i and P_i is linear, we can write, for the SAR case:

$$z_i = a_0 + a_1 P_i + \sum_{j=1}^{n} b_{ij}\left(z_j - a_0 - a_1 P_i\right) + \varepsilon_i \tag{7.13}$$

where a_0 and a_1 are effectively intercept and slope terms in a regression model. The key difference between this kind of model and a standard ordinary least squares (OLS) model is that for the OLS case the z_i values are assumed to be independent, whereas here nearby z_j values influence z_i as well as the predictor variable.

Calibrating models such as that in equation (7.13) in R is straigh forward, and involves including predictor variables in the model argument for spautolm. In the following example, a new data item, the per-county lung cancer rate for Pennsylvania in 2002, is computed and used as the z_i variable. This time the role of the smoking uptake variable is changed to that of the predictor variable, P_i. This is acheived via a two-stage process:

- Compute the per-county lung cancer rates

- Compute the regression model

For stage 1, the plyr package is used to manipulate the data. Recall that pennLC is a list, and one of the elements (called data) is a data frame giving the counts of population, and lung cancer incidence, for each county in Pennsylvania subdivided by race ('white' or 'other'), gender ('male' or 'female') and age ('under 40', '40 to 59', '60 to 69', and 'over 70'). The format of the data frame uses a county column and three *substrata* columns – together specifying a combination of county, age, gender and ethnicity. Two further columns then specify the count of cases for that county–substrata combination, and also the overall population for the same county–substrata combination:

```
head(pennLC$data)
```

```
##      county   cases   population   race   gender        age
## 1     adams       0         1492      o        f   Under.40
## 2     adams       0          365      o        f      40.59
## 3     adams       1           68      o        f      60.69
## 4     adams       0           73      o        f        70+
## 5     adams       0        23351      w        f   Under.40
## 6     adams       5        12136      w        f      40.59
```

For example, it may be seen that Adams County has 0 incidents of lung cancer for non-white[7] females under 40 out of a total population of 1492 female non-white people under 40 in Adams County. Using the `plyr` package, it is possible to create a data frame showing the total number of cases over all combinations of age, race and gender for each county:

```
require(plyr)
totcases <- ddply(pennLC$data,c("county"),numcolwise(sum))
```

`plyr` is a very powerful package very much worth reading more about – see Wickham (2011). It applies a *split-apply-combine* approach to data manipulation. A number of functions are supplied to apply this approach for various formats of variable. Here, `ddply` is used. A dataset is supplied, `pennLC$data`, and one of the factor (or character) column names is given (`county`) in this example. The data frame is *split* into a list of smaller data frames, one for each value of the `county` variable. Next, a function is *applied* to each of these data frames, giving a list of transformed data frames - quite often the new data frame is a smaller one, often having only one row consisting of summary statistics (or sums or counts) for some selected rows of the data frames arising from the split. Finally, the list of transformed data frames is *combined* by row-wise stacking to create a new data frame. Hence *split-apply-combine*.

In the code above, the function applied to a subset data frame for each county is created via `numcolwise(sum)`. This transforms the basic sum function, which applies to vectors, to a new function which sums all numeric columns in a data frame, yielding a one-row data frame with sums of numeric columns. Here these columns are the number of incidents of lung cancer, and the population. After applying this function to each subset of the data, the countywise totals for lung cancer incidents and populations are recombined to give a data frame with county name, county total lung cancer cases, and county total population – in the data frame `totcases`:

```
head(totcases)
```

```
##          county      cases      population
## 1         adams         55           91292
```

---

7 Here 'o' denotes 'other' – that is, 'non-white'.

```
##   2   allegheny        1275        1281666
##   3   armstrong          49          72392
##   4      beaver         172         181412
##   5     bedford          37          49984
##   6       berks         308         373638
```

The expression `numcolwise(sum)` may look a little strange. `numcol-`
`wise` is a function, but, unusually, it takes another function as its input, and
returns yet another function as output. The input function is assumed to
apply to standard R numerical vectors – it is modified by `numcolwise` to
produce a new function that applies the input function to data frames on a
row-by-row basis, and returns a single row data frame of the results. Note
that since in this example `sum` is the input function, it is only valid for numerical data columns. The `numcolwise` column allows for this, and the modified function only returns entries in the output data frame for numerical
columns. Although it would not make much sense in this example, functions
like `mean` and `median` could also be used as inputs to `numcolwise` – or
indeed user-defined numeric functions.

In the example the output function is then fed into `ddply` to provide the
apply stage function in the *split–apply–combine* procedure.

Having created a data frame of county-based lung cancer incident and population
counts, the cancer rates per 10,000 population are computed. These are added as a
new column to the `totcases` data frame:

```
totcases <- transform(totcases,rate=10000*cases/
population)
```

Thus, `totcases` now has three columns, and is ready to provide input to the
regression model – below this variable is inspected (using `head`) and a box-and-
whisker plot drawn in Figure 7.9:

```
head(totcases)
```

```
##            county   cases   population    rate
##   1         adams      55        91292   6.025
##   2     allegheny    1275      1281666   9.948
##   3     armstrong      49        72392   6.769
##   4        beaver     172       181412   9.481
```

```
##    5      bedford      37      49984    7.402
##    6        berks     308     373638    8.243
```

```
# Check the distribution of rates
boxplot(totcases$rate,horizontal=TRUE,
        xlab='Cancer Rate (Cases per 10,000 Popn.)')
```

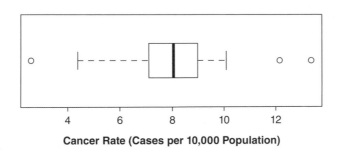

Cancer Rate (Cases per 10,000 Population)

Figure 7.9 Boxplot of cancer rates, Pennsylvania, 2002

It is now possible to calibrate the spatial regression model. As stated earlier, the z_i variable here is related to the cancer rate, and the predictor is smoking uptake. Note that in this case an additional weighting variable is added, based on the population variable, and also that z_i is actually the square root of the cancer rate. This allows for the fact that the random variable here is actually the count of cancer cases – and that this is possibly a Poisson distributed variable – since the square root transform can stabilise the variance of Poisson count data (Bartlett, 1936). Since the square root rate is essentially

$$\sqrt{\frac{\text{No. of cases}}{\text{Population}}} \tag{7.14}$$

and population is assumed a fixed quantity, the numerator above will have an approximately fixed variance and be reasonably approximated by a normal distribution. Dividing this by the square root of population then makes the variance inversely proportional to the population. Hence, weighting by population is also appropriate here. Taking these facts into account, the SAR model may be calibrated and assessed:

```
sar.mod <- spautolm(rate~sqrt(smk),listw=penn.state.lw,
                    weight=population,data=totcases)
```

```
summary(sar.mod)
```

```
##
## Call:
## spautolm(formula = rate ~ sqrt(smk), data = totcases,
    listw = penn.state.lw,
## weights = population)
##
## Residuals:
##      Min         1Q     Median        3Q        Max
## -5.45183   -1.10235   -0.31549   0.59901    5.00115
##
## Coefficients:
##                  Estimate  Std. Error  z value    Pr(>|z|)
## (Intercept)      -0.35263     2.26795  -0.1555      0.8764
## sqrt(smk)         1.80976     0.46064   3.9288   8.537e-05
##
## Lambda: 0.3806 LR test value: 6.312 p-value: 0.01199
## Numerical Hessian standard error of lambda: 0.1398
##
## Log likelihood: -123.3
## ML residual variance (sigma squared): 209030,
    (sigma: 457.2)
## Number of observations: 67
## Number of parameters estimated: 4
## AIC: 254.6
```

The 'coefficients' section in the output may be interpreted in a similar way to a standard regression model. From this it can be seen that the rate of smoking does influence the rate of occurrence of lung cancer, or at least that there is evidence to reject a null hypothesis that it does not effect cancer rates, with $p = 8.537 \times 10^{-5}$. The 'lambda' section provides a p-value for the null hypothesis that $\lambda = 0$ – that is, that there is a degree of spatial autocorrelation in the cancer rates. Here, $p = 0.01199$, so that at the 5% level there is evidence to reject the null hypothesis, although the strength of evidence just falls short of the 1% level.

Thus, the analysis here suggests that smoking is linked to lung cancer, but that lung cancer rates are spatially autocorrelated. This is possibly because other factors that influence lung cancer (possibly age, or risk associated with occupation) are geographically clustered. Since these factors are not included in the model, information about their spatial arrangement might be inferred via nearby occurrence of lung cancer.

7.6.2 Further Issues

The above analysis gave a reasonable insight into the occurrence of lung cancer in Pennsylvania as a spatial process. However, a number of approximations were made. A more exact model could have been achieved if a direct Poisson model had been used, rather than using an approximation via square roots. Indeed, if an independent z_i model were required, where the z_i were case counts, then a straighforward Poisson regression via `glm` could have achieved this. However, a Poisson model with an autocorrelated error term is less straightforward. One approach might be to use a Bayesian Markov chain Monte Carlo approach for this kind of model – see Wolpert and Ickstadt (1998) for an example. In R, this type of approach can be achieved using the `RJags` package.[8]

7.6.3 Troubleshooting Spatial Regression

In this section, a set of the issues with spatial models based on **W** matrices will be explored. These issues are identified in Wall (2004). The issues identify certain strange characteristics in some spatial models – and possibly interactive exploration via R is an important way of identifying whether these issues affect a particular study. For this exercise you will look at the Columbus crime data supplied with the `spdep` package.[9] Typing in the following will load the shapefile of neighbourhoods in Columbus, Ohio, and create a map (Figure 7.10):

```
columbus <- readShapePoly(
          system.file("etc/shapes/columbus.shp",
          package="spdep")[1])
# Create a plot of columbus
plot(columbus, col = "wheat")
# Add labels for each of the zones
text(coordinates(columbus), as.character(1:49), cex = 0.8)
# The box just makes things look neater
box(which = "outer", lwd = 2)
```

This dataset has been used in a number of studies. For each neighbourhood, a number of attributes are provided, including 'average house price', 'burglary rate' and 'average income'. However, here these will not be considered, as the focus will be on the correlation structure implied by the **W** matrix. Here, a queen's case matrix is extracted from the data. The adjacency plays an important role in a SAR model. Recall there are also several options in terms of specifying the definition of polygon adjacency – in particular the rook's case and queen's case. Both of these can be computed from `columbus`, which is a `SpatialPolygonsDataFrame` object.

```
# Extract a 'queen's case' adjacency object and print it out
col.queen.nb <- poly2nb(columbus,queen=TRUE)
col.queen.nb
```

8 http://cran.r-project.org/web/packages/rjags/index.html
9 http://www.rri.wvu.edu/WebBook/LeSage/spatial/anselin.html, http://dae.unizar.es/docencia/regional/spacestat\%20Tutorial.pdf

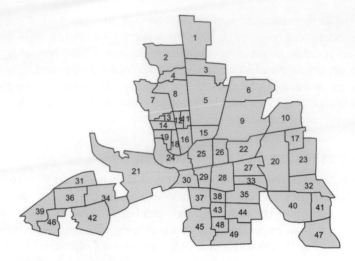

Figure 7.10 Shapefile of neighbourhoods in Columbus, Ohio, with labels

```
## Neighbour list object:
## Number of regions: 49
## Number of nonzero links: 236
## Percentage nonzero weights: 9.829
## Average number of links: 4.816

# Extract a 'rook's case' adjacency object and print it
out
col.rook.nb <- poly2nb(columbus,queen=FALSE)
col.rook.nb

## Neighbour list object:
## Number of regions: 49
## Number of nonzero links: 200
## Percentage nonzero weights: 8.33
## Average number of links: 4.082
```

The two variables `col.queen.nb` and `col.rook.nb` respectively contain the adjacency information for the queen's and rook's case adjacency. It can be seen that the queen's case has 36 more adjacencies than the rook's case.

Wall (2004) and others demonstrate that for the SAR model with a constant σ^2 term,

$$\text{Var}(\mathbf{z}) = (\mathbf{I} - \lambda \mathbf{W})^{-1} \left[(\mathbf{I} - \lambda \mathbf{W})^{-1} \right]^T \sigma^2 \qquad (7.15)$$

provided $(\mathbf{I} - \lambda \mathbf{W})$ is invertible. Thus, as stated before, the spatial autoregressive model is essentially a regression model with non-independent error terms, unless

$\lambda = 0$ in which case it is equivalent to a model with independent observations. The variance–covariance matrix is therefore a function of the variables $\mathbf{W}$, σ^2 and λ. Without loss of generality, we can assume that Y is scaled so that $\sigma^2 = 1$. Then, for any given definition of adjacency for the study area, it is possible to investigate the correlation structure for various values of λ. In R, the following defines a function to compute a variance–covariance matrix from λ and $\mathbf{W}$. Here, the adjacency object is used (rather than supplying a $\mathbf{W}$ matrix), but this contains the same information.

```
covmat <- function(lambda,adj) {
      solve(tcrossprod(diag(length(adj)) - lambda*
listw2mat(nb2listw(adj))))
}
```

The `tcrossprod` function takes a matrix $\mathbf{X}$ and returns $\mathbf{XX^T}$. The function `solve` finds the inverse of a matrix. This can also be used as the basis for finding the *correlation* matrix (rather than the variance–covariance matrix):

```
cormat <- function(lambda,adj) {
      cov2cor(covmat(lambda,adj))
}
```

We can now examine the relationship between, say, the correlation between zones 41 and 47, and λ the plot created is shown in Figure 7.11.

```
# Create a range of valid lambda values
lambda.range <- seq(-1.3,0.99,l=101)
# Create an array to store the corresponding correlations
cor.41.47 <- lambda.range*0
#... store them
for (i in 1:101) cor.41.47[i] <- cormat(
      lambda.range[i],col.rook.nb)[41,47]
#... plot the relationship
plot(lambda.range,cor.41.47,type='l')
```

This seems reasonable – larger values of λ lead to higher correlation between the zones, $\lambda = 0$ implies no correlation, and the sign of λ implies the sign of the correlation. However, now consider the same curve, but between zones 40 and 41 (see Figure 7.12).

```
# First, add the line from the previous figure for
reference
plot(lambda.range,cor.41.47,type='l',xlab=expression
(lambda),ylab='Correlation',lty=2)
```

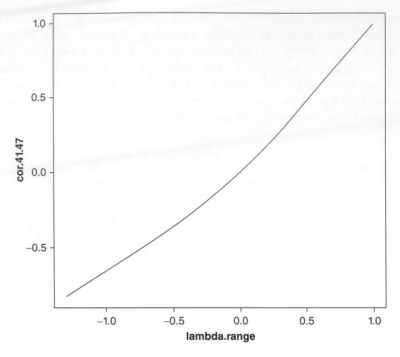

Figure 7.11 Relationship between λ and the correlation between zones 40 and 41

```
# Now compute the correlation between zones 40 and 41.
cor.40.41 <- lambda.range*0
for (i in 1:101) cor.40.41[i] <- cormat(
lambda.range[i],col.rook.nb)[40,41]
#... and add these to the plot
lines(lambda.range,cor.40.41)
```

Here, something strange is happening. When λ drops below around –0.5 the correlation between zones 40 and 41 begins to increase, and at a point at around –0.7 it becomes positive again. This is somewhat counter-intuitive, particularly as λ is often referred to as an indicator of spatial association. For example, Ord (1975) states that w_{ij} 'represents the degree of possible interaction of location j on location i'. Although initially for positive λ the correlation between zones 40 and 41 is less than that for zones 41 and 47, when λ exceeds around 0.5 the situation is reversed (although this is a less pronounced effect than the sign change noted earlier). A useful diagnostic plot is a parametric curve of the two correlations, with parameter λ (see Figure 7.13):

```
# First, plot the empty canvas (type='n')
plot(c(-1,1),c(-1,1),type='n',xlim=c(-1,1),ylim=c(-1,1),
xlab='Corr1',ylab='Corr2')
```

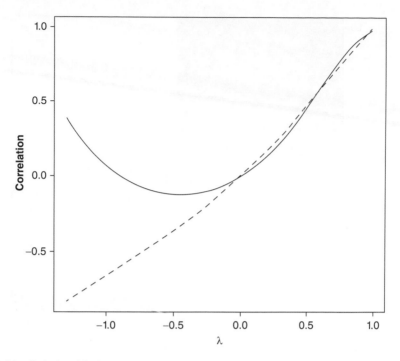

Figure 7.12   Relationship between λ and the correlation between zones 41 and 47

```
# Then the quadrants
rect(-1.2,-1.2,1.2,1.2,col='pink',border=NA)
rect(-1.2,-1.2,0,0,col='lightyellow',border=NA)
rect(0,0,1.2,1.2,col='lightyellow',border=NA)
# Then the x=y reference line
abline(a=0,b=1,lty=3)
# Then the curve
lines(cor.40.41,cor.41.47)
```

We term this a *Battenburg*[10] plot. Tracing along this line from top right shows the relationship between the two correlations as λ decreases from its maximum value. The dotted line is the $x = y$ reference point – whenever the curve crosses this, the values of the two correlations change order. Perhaps the key feature is that the curve 'doubles back' on itself – so that for some ranges of λ one of the correlations increases while the other decreases. The quadrants are also important – if a curve enters one of the pink quadrants, this suggests that one of the correlations is positive while the other is negative. Again this is perhaps counter-intuitive, given the

---

10   http://britishfood.about.com/b/2011/08/17/british-bake-off-and-a-battenburg-cake.htm

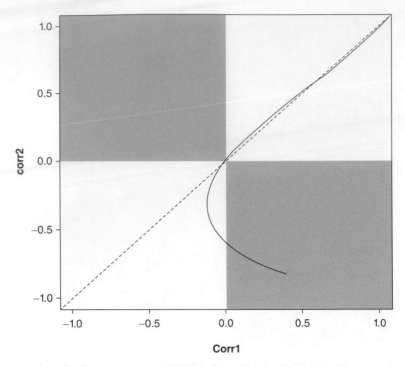

Figure 7.13 Parametric plot of correlations between two polygon pairs (40,41) and (41,47)

interpretation of λ as a measure of spatial association. Note in this case after the 'doubling back' of the curve it does enter the pink quadrant.

A selection of 100 random pairs of correlations (chosen so that each pair has one zone in common) can be drawn (see Figure 7.14). This seems to suggest that 'doubling back' and curves going inside the pink quadrants are not uncommon problems. In addition, for positive λ values, there is a fair deal of variation in the values of correlation for given λ values. In addition, the variability is not consistent, so that the order of values of correlation changes frequently.

```
# First, plot the empty canvas (type='n')
plot(c(-1,1),c(-1,1),type='n',xlim=c(-1,1),ylim=c(-1,1),
    xlab='Corr1',ylab='Corr2')
# Then the quadrants
rect(-1.2,-1.2,1.2,1.2,col='pink',border=NA)
rect(-1.2,-1.2,0,0,col='lightyellow',border=NA)
rect(0,0,1.2,1.2,col='lightyellow',border=NA)
# Then the x=y reference line
```

```
abline(a=0,b=1,lty=3)
# Then the curves
# First, set a seed for reproducibility
set.seed(310712)
for (i in 1:100) {
  r1 <- sample(1:length(col.rook.nb),1)
  r2 <- sample(col.rook.nb[[r1]],2)
  cor.ij1 <- lambda.range*0
  cor.ij2 <- lambda.range*0
  for (k in 1:101)
    cor.ij1[k] <- cormat(lambda.range[k],
    col.rook.nb)[r1,r2[1]]
  for (k in 1:101)
    cor.ij2[k] <- cormat(lambda.range[k],
    col.rook.nb)[r1,r2[2]]
  lines(cor.ij1,cor.ij2)
}
```

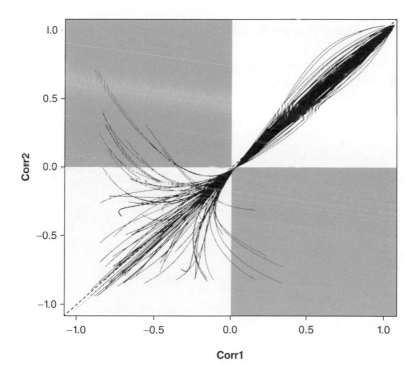

Figure 7.14 Parametric plots of 100 sampled correlations

This shows a pattern very similar to those seen in Wall (2004). Essentially, for negative λ values, some correlations become positive while others remain negative. The ordering can also change as λ changes, as noted earlier, so that some adjacent zones are more correlated than others for certain λ values, but this situation can alter. Finally, some adjacent zone pairs experience a sign change for negative values of λ, while others do not. The aim of this section has been in part to highlight the issues in Wall (2004), but also to suggest some visual techniques in R that could be used to explore these – and identify situations in which the counter-intuitive behaviour seen here may be occurring. As a general rule, the authors have found this not to happen a great deal when working with zones based on a *regular* grid, but that the problems seen here occur quite often for irregular lattices. This provides empirical back-up to the more theoretical arguments of Besag and Kooperberg (1995) for CAR models.

ANSWER TO SELF-TEST QUESTION

The following code will apply the modified approach asked for in the question:

```
# Set up the parameters - six plots in 3 rows by 2 cols
# set margins as smaller than usual to allow bigger
maps
par(mfrow=c(3,2),mar=c(1,1,1,1)/2)

# Which one will be the real data?
real.data.i <- sample(1:6,1)

# Draw six plots.   Five will be random, one will be the
real data
for (i in 1:6) {
  if (i == real.data.i) {
    choropleth(penn.state.utm,smk,shades)}
  else {
    choropleth(penn.state.utm,sample(smk,replace=TRUE),
    shades)}
}
```

Figure 7.16 Bootstrap randomisation of smoking uptake rates

The only difference between this and the previous code block is the inclusion of the optional parameter replace=TRUE in the sample function, which tells the function to return *n* random samples from the list of smoking take-up rates *with* replacement. This is essentially the technique to simulate the drawing of random samples used by Efron (1979) to carry out the *bootstrap* approach to non-parametric estimations of standard error. Thus, here it is referred to as 'bootstrap randomisation'.

REFERENCES

Anselin, L. (1995) Local indicators of spatial association – LISA. *Geographical Analysis*, 27: 93–115.

Anselin, L. (1996) The Moran scatterplot as an ESDA tool to assess local instability in spatial association. In M.M. Fischer, H.J. Scholten and D. Unwin (eds), *Spatial Analytical Perspectives on GIS*, pp. 111–125. London: Taylor & Francis.

Bartlett, M.S. (1936) The square root transformation in analysis of variance. *Supplement to the Journal of the Royal Statistical Society*, 3(1): 68–78.

Belsley, D.A., Kuh, E. and Welsch, R.E. (1980) *Regression Diagnostics*. New York: John Wiley & Sons.

Besag, J. (1974) Spatial interaction and the statistical analysis of lattice systems (with discussion). *Journal of the Royal Statistical Society, Series B*, 36: 192–236.

Besag, J. and Kooperberg, C. (1995) On conditional and intrinsic autoregressions. *Biometrika*, 82(4): 733–746.

Cliff, A.D. and Ord, J. K. (1973) *Spatial Autocorrelation*. London: Pion.

Cliff, A.D. and Ord, J.K. (1981) *Spatial Processes: Methods and Applications*. London: Pion.

Cook, R.D. and Weisberg, S. (1982) *Residuals and Influence in Regression*. London: Chapman & Hall.

Cressie, N. (1991) *Statistics for Spatial Data*. New York: John Wiley & Sons.

de Jong, P., Sprenger, C. and van Veen, F. (1984) On extreme values of Moran's *I* and Geary's *C*. *Geographical Analysis*, 16(1): 17–24.

Efron, B. (1979) Bootstrap methods: Another look at the jackknife. *Annals of Statistics*, 7: 1–26.

Fotheringham, A., Brunsdon, C. and Charlton, M. (2000). *Quantitative Geography: Perspectives on Spatial Analysis*. London: Sage.

Hope, A.C.A. (1968). A simplified Monte Carlo significance test procedure. *Journal of the Royal Statistical Society, Series B*, 30(3): 582–598.

Marcus, H. and Minc, H. (1988) *Introduction to Linear Algebra*. New York: Dover.

Moran, P. (1950) Notes on continuous stochastic phenomena. *Biometrika*, 37: 17–23.

Ord, J. K. (1975) Estimation methods for models of spatial interaction. *Journal of the American Statistical Association*, 70(349): 120–126.

Wall, M. M. (2004) A close look at the spatial structure implied by the CAR and SAR models. *Journal of Statistical Planning and Inference*, 121(2): 311–324.

Wickham, H. (2011) The split–apply–combine strategy for data analysis. *Journal of Statistical Software*, 40(1): 1–29.

Wickham, H., Cook, D., Hofmann, H. and Buja, A. (2010) Graphical inference for infovis. *IEEE Transactions on Visualization and Computer Graphics*, 16(6): 973–979.

Wolpert, R. and Ickstadt, K. (1998) Poisson/gamma random field models for spatial statistics. *Biometrika*, 85(2): 251–267.

LOCALISED SPATIAL ANALYSIS

8.1 INTRODUCTION

In the previous chapters, a number of models of spatial processes have been used to analyse data. One characteristic of many of the models used was an assumption of homogeneity in the way that spatial data interacted. For example, K-functions and related ideas model the interdependence *between* points, in terms of the distance between them – K-functions themselves model the number of points one might encounter within a radius r from a particular point. However, a general assumption is that these relations depend only on *relative* distance. Thus, the expected number of points within a circle of radius r centred around a point at location x will depend only on the value of r and not on x. Similarly, in the SAR models considered in the previous chapter, the coefficient λ specified the degree to which an attribute at polygon i depended on the values of nearby polygons. However, λ takes the same value for all polygons – suggesting again that the degree of spatial interdependency is the same regardless of location.

This has an effect on the kind of hypothesis testing that may take place. For example, in the previous chapter, the hypothesis that $\lambda = 0$ was tested – and in the examples given it was rejected at the 5% level. This tells us that there is spatial dependency in the process under investigation (in the example, rates of smoking) – but of itself it supplies no inference as to where high or low levels occur geographically, or whether the dependency occurs in some regions but not in others.[1] In this chapter, a number of approaches that attempt to highlight geographical variation in spatial processes will be introduced. Two key ideas here are *index decomposition*, in which indices such as Moran's I are decomposed according to the contribution of data from each locality to identify local effects, and moving window approaches, where data will be analysed in a moving circular window, to identify variation in relationships within the data over space.

8.2 SETTING UP THE DATA USED IN THIS CHAPTER

The main dataset used in this chapter will be the North Carolina sudden infant death syndrome (SIDS) data, appearing in Getis and Ord (1992). The data are

---

1 Indeed, adopting this model requires a prior assumption of homogeneity in spatial dependency.

supplied with the spdep package. The package supplies this as a shapefile, and readShapePoly is used to read it in. Initially, the shapefile is supplied in geographical (i.e. latitude and longitude) coordinates. However, some of the examples in this chapter will require distances between county centroids and so a projected coordinate system should be used. Here the geodetic parameters with ID 2264 from the European Petroleum Survey Group (EPSG) are used – with units expressed in miles. The code to carry out this operations follows. The map (in projected coordinates) is shown in Figure 8.1.

```
# Load spdep and rgdal packages
require(maptools)
require(spdep)
require(rgdal)
# Read in the North Carolina shapefile
nc.sids <- readShapePoly(
  system.file("etc/shapes/sids.shp",
  package="spdep")[1],
  ID="FIPSNO",
  proj4string=CRS("+proj=longlat +ellps=clrk66"))
# Transform to EPSG 2264 (with distances in miles)
nc.sids.p <- spTransform(nc.sids,CRS("+init=epsg:2264
                                   +units=mi"))
# Plot North Carolina
plot(nc.sids.p)
# add a scale
lines(c(480,480,530,530),c(25,20,20,25))
text(505,10, "50 Miles")
```

Figure 8.1 North Carolina county map

The last two commands add a scale to the map. Note that the coordinates are specified to be in miles, hence the base line of the scale bar runs from 480 to 530. This scale bar will recur in several maps. One of the advantages of R is that it is a programming language – and so the scale bar commands can be made into a function, to simplify the drawing of the scale bar in other maps in this chapter:

```
add.scale <- function() {
  lines(c(480,480,530,530),c(25,20,20,25))
  text(505,10,"50 Miles")
}
```

8.3 LOCAL INDICATORS OF SPATIAL ASSOCIATION

Recalling that the purpose of this chapter is to consider localised forms of spatial data analysis, Anselin (1995) proposed the idea of *local indicators of spatial association* (LISAs). He states two requirements for a LISA:

- The LISA for each observation gives an indication of the extent of significant spatial clustering of similar values around that observation;

- The sum of LISAs for all observations is proportional to a global indicator of spatial association.

It should be possible to apply a statistical test to the LISA for each observation, and thus test whether the local contribution to clustering around observation i is significantly different from zero. This provides a framework for identifying localities where there is a significant degree of spatial clustering (or repulsion). A good initial example of a LISA may be derived from the Moran's I Index. Recall that this is defined by

$$I = \frac{n}{\sum_j \sum_j w_{ij}} \frac{\sum_i \sum_j w_{ij}(z_i - \bar{z})(z_j - \bar{z})}{\sum_i (z_i - \bar{z})^2} \tag{8.1}$$

where z_i is a measurement associated with polygon i; and w_{ij} is a binary indicator as to whether polygons i and j are neighbours, taking the value 0 if they are not, and the value $\frac{1}{|\delta_i|}$ if they are, with $|\delta_i|$ being the number of polygon neighbours that polygon i has. This expression can be written as

$$I = n \left(\sum_k (z_k - \bar{z})^2 \right)^{-1} \left[\sum_k \sum_j w_{kj} \right]^{-1} \sum_i I_i \tag{8.2}$$

where

$$I_i = (z_i - \bar{z}) \sum_j w_{ij}(z_j - \bar{z}) \tag{8.3}$$

Noting that $n(\sum_k (z_k - \bar{z})^2)^{-1}\left[\sum_k \sum_j w_{kj}\right]^{-1}$ does not depend on i, so that for a given set of z_i it may be regarded as a constant, we have

$$I = \text{const.} \times \sum_i I_i \tag{8.4}$$

so that Ii is a LISA. As previously, writing $q_i = z_i - \bar{z}$ – so that the qi are mean centred values, we can write

$$I_i = q_i \sum_j w_{ij} q_j \tag{8.5}$$

so that Ii is the product of q_i and the mean of the q_j values for the neighbours of polygon i. If both q_i and the average value of q_j for polygon i's neighbours are all above average, this quantity will be large, indicating a cluster of above average values focused on polygon i. This is also the case if polygon i and its neighbours all have values below average. Thus, it can be seen that Ii is a local measure of clustering (either above or below the average value). Also, if the signs of q_i and $\sum_j w_{ij} q_j$ differ, and I_i is a large negative value, this suggests that a local 'repulsion' effect may be occurring, where neighbouring values take opposite extremes. Finally, if the magnitude of I_i is not particularly large (for either positive or negative values) this suggests that there is little evidence for either clustering or repulsion.

For each Ii, a significance test may be carried out against a hypothesis of no spatial association. Anselin (1995) provides formulae for the sampling mean and variance of Ii given a randomisation hypothesis as discussed in the previous chapter (essentially this assumes that any permutation of z_i values among polygons is equally likely), and from these, the quantity

$$\frac{I_i - \mathrm{E}[I_i]}{\mathrm{Var}[I_i]^{0.5}} \tag{8.6}$$

may be used as a test statistic. The R function `localmoran` in `spdep` computes Ii values, given a set of z_i values and a `listw` object providing neighbour weighting information for the polygons associated with the z_i. This function returns a matrix of values whose columns are:

1. the local Moran's I statistic – I_i

2. E(Ii) under the randomisation hypothesis

3. Var(I_i) under the randomisation hypothesis

4. the test statistic from equation (8.6)

5. the p-value of the above statistic, assuming an approximate normal distribution

The following code computes the SIDS rates for 1979 per 1000 births, then computes the local Moran's I and then produces a map (Figure 8.2) – here the basic I_i values are plotted.

```
# Use GISTools to draw maps
require(GISTools)
# Compute the listw object for the North Carolina polygons
nc.lw <- nb2listw(poly2nb(nc.sids.p))
# Compute the SIDS rates (per 1000 births) for 1979
sids79 <- 1000*nc.sids.p$SID79/nc.sids.p$BIR79
# Compute the local Moran's I
nc.lI <- localmoran(sids79,nc.lw)
# Compute a shading scheme
sids.shade <- auto.shading(c(nc.lI[,1],-nc.lI[,1]),
                           cols=brewer.pal(5,"PRGn"))
# Draw the map
choropleth(nc.sids.p,nc.lI[,1],shading=sids.shade)
# Add legends + title + scale
choro.legend(120.3,54.9,sids.shade,fmt="%6.2f")
title("Sudden Infant Death Syndrome (Local Moran's I)",
      cex.main=2)
add.scale()
```

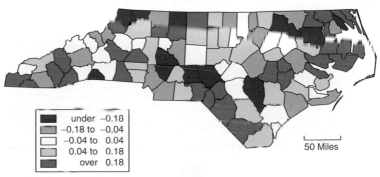

Figure 8.2   Standardised local Moran's I-values

The auto.shading(c(nc.lI[,5],-nc.lI[,5]),...) command in the previous code block perhaps needs some explanation. The aim here is to create a set of shading categories that are symmetric about zero. The

(Continued)

(Continued)

legend in Figure 8.2 shows that this has happened. This works because, for a vector x, the expression c(x,-x) returns a symmetrical list, in the sense that if $x_i \in X$ then $-x_i \in X$. This ensures that computing regular quantiles will also lead to a symmetric set of values – and the default for auto. shading returns regular quantiles as shading interval boundaries. Note that although this creates shading *categories* that run from -max(abs(x)) to max(abs(x)), the values of x may not fall into *all* of these categories. The idea of using categories that are symmetrical about zero is in part to identify whether positive and negative values of x are equally balanced.

The map shows there is some evidence for both positive and negative *Ii* values. However, it is useful to consider the *p*-values for each of these values, as considered above. These are mapped below. In this case a manual shading scheme (i.e. one in which the shading intervals are specified directly) is used, based on conventional 'critical' *p*-values. The code below produces this (see Figure 8.3).

```
# Create a manual shading scheme
pval.shade <- shading(c(0.01,0.05,0.1),
                      cols=rev(brewer.pal(4,'PuRd')))
# Draw the map
choropleth(nc.sids.p,nc.lI[,5],shading=pval.shade)
# Add legends + title + scale
choro.legend(120.3,54.9,pval.shade,fmt="%6.2f")
title("Sudden Infant Death Syndrome (Local p-value)",
      cex.main=2)
add.scale()
```

The use of rev in the above code chunk reverses the items in a list. In this case, it reverses the colours in the Brewer palette PuRd. The palette runs from purple to red – starting with a light purple and progressing to a dark red. All of the Brewer palettes from the *RColorBrewer* package run from light to dark. Normally this is useful, with the darker colours corresponding to higher attribute values on a choropleth map. However, for *p*-values the 'strongest' effects are associated with *low* values, and so a palette running from dark to light is appropriate – hence the use of rev.

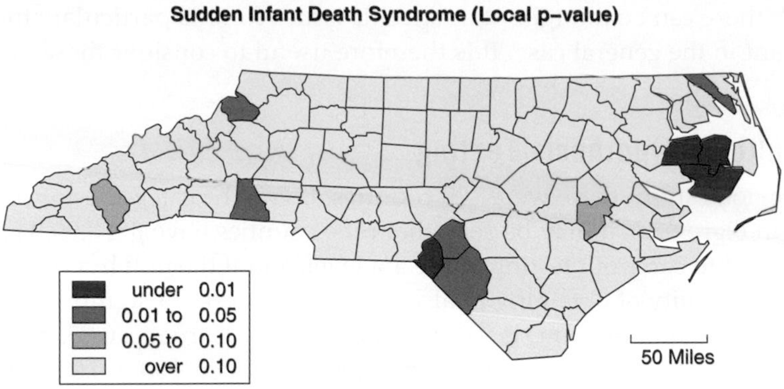

Sudden Infant Death Syndrome (Local p–value)

Figure 8.3 Local Moran's *I* *p*-values

Figure 8.3 shows a number of places where the *p*-value is notably low (for example, Washington County), suggesting the possibility of a cluster of either high or low values. Inspecting the actual rate for Washington (which is zero) suggests there may be a cluster of very low rates here. Another region where the *p*-value is low is Scotland County – although in this case the rate is very high – suggesting a cluster of higher values here.

Self Test Question. Verify the significance figures above by selecting and listing the counties for which $p < 0.05$. To help identify locations, the identify function can be used. At the R prompt, enter

```
identify(coordinates(nc.sids.p),labels=nc.sids.p$NAME)
```

and then click on locations of interest. When you have selected all of these, press the Escape key. This should result in the names of the counties in which you have clicked appearing on the map.

8.4 FURTHER ISSUES WITH THE ABOVE ANALYSIS

The above analysis shows a way in which notable counties – or possibly clusters of neighbouring counties (in terms of their SIDS rates) can be identified via mapping the *p*-values of local Moran's *I* statistics. However, there are two notable difficulties with using this approach in an unmodified form. These are:

- Multiple hypothesis testing
- Assuming that the I_i are normally distributed

Although these can be thought of as specific issues for this particular study, many are relevant in the general case. It is therefore useful to consider these in turn.

8.4.1 Multiple Hypothesis Testing

In the previous study, there were 100 counties. Using the categories of shading for the map in Figure 8.3, it may be seen that nine counties have $p \leq 0.05$. However, if it is proposed to carry out testing at the 5% level, and if the null hypothesis is true, then the probability of obtaining a false positive result (i.e. a significant value of I_i when in fact the null hypothesis – of randomisation – is true) is 0.05. Thus, even if no spatial process is occurring, we can expect to obtain $100 \times 0.05 = 5$ counties flagged as 'significant'. Thus, even when no effect is present, this approach can generate several false positives. One way this could be dealt with is by comparing the number of significant results observed in the data to the binomial distribution – but ultimately this loses sight of the main objective of the local Moran's I approach, since it then just provides a 'whole-study-area' test of whether a spatial process occurs, rather than considering specific localities. If that is all that is required, there is no advantage in the suggested approach over a test based on the standard Moran's I.

However, the advertised advantage of a LISA-based approach is its ability to identify *where* clustering is occurring, not just *whether* it occurs. The problem happens because often the method is required to answer both of these questions. If the 'false positive rate' – the probability of detecting a significant I_i if the null hypothesis were true – were zero, then *any* significant I_i would imply with certainty that clustering does occur. But the false positive rate is not zero – and given that inconvenient fact, one useful approach is to determine the probability of falsely stating that clustering exists on the basis of finding one or more significant I_i. The individual p-values, and associated tests, apply to individual counties. Assuming the tests are applied independently, and each has a false positive probability p, then the probability of not getting a false positive is $1 - p$ for each county. If there are n counties, then the probability of getting *no* false positives is $(1-p)^n$, and therefore the probability of getting one or more false positives when looking at *all* counties denoted by p^*, is the complement of this, so that

$$p^* = 1 - (1 - p)^n \tag{8.7}$$

Thus, p^* can be regarded as a p-value for the ensemble of tests on each county – and as a false positive rate for a general test of a 'no clustering' null hypothesis. A further simplification may be made by noting that for small p,

$$p^* \approx np \tag{8.8}$$

Now, if it were desired to find the individual county p-value required to give a specified overall p^*-value, equation (8.7) can be rearranged to give

$$p = 1 - (1 - p^*)^{\frac{1}{n}} \tag{8.9}$$

or using the approximation above,

$$p \approx \frac{p^*}{n} \tag{8.10}$$

Here, $n = 100$ and so if a p^*-value of 0.05 is required, R can be used as a desk calculator to obtain the countywise p:

```
1 - (1 - 0.05)^(1/100)

## [1] 0.0005128
```

Thus, to make the overall chance of falsely rejecting the null hypothesis of no clustering anywhere equal to 0.05, individual counties should be tested against a p-value of approximately 5×10^{-4}. The approach using the approximation in equations (8.8) and (8.10) is known as the Bonferroni p-value adjustment (see Šidák, 1967, for example). In R, instead of the 'desktop calculator' approach set out above, the function p.adjust may be used. This takes a slightly different approach – instead of adjusting the threshold for countywise p-values to be significant, it adjusts the p-values themselves, so they may be compared to the critical value of p^* required. Thus to apply the test above, using p.adjust(pvals, method='bonferroni') on a set of countywise p-values returns a set of *adjusted countywise* p-values that may be compared against the critical value for p^*. Using this approach, anomalous localities can be identified, but the overall probability of any false positives is controlled. For example, comparing adjusted county p-values against 0.05 will provide a test where the overall chance of erroneously rejecting the overall hypothesis of no spatial pattern is 0.05.

This idea may now be used to provide a map of *adjusted* local Moran's I p-values for the SIDS data analysed earlier (see Figure 8.4).

```
# Create a manual shading scheme
pval.shade <- shading(c(0.01,0.05,0.1),
                    cols=rev(brewer.pal(4,'PuRd')))
# Draw the map - note the p.adjust function
choropleth(nc.sids.p,
           p.adjust(nc.lI[,5],
           method='bonferroni'),
           shading=pval.shade)
# Add legends + title + scale
choro.legend(120.3,54.9,pval.shade,fmt="%6.2f")
title("Sudden Infant Death Syndrome (Bonferroni Adjusted
       p-value)",
       cex.main=2)
add.scale()
```

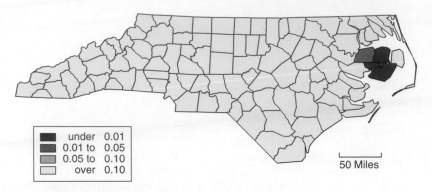

Sudden Infant Death Syndrome (Bonferroni Adjusted p–value)

■	under 0.01
■	0.01 to 0.05
■	0.05 to 0.10
□	over 0.10

50 Miles

Figure 8.4   Local Moran's *I* Bonferroni adjusted *p*-values

This reveals that there is in fact a significant pattern (some counties are still significant even after *p*-values are adjusted), and that it is the pattern around Washington County that contributes notably to the departure from an aspatial process. Interestingly, it is a group of very low rates that is detected here.

A slightly different approach to explaining the idea of *p** is to note that the probability of erroneously rejecting a null hypothesis of no spatial association is equivalent to the probability of erroneously rejecting the smallest *p*-value of all of the counties. Assuming the same threshold is applied to all tests, if the smallest *p*-value falls below this threshold, this is equivalent to the event that at least one county is erroneously flagged as significant. Noting that typically one is testing with a one-tailed (upper-tail) alternative hypothesis, so that large I_i values relate to small *p*-values, an alternative way to compute adjusted *p*-values is to compare local standardised Moran's *I* against the distribution of the largest of *n* standard normal variates.

8.4.2 Issues with the Bonferroni Approach

The Bonferroni approach is very helpful if a major concern is falsely identifying even one false case – as is the case in a situation where a single counter-example from several tests is considered notable. However, in some other situations, alternative approaches may be more appropriate. Permeger (1998) cites a number of issues with Bonferroni corrections. One of particular note is related to *Type II errors*. Until now this chapter has focused on so-called *Type I errors* – these occur when falsely rejecting a true null hypothesis. Type II errors occur when a null hypothesis is true, but the testing procedure fails to reject it. As Permeger states, 'Type I errors cannot decrease ... without inflating type II errors ... And type II errors are no less false than type I errors.'

An inconvenient side effect of using the Bonferroni procedure – which places tight control on overall Type II error – is that it reduces the power of the test to detect anomalies. A number of alternative procedures exist which have a greater chance of detecting genuine anomalies, albeit with more chance of obtaining false positive results. However, one notable alternative approach, due to Holm (1979), guarantees a false positive rate no higher than the Bonferroni procedure – but always has a lower Type II error. The procedure is set out below:

1. Sort the basic p-values, labelling them $\{p_{[1]}, p_{[2]}, \cdots, p_{[n]}\}$, where $p_{[1]}$ is the lowest value, and $p_{[n]}$ the highest.

2. Apply the adjustment $p'_{[1]} = 1 - (1 - p_{[1]})^n$ to $p_{[1]}$ (or use the approximate form)

3. Apply the adjustment $p'_{[2]} = 1 - (1 - p_{[2]})^{n-1}$ to $p_{[2]}$ (or use the approximate form)

4. Continue in this way so that $p'_{[m]} = 1 - (1 - p_{[m]})^{n-m+1}$ for $m = 2, ..., n$ (or use the approximate form)

5. If α is the overall maximum acceptable Type I error, reject the null hypothesis for all $p'_{[i]} < \alpha$

The logic behind this approach is to note that, for the Bonferroni procedure, if k of the counties (or more generally polygons) are genuinely anomalous then the false positive rate is overestimated using the standard Bonferroni adjustment. In this situation there is only a need to adjust for $n - k$ multiple tests rather than n. This is because the remaining k tests actually take place where the null hypothesis is false, so any significant results are *true* positives, rather than *false* positives. Thus, if one accepts the possibility that there may be some genuine departures from the null hypothesis in the data, then the Bonferroni adjustment is *conservative* – that is, it provides an upper limit to the Type I error, but does not specify it exactly. Since it is not known *which* k tests are associated with genuine anomalies, or indeed the value of k, all that

(Continued)

(Continued)

the previous discussion demonstrates is the conservatism of Bonferroni's procedure. The Holm adjustment is also conservative, but notes that if the smallest *p*-value $p_{[1]}$, is associated with an observation for which the null hypothesis is true, then adjusting for *n* multiple tests will ensure the upper limit of α for the Type I error applies, regardless of the outcome of tests for the other *p*-values. However, suppose the lowest *p*-value *is* associated with one of the *k* tests where there really is an anomaly; then the outcome of the test does not affect the false positive rate. In this case we consider the remaining $n-1$ *p*-values. We can apply the previous arguments to this reduced dataset, and in particular consider the smallest remaining *p*-value, $p_{[2]}$. In this case, again the Bonferroni adjustment can be applied, but this time with just $n-1$ multiple tests, not *n*. Repeatedly applying the same logic, $p_{[3]}$ can be corrected with $n-2$ multiple tests, and so on. This description rather loosely demonstrates the justification for Holm's procedure. Note that apart from p[1], the Holm adjusted values lead to a greater range of values for which locations would be flagged as significant than those associated with the Bonferroni method. However, both methods have the same upper limit for the Type I error – this implies that there is a greater chance of detecting an I_i value that is genuinely anomalous with the Holm approach.

The Holm adjustment may be used in R via the p.adjust function again, this time using the argument method='holm'. Thus, a revised map (Figure 8.5) of adjusted *p*-values may be obtained by the following code:

```
# Create a manual shading scheme
pval.shade <- shading(c(0.01,0.05,0.1),
                    cols=rev(brewer.pal(4,'PuRd')))
# Draw the map - note the p.adjust function -
# this time using Holm's approach
choropleth(nc.sids.p,
          p.adjust(nc.lI[,5],
              method='holm'),
          shading=pval.shade)
# Add legends + title + scale
choro.legend(120.3,54.9,pval.shade,fmt="%6.2f")
title("Sudden Infant Death Syndrome (Holm Adjusted
      p-value)",
      cex.main=2)
add.scale()
```

Sudden Infant Death Syndrome (Holm Adjusted p–value)

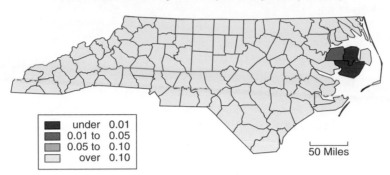

■	under 0.01
■	0.01 to 0.05
▨	0.05 to 0.10
□	over 0.10

50 Miles

Figure 8.5   Local Moran's *I* Holm adjusted *p*-values

In fact, in this instance it is still the same areas that are highlighted – this may seem a little disappointing, but it can at least be stated that this version of the procedure had a greater chance of detecting other anomalies, had they been present.

It is perhaps also worth noting that for the local Moran's *I* there are two further reasons for conservatism – the calculations for adjustments are based on the assumption that each test is independent. In fact, due to the fact that I_i depends not only z_i but also on z_j values for neighbours, there is in fact positive correlation between tests focussed on polygon pairs where the polygons share one or more neighbours. In fact Šidák (1967) demonstrates that where the individual test results are correlated the Bonferroni adjusted *p*-values still provide a conservative test – although it is no longer exact. This is also the case for the Holm procedure. The second reason for conservatism is the use of the approximation in equations (0,0) and (8.10) - it may be seen that the approximate adjusted *p*-value is always higher than the exact one.

8.4.3 The False Discovery Rate

An entirely different approach to multiple testing is based on the work of Benjamini and Hochberg (1995), which introduces the concept of the *false discovery rate* (FDR). Instead of considering Type I error as the quantity to control, they suggest controlling for the proportion of tests flagged as significant that are false alarms. For this proportion, the denominator is actually the number of flagged tests, rather than the number of tests for which the null hypothesis is true, as it is for the Type I error. They provide a stepwise testing procedure, similar to Holm's procedure. Given a desired FDR level (denoted FDR here):

1. Sort the *p*-values into an ordered list $\{p_{[1]}, p_{[2]}, ..., p_{[n]}\}$ as with Holm's procedure

2. Find the largest integer *k* such that $p_{[k]} \leq \frac{k}{n} \times \text{FDR}$

3. Declare as significant all results $p_{[j]}$ for *j* = 1, ... , *k*

Computing the FDR adjustment is R is also via p.adjust, this time with the argument method='fdr':

```
# Create a manual shading scheme
pval.shade <- shading(c(0.01,0.05,0.1),
                        cols=rev(brewer.pal(4,'PuRd')))
# Draw the map - note the p.adjust function -
# this time using the FDR approach
choropleth(nc.sids.p,
            p.adjust(nc.lI[,5],
                method='fdr'),
            shading=pval.shade)
# Add legends + title + scale
choro.legend(120.3,54.9,pval.shade,fmt="%6.2f")
title("Sudden Infant Death Syndrome (FDR Adjusted
p-value)",
      cex.main=2)
add.scale()
```

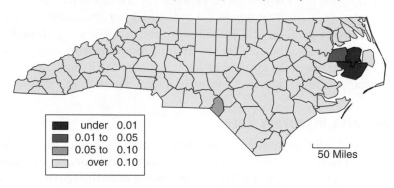

Figure 8.6 Local Moran's I FDR adjusted p-values

Here the resultant map is in Figure 8.6 – this time Scotland County is also flagged, albeit at the relatively mild 10% level.

8.4.4 Which Method to Use?

In summary, there are a number of ways of dealing with multiple hypothesis testing – fortunately several are available in R via the p.adjust function. However, it is perhaps worth noting that Bonferroni's method is generally inferior to Holm's – both set out to control the overall Type I error but Holm's always has a lower (or at worst equal) Type II error. To quote from the R help page for p.adjust: 'There seems no reason to use the unmodified Bonferroni correction because it is dominated by Holm's method, which is also valid under arbitrary assumptions.' Bonferroni's method is of historical importance – and arguably helpful pedagogically in developing the ideas of multiple hypothesis testing – but in current practice should be superseded by Holm's method.

Thus, of the methods covered here, the choice is generally between Holm's – which controls the Type I error, and Benjamini and Hochberg's, which controls the FDR. Perhaps the choice depends on the purpose of the analyses. We classify the analyses here into two key kinds:

- **Existence** Here the intention is to detect whether clustering *exists* at all. The local approach has the added advantage of locating any clusters that are found. Here the Type I error (and Holm's approach) is appropriate, as this is the probability of erroneously declaring that any clustering is present. As an example, this approach is helpful in an epidemiological study with the aim of testing whether a certain kind of illness exhibits spatial clustering.

- **Screening** In this case it may well be accepted that clustering exists, and the focus is on screening for potential clusters. In this case the consequence of a single false positive is less problematic, and the FDR, which controls the number of false alarms to a small proportion (say 5%) is appropriate.

One final note of caution is that the standard Benjamini and Hochberg (1995) approach to controlling for FDR is valid only for p-values that are either independent or positively correlated. However, a slightly less powerful test by Benjamini and Yekutieli (2001) will work in all circumstances. In p.adjust, the method `BY` option uses this approach

8.5 THE NORMALITY ASSUMPTION AND LOCAL MORAN'S I

As well as considering the most appropriate way to deal with multiple significance tests, it is perhaps important to question the distributional assumptions underlying the countywise calculations of the p-values. In the above examples, it has been assumed that the standardised I_i values are approximately normally distributed, under a randomisation hypothesis. While this asymptotic assumption may be reasonable when the I_i depend on a large number of z_i values, for smaller numbers of z_i values, it may be quite inaccurate for smaller numbers of z_i values. Fortunately, this can be examined using R, by simulating draws from a randomisation distribution:

```
# Create a matrix to place the simulated local Moran's I
sim.I <- matrix(0,1000,100)
# Run the simulations - use column 4 - standardised local
                                        Moran's i -
# to evaluate the simulated distributions.
for (i in 1:1000) sim.I[i,] <- localmoran(sample(sids79),
    nc.lw)[,4]
```

Having obtained the simulated values, it is possible to check individual polygon simulated values for normality. Each row contains a set of simulated local Moran's *I* values for each county. Thus, column 1 contains the simulated local Moran's *I* value for Alamance County. A useful graphical check for normality is the *quantile-quantile (QQ)* plot (Wilk and Gnanadesikan, 1968). Here the sampled values are plotted against their corresponding quantiles on the standard normal distribution. If the values follow a normal distribution (or something close to it) the resultant plot should be a straight line. Here, a *QQ* plot of the simulated I_i value is created, together with a reference line (Figure 8.7).

```
qqnorm(sim.I[,1],main="Alamance County")
qqline(sim.I[,1])
```

From this, it seems that the distribution of the standardised local Moran's *I* for Alamance County is a long way from being a normal distribution. The figure shows higher simulated values above the reference line, and lower ones below it – suggesting that high-end quantiles are higher than the normal distribution,

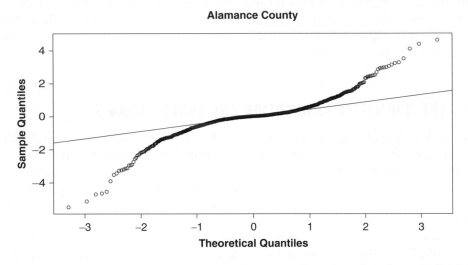

Figure 8.7 *QQ* plot used to evaluate deviation from normality assumption of standardised I_i

and lower quantiles are lower than the normal. Although the distribution of the local Moran's I appears symmetric, it would appear to have notably heavier tails than the normal distribution. In general, this implies that p-values based on normal approximations are likely to be lower than the exact ones – unfortunately, this suggests that the Type I error rates may be higher than expected.

Let us repeat this check – on a random sample of nine more counties. The mfrow parameter may be used to create a 3 × 3 matrix of QQ plots, displayed in Figure 8.8.

```
# Set up the 3 x 3 multiple window
par(mfrow=c(3,3))
# Create a random sample of 9 counties from 100
samp <- sample(100,9)
# For county in the each sample,  create a QQ-plot
for (cty in samp) {
    place <- nc.sids.p@data$NAME[cty] # County name
    qqnorm(sim.I[,cty],main=place) # QQ-plot
    qqline(sim.I[,cty]) # Reference line
}
```

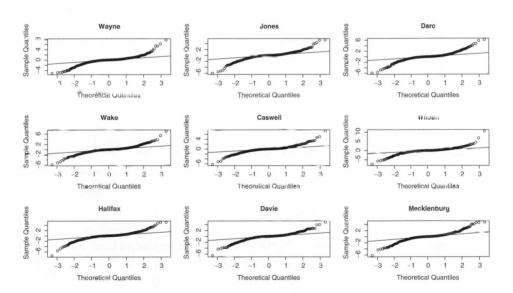

Figure 8.8 Matrix of *QQ* plots for nine randomly selected counties.

Although there is some variation, all of the selected counties' standardised Moran's I exhibit the same heavy-tailed pattern. Note that since the sample of nine counties is chosen randomly, entering the above code is likely to result in a different sample of counties than those illustrated above. As an exercise, the reader may wish to examine all of the counties.

For this reason, it may not be a good idea to trust an analysis based on normal approximation for the standardised local Moran's *I*. However, the simulation technique used to investigate the true distributions above could also be used as the basis for a Monte Carlo Hope test (as set out in Chapter 7). This is done by counting, for each county, the number of simulated standardised local Moran's *I* statistics that are equal to, or larger than, the measured value from the data. One way of achieving this is via the sweep function:

```
mc.pvals <- (colSums(sweep(sim.I,2,nc.lI[,4],'>='))  +  1) /
            (nrow(sim.I)  +  1)
```

sweep is typically called in the form

```
sweep(X,margin,sweepvals,fun)
```

It takes a matrix X, an indicator (margin) referring to either rows (1)or columns (2), a vector sweepvals which has the same length as the number of rows (if margin=1) or columns (if margin=2), and finally a bivariate function such as − or *, with the variable name (fun). The idea is that the each element of sweepvals is subtracted (or whatever function is supplied to fun) from each corresponding row (or column) of X. This is often used for example, as a way to mean-centre columns in a matrix X:

```
sweep(X,2,colMeans(X),'-')
```

Note that colMeans returns the mean of each column of X, and it is possible to refer to a bivariate function in quoted form (i.e. '−' for minus). Similarly, the following rescales the rows of X to sum to 1:

```
sweep(X,1,rowSums(X),'/')
```

To return a *logical* matrix which checks whether each simulated local Moran's *I* in a column is greater than or equal to the actual one, use

```
sweep(sim.I,2,nc.lI[,4],'>=')
```

Note that the bivariate function here is '>=', which returns a logical value. Finally, note that logicals in R can be treated as 0–1 values, so summing a logical vector counts the number of TRUE values. Thus, using colSums on this matrix gives a vector counting the number of times the simulated value is more extreme than the observed one on a per column (i.e. per county)

basis. The counts can then be converted into *p*-values using the Hope
approach outlined in Chapter 7.

This then gives a set of individual *p*-values for each county, based on randomisation.
These may then be adjusted, using either Holm's method or an FDR approach, and
mapped as in the previous sections. In this case, suppose there was an interest in
the scanning approach for local SIDS anomalies. Then the following produces an
appropriate map

```
# reset par(mfrow)
par(mfrow=c(1,1))

# Create a manual shading scheme
pval.shade <- shading(c(0.01,0.05,0.1),
                      cols=rev(brewer.pal(4,'PuRd')))
# Draw the map - note the p.adjust function -
# this time using the FDR approach
choropleth(nc.sids.p,
          p.adjust(mc.pvals,
               method='fdr'),
          shading=pval.shade)
# Add legends + title + scale
choro.legend(124 7,94.0,pval.shade,fmt="%6.2f")
title("Sudden Infant Death Syndrome (FDR Adjusted p-value)",
     cex.main=2)
add.scale()
```

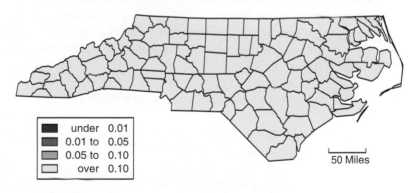

Sudden Infant Death Syndrome (FDR Adjusted p-value)

- ■ under 0.01
- ■ 0.01 to 0.05
- ▢ 0.05 to 0.10
- □ over 0.10

50 Miles

Figure 8.9 Local Moran's *I* FDR adjusted simulated *p*-values

As can be seen, when simulation is used to allow for problems in the normal approximation, the resultant heavy-tailed distributions now show imply that the approach fails to detect any anomalous results.

8.6 GETIS AND ORD'S *G*-STATISTIC

An alternative statistic used to detect spatial anomalies is the G-statistic (Getis and Ord, 1992; Ord and Getis, 2010). Like the local Moran's *I*, for each of polygon *i*, there is an associated statistic G_i. This is defined as follows:

$$G_i = \frac{\sum_{j=1}^{n} z_j v_{ij}(d)}{\sum_{j=1}^{n} z_j} \tag{8.11}$$

where $v_{ij}(d)$ is 1 if the distance between the centroids of polygons *i* and *j* is less than *d*, and 0 otherwise.[2] This can be thought of as the proportion of the total z_i concentrated at a distance *d* around polygon *i*. Note that this quantity is only meaningful if z_i is a non-negative quantity with a natural zero – for example, the SIDS rates used before satisfy this requirement. Clearly they cannot be negative, and the zero value corresponds to the situation where no sudden infant deaths were recorded in the study period. A counter-example might be net migration in each county, which could be either negative or positive. Some further discussion on the differences bewtween Moran's *I* and the G-statistic can be found in Getis and Ord (1992).

The G-statistic may be computed in R via the spdep package – using the localG function. The v_{ij} information is represented by a listw object as with Moran's *I*, although here the weights are always 0 or 1 – and it is distance between polygon centroids, rather than adjacency, that defines the values. An nb object is first created from the Spatial Polygons Data Frame nc.sids.p using the dnear-neigh function; this takes the centroid coordinates of nc.sids.p and then two further arguments, the minimum and maximum distances. This is then converted to a listw object – the style='B' option selects a 0–1 weighting system (rather than standardising rows to sum to 1, for example) – the 'B' stands for 'binary'. The following code does this conversion, for *d* = 30 miles, and plots the connected centroids in Figure 8.10:

```
nc.nb.g <- dnearneigh(coordinates(nc.sids.p),0,30)
                                # Create the nb object
nc.lw.g <- nb2listw(nc.nb.g,style='B')
                            # Create the associated listw object
plot(nc.sids.p) # Plot the counties
```

2 In the original paper, w_{ij} was used, but we have already used this to define Moran's *I*.

```
plot(nc.nb.g,coordinates(nc.sids.p),add=TRUE,col='red')
                              # Add the v[i,j] information
add.scale() # Add scale
```

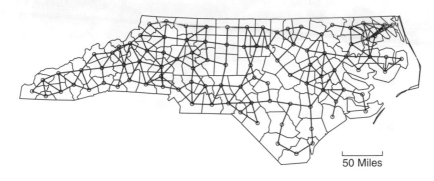

Figure 8.10 Connectivity between counties for d = 30 miles.

Once the v_{ij} information has been created, it is possible to compute the local G statistics. As with local Moran's I, the values of $E(G_i)$ and $Var(G_i)$ under a randomisation null hypothesis can be deduced – and again these could be compared against a theoretical normal distribution, or (if more appropriate) subjected to a Monte Carlo test. Expressions for $Var(G_i)$ and $E(G_i)$ are given in Getis and Ord (1992) The localG function in spdep returns these standardised G_i statistics – the following example creates a choropleth map (Figure 8.11) using this function:

```
nc.1G <- localG(sids79,nc.lw.g)  # Create local G
                           # Create a shading scheme
sids.shade <- auto.shading(c(nc.1G,-nc.1G),
cols=brewer.pal(5,"PRGn"))
choropleth(nc.sids.p,nc.1G,shading=sids.shade)
                            # Draw choropleth map
choro.legend(120.3,54.9,sids.shade,fmt="%5.2f")  # Add
legend
title("Sudden Infant Death Syndrome (Cases per 1000 Popn)",
      cex.main=2)  # Add title
add.scale() # Add scale
```

Generally this highlights areas where there are relatively high or low values of the SIDS rate. As with local Moran's I, however, it is important to consider this in a more formal inferential framework. For this we can make use of the ideas already set out regarding multiple testing in the earlier sections. A first question is whether the assumption of normality for the standardised G_I statistics is reasonable.

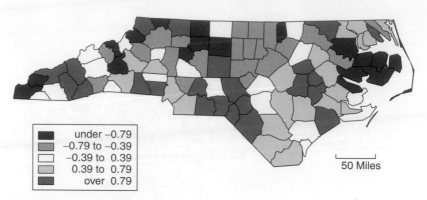

Figure 8.11 Map of standardised *Gi*

To investigate this, *QQ* plots will be used, as before. Again we take a Monte Carlo approach and generate a set of randomised simulated datasets:

```
# Create a matrix to place the simulated local G
sim.G <- matrix(0,1000,100)
# Run the simulations
# to evaluate the simulated distributions.
for (i in 1:1000) sim.G[i,] <- localG(sample(sids79),nc.lw.g)
```

Then we take a random sample of counties and examine their QQ plots (Figure 8.12). Again, recall that due to its random nature, running the following code is likely to produce a different sample of counties than the ones illustrated.

```
# Set up the 3 x 3 multiple window
par(mfrow=c(3,3))
# Create a random sample of 9 counties from 100
samp <- sample(100,9)
# For county in the each sample,  create a qq plot
for (cty in samp) {
  place <- nc.sids.p@data$NAME[cty] # County name
  qqnorm(sim.G[,cty],main=place) # QQ-plot
  qqline(sim.G[,cty]) # Reference line
}
```

Although perhaps there is some evidence of departure, the normal approximation appears to be less problematic for G_i than it was for I_i. The authors would speculate that this may be because G_i is a linear expression, whilst I_i is quadratic – however, this requires further investigation before a more rigorous explanation

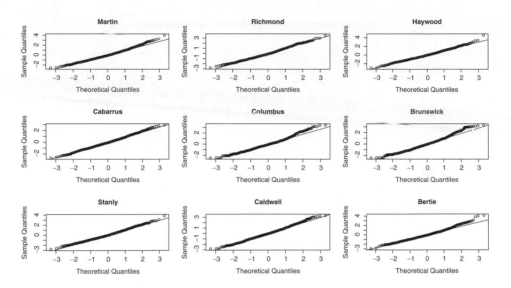

Figure 8.12 Matrix of *QQ*-plots for G_i for nine randomly selected counties.

is possible. Since a few of the randomly selected examples appear to have an slightly heavy upper tail, and an upper-tail *p*-value is used here, a precautionary approach may be to use Monte Carlo estimates for the per-county *p*-values:

```
mc.pvals.g <- (colSums(sweep(sim.G,2,nc.lG,'>=')) + 1) /
                (nrow(sim.G) + 1)
```

Again working with an FDR approach, the adjusted local *p*-values may be mapped (see Figure 8.13):

```
# reset par(mfrow)
par(mfrow=c(1,1))
nc.lpv.g <- p.adjust(mc.pvals.g,method="fdr")
lpv.shade <- shading(c(0.001,0.01,0.05,0.10),
    cols=rev(brewer.pal(5,"BuGn")))
choropleth(nc.sids.p,nc.lpv.g,shading=lpv.shade)
choro.legend(120.3,54.9,lpv.shade,fmt="%5.3f")
title("Sudden Infant Death Syndrome (Local p-values)",
    cex.main=2)
add.scale()
```

Again, this map suggests that the method has failed to identify any counties that could be flagged as having a high SIDS rate under a randomisation null hypothesis.

Sudden Infant Death Syndrome (Local *p*-values)

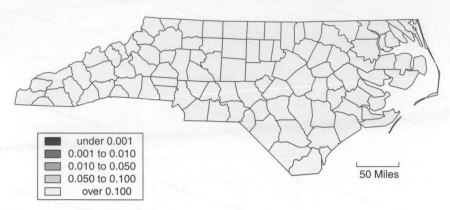

■	under 0.001
■	0.001 to 0.010
■	0.010 to 0.050
■	0.050 to 0.100
□	over 0.100

50 Miles

Figure 8.13   FDR-adjusted local *p*-values for local *G* statistics

---

Perhaps drawing a map when *none* of the counties are flagged may seem like overkill. A quicker method of testing this might be to use `all` – this function returns a logical value of TRUE only if all of the logical elements in an input array are TRUE:

```
all(c(TRUE,FALSE,TRUE,TRUE))
## [1] FALSE
all(c(TRUE,TRUE,TRUE))
## [1] TRUE
```

This could be used with a general test as to whether each adjusted *p*-value was greater than or equal to 0.05:

```
all(nc.lpv.g >= 0.05)
## [1] TRUE
```

Only if this expression is FALSE is it necessary to map the *p*-values.
   Another related function is `any`, which works in the same way, but returns TRUE if *any* input value is TRUE. This may also be used in a similar way:

```
any(nc.lpv.g < 0.05)
## [1] FALSE
```

In this case, only if this expression is TRUE is it necessary to map the *p*-values.

Another way the G statistic may be used is to vary the value of d and investigate whether this changes the identification of potential clusters, and therefore idenitify the scale of any clustering. One way this can be achieved in R is to create a function to carry out the local G_i testing as above, given a distance d, and then to loop through a set of distances. Such a function is defined here:

```
g.test <- function(d,spdf, var) {
  spdf.nb <- dnearneigh(coordinates(spdf),0,d)
  spdf.lw <- nb2listw(spdf.nb,style='B')
  true.G <- localG(var,spdf.lw)
  sim.G <- matrix(0,10000,length(var))
  for (i in 1:10000) sim.G[i,] <- localG(sample(var),spdf.lw)
  return((colSums(sweep(sim.G,2,nc.lI[,4],'>='))) + 1) /
          (nrow(sim.I) + 1))
}
```

This function takes a distance, a Spatial Points Data Frame and a variable associated with each polygon (i.e. a z_i vector) and returns a set of per-polygon p-values (which will require either Holm or FDR adjustment) based on a Monte Carlo simulation with 10,000 replications. As an initial exploration, it is possible using the `all` function set out above to detect whether *any* counties are flagged for the North Carolina data, over a range of d-values:

```
dists <- seq(10,100,by=5) # 30 to 100 miles, in steps of 5
p.results <- matrix(0,100,15)
i <- 1 # Counter for p.results vector
for (d in dists) {
  p.results[,i] <- p.adjust(
    g.test(d,nc.sids.p,sids79),method='fdr')
  i <- i + 1 }
flag.p <- p.results < 0.05
apply(flag.p,2,any)

##   [1] FALSE FALSE FALSE FALSE FALSE FALSE FALSE FALSE
           TRUE TRUE TRUE
## [12] TRUE   TRUE   TRUE   TRUE
```

Here it can be seen that there are some distances where some counties were flagged. The distances are:

```
dists[apply(flag.p,2,any)]

## [1]   70   75   80   85   90   95   100
```

It is then possible to map the *p*-values for one of the distances at which some counties are flagged – for example, the following code yields Figure 8.14:

```
choropleth(nc.sids.p,p.results[,dists==100],
          shading=lpv.shade)
choro.legend(120.3,54.9,lpv.shade,fmt="%5.3f")
title(
      "Sudden Infant Death Syndrome d=100 miles (Local
      p-values)",cex.main=2)
add.scale()
```

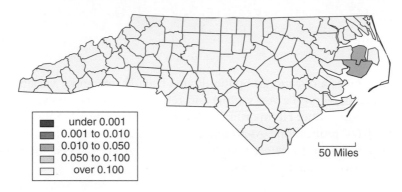

Sudden Infant Death Syndrome, d = 100 Miles (Local *p*-values)

Figure 8.14 FDR-adjusted local *p*-values for local *G* statistics, *d* = 100 miles

Note that although several sets of tests were carried out here, the FDR will not be altered – essentially this quantity is a rate, so adding together all of the tagged counties in all of the tests (all carried out with a FDR capped at 0.05) will still result in a process with a FDR capped at this level. Therefore one advantage of the *G* statistic combined with FDR adjustment is that it allows testing to be carried out over a range of distances. It seems here that clusters tend to become apparent only when larger values of *d* are considered.

8.7 GEOGRAPHICALLY WEIGHTED APPROACHES

A different – and arguably more exploratory – approach is to use *geographical weighting* (see Brunsdon et al., 1996, for example). The idea here is to take some kind of statistical technique to which weighting may be applied (for example, regression) and at a number of *sample points* to compute the weighted version of this technique using a weighted scheme centred on each sample point. The weighting schemes are similar to those used in kernel density estimation (see Chapter 6). This moving kernel approach is used to identify regional variation in the relationships between variables, or in some cases to investigate changes in the distributional characteristic of a single variable – for example, whether the standard deviation of some quantity (say, house price) is higher in some regions than in others.

8.7.1 Review of Summary Statistics

To introduce the geographically weighted (GW) approach, it is useful to recall the general ideas surrounding summary statistics – these are basic statistics used to summarise a large dataset. For example, when looking at a dataset of, say, 10,000 house prices, you might wish to calculate the mean of these, to obtain an idea of what a typical house price might be. Similarly, you may use a standard deviation to see the extent to which house prices are spread around this mean. Finally (and perhaps a bit more obsure), you can use the skewness to measure the symmetry of distribution (i.e. whether there is a long upper or lower tail to the distribution, or whether values are fairly evenly distributed around the mean). Generally these are useful – although not comprehensive – techniques for what is sometimes called 'data reduction' (Ehrenberg, 1982). They are useful in that, with a small number of quantities, it is possible to summarise note only typical values, but also distributional properties of variables of interest in very large datasets. Geographically weighted summary statistics (Brunsdon et al., 2002) are similar, but, as stated above, they apply summary statistics using a moving window, so that the above characteristics can be mapped as you move through different geographical regions in a dataset. Thus, you can see whether the mean house price in London, UK, is different from that in Liverpool, UK. Looking at means in this way is not unusual. However, although mean levels are often considered in that way, it is also possible to think about moving windows to estimate geographical variations in standard deviation – and see whether house prices are more *variable* in some places than others, or local skewness – to see whether the lopsidedness of house price distribution changes from place to place.

Also, correlation is a useful bivariate summary statistic, as it measures the degree to which two variables are associated. The most commonly used measure of this is the *Pearson correlation coefficient*. Again, the idea with a geographically weighted correlation is to use a moving window approach to see whether this degree of association varies geographically – for example, in some places floor area may be strongly correlated with house price, but in others less so, if, say, being of historical or cultural interest might make a smaller house more valuable than it would otherwise be.

Finally, the mean, standard deviation, skewness and correlation coefficient all have *robust* equivalents: the median, interquartile range and quantile imbalance. These are robust in the sense that they are based on the sorted order of values. For the univariate summary statistics, if we sort a variable in ascending order, let the halfway point be Q_2, the first quarter point be Q_1 and the third quarter point be Q_3, then the median is Q_2, the interquartile range is $Q_3 - Q_1$ and the quantile imbalance is

$$\frac{Q_3 - 2Q_2 + Q_1}{Q_3 - Q_1}$$

The last one may be less familiar, but it basically measures the difference between the first quartile and the median and the median and the second quartile – leading to a measure of lopsidedness. The measures are seen as robust because one or two very high or very low values do not 'throw' the summary statistics, since they will not alter the values of Q_1, Q_2 or Q_3. Again, these can be geographically weighted (see Brunsdon et al., 2002).

Finally, Spearman's rank correlation coefficient is a robust version of the Pearson coefficient. Each value of each variable is replaced by its rank. The smallest value of the first variable is replaced by 1, the next smallest by 2 and so on. The same is then done for the second variable, Then the Pearson correlation coefficient is computed for these rank-based variables.

The package GWmodel provides a number of tools for geographically weighted approaches. The geographically weighted summary statistics it provides are listed below:

Statistic	What it Measures	Robust	Bivariate or Univariate
Mean	Overall level	No	Univariate
Standard deviation	Spread	No	Univariate
Skewness	Asymmetry	No	Univariate
Median	Overall level	Yes	Univariate
Interquartile range	Spread	Yes	Univariate
Quantile imbalance	Asymmetry	Yes	Univariate
Pearson correlation	Association	No	Bivariate
Spearman correlation	Association	Yes	Bivariate

8.7.2 Geographically Weighted Summary Statistics in R

In this example house price data will be used, obtained from the Nationwide Building Society in the UK; this is a sample of houses sold in 1991 with mortgages arranged by this building society.

```
library(GWmodel)
data(EWHP)
head(ewhp)
```

```
##   Easting  Northing  PurPrice  BldIntWr  BldPostW  Bld60s  Bld70s  Bld80s
## 1  599500    142200     65000         0         0       0       0       1
## 2  575400    167200     45000         0         0       0       0       0
## 3  530300    177300     50000         1         0       0       0       0
## 4  524100    170300    105000         0         0       0       0       0
## 5  426900    514600    175000         0         0       0       0       1
## 6  508000    190400    250000         0         1       0       0       0
##   TypDetch  TypSemiD  TypFlat   FlrArea
## 1        0         1        0     78.95
## 2        0         0        1     94.37
## 3        0         0        0     41.33
## 4        0         0        0     92.88
## 5        1         0        0    200.53
## 6        1         0        0    148.61
```

From this, it can be seen that the house purchase price PurPrice is recorded together with a number of other artefacts of the house – for example, its floor area in square metres ('FlrArea').

Also, house prices can be divided by 1000 since this tends to make graphs, map keys and so on less cluttered – as well as avoiding some numerical rounding errors when doing some fairly complex calculations:

```
ewhp$PurPrice <- ewhp$PurPrice / 1000
```

We can look at the relation of floor area and purchase price using the standard plot command in R.

```
plot(ewhp$FlrArea,ewhp$PurPrice, xlab='Floor Area',
     ylab='Purchase Price (1000\'s UK Pounds)')
```

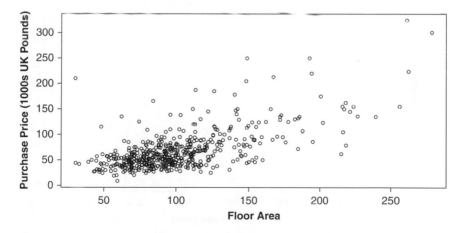

Figure 8.15 Purchase price plotted against floor area

This is shown in Figure 8.15 and demonstrates that there a few quite expensive houses with small floor areas, and also some quite large houses with relatively low price. The summary statistics can also be viewed. First, the mean and standard deviation:

```
mean(ewhp$PurPrice)

## [1]  67.35

sd(ewhp$PurPrice)

## [1]  38.75
```

Skewness can be calculated via a function in the package e1071:

```
library(e1071)
skewness(ewhp$PurPrice)

## [1]  2.441
```

From this value it can be seen that this distribution is strongly positively skewed – suggesting a large upper tail – that is, a central group of typically priced houses together with a long tail of relatively expensive ones. A histogram command should verify this (see Figure 8.16):

```
hist(ewhp$PurPrice,xlab='Purchase Price',
     main='Housing Cost Distribution')
```

Figure 8.16 Histogram of UK house prices

Having examined the aspatial aspects of the houses, we may now explore the geo-graphically weighted statistics. As noted earlier, GWmodel provides a number of geographically weighted methods – each of these operates on a SpatialPoints DataFrame (or possibly a SpatialPolygonsDataFrame) object. Taking the eastings and northings from the ewhp data frame, a SpatialPointsDataFrame called houses.spdf is created:

```
houses.spdf <- SpatialPointsDataFrame(ewhp[,1:2],ewhp)
```

Next load the border around England and Wales as a *SpatialPolygon* and plot this as well as the points where the houses are:

```
data(EWOutline)
plot(ewoutline)
plot(houses.spdf,add=T,pch=16)
```

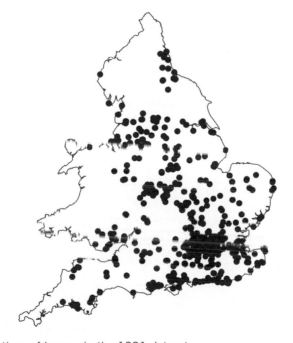

Figure 8.17 Locations of houses in the 1991 dataset

Your plot should look like Figure 8.17.

Now you can compute the geographically weighted summary statistics. The function to do this is called gwss and can be called with arguments giving the spatial points data frame, the variables that you want to compute the statistics for, and the bandwidth for the moving window. Use a 50 km bandwidth here. All of the statistics discussed above are returned in a single object, stored in a variable called `localstats1`:

```
localstats1 <- gwss(houses.spdf,vars=c("PurPrice",
                    "FlrArea"),bw=50000)
```

This object has a number of components. The most important one is probably a spatial data frame containing the results of local summary statistics for each data point location. These are stored in `localstats1$SDF` (this itself is a spatial points data frame). To access just the data frame component of it, use the expression `data.frame(localstats1$SDF)`. To see just the first few observations, enter

```
head(data.frame(localstats1$SDF))
##   PurPrice_LM FlrArea_LM PurPrice_LSD FlrArea_LSD PurPrice_LVar
## 1       61.48     101.44        30.38       38.78         923.2
## 2       62.57      96.73        32.68       39.75        1068.1
## 3       86.37      94.38        40.72       37.60        1658.3
## 4       87.81      94.92        41.54       37.66        1725.4
## 5       67.75     117.02        53.57       43.04        2870.0
## 6       89.51      95.37        49.56       38.41        2455.7
##   FlrArea_LVar PurPrice_LSKe FlrArea_LSKe PurPrice_LCV FlrArea_LCV
## 1         1504         1.466        1.328       0.4942      0.3823
## 2         1580         2.498        1.791       0.5223      0.4110
## 3         1414         1.954        1.688       0.4715      0.3984
## 4         1418         2.037        1.657       0.4730      0.3968
## 5         1852         1.239        1.058       0.7908      0.3678
## 6         1475         2.380        1.581       0.5536      0.4028
## Cov_PurPrice.FlrArea Corr_PurPrice.FlrArea Spearman_rho_PurPrice.FlrArea
## 1                858.6                0.6969                        0.5158
## 2               1078.7                0.8063                        0.7290
## 3               1104.6                0.7146                        0.6176
## 4               1139.6                0.7219                        0.6294
## 5               2459.2                0.9532                        0.8161
## 6               1482.4                0.7716                        0.6829
##   Easting Northing
## 1  599500   142200
## 2  575400   167200
## 3  530300   177300
## 4  524100   170300
## 5  426900   514600
## 6  508000   190400
```

A guide to the variable names is below:

Variable name	Statistic referred to
X_LM	GW mean
X_LSD	GW standard deviation
X_Lvar	GW variance
X_LSKe	GW skewness
X_LCV	GW coefficient of variation
Cov_X.Y	GW covariance
Corr_X.Y	GW Pearson correlation
Spearman_rho_X.Y	GW Spearman correlation

Note that the GW coefficient of variation is the GW standard deviation divided by the GW mean. Also note that X and Y should be replaced by the names of the actual variables being investigated.

Next, enter a small R function definition to produce a map of the local geographically weighted summary statistic of your choice. Firstly, load the RColorBrewer package – a useful tool for designing map colour palettes:

```
require(RColorBrewer)
```

Now type in the function definition:

```
quick.map <- function(spdf,var,legend.title,main.title) {
  x <- spdf@data[,var]
  cut.vals <- pretty(x)
  x.cut <- cut(x,cut.vals)
  cut.levels <- levels(x.cut)
  cut.band <- match(x.cut,cut.levels)
  colors <- brewer.pal(length(cut.levels),'Reds')
  par(mar=c(1,1,1,1))
  plot(ewoutline,col='grey85')
  title(main.title)
  plot(spdf,add=TRUE,col=colors[cut.band],pch=16)
  legend('topleft',cut.levels,col=colors,pch=16,bty='n',
  title=legend.title)
}
```

In short, the function does the following things:

1. Extracts the GW summary statistic of interest from the `gwss` object

2. Finds a 'nice' set of regularly spaced class intervals

3. Works out which class interval the GW summary statistic at each point falls into

4. Defines a colour palette to show the intervals

5. Defines the size of the margin around the map

6. Plots the UK border

7. Adds a title

8. Plots the colour-coded gwss points

9. Draws a legend

The function is called by entering:

```
quick.map(gwss.object,variable.name,legend.title,
          main.map.title)
```

Thus, to create a map of the geographically weighted mean (Figure 8.18), enter:

```
quick.map(localstats1$SDF,"PurPrice_LM",
          "1000's Uk Pounds","Geographically Weighted Mean")
```

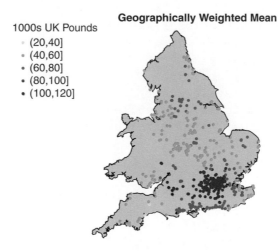

Figure 8.18 Geographically weighted mean

Next, look at the locally weighted standard deviation and skewness (Figure 8.19):

```
par(mfrow=c(1,2))
quick.map(localstats1$SDF,"PurPrice_LSKe",
          "Skewness Level","Local Skewness")
quick.map(localstats1$SDF,"PurPrice_LSD",
          "1000's Pounds","Local Standard Deviation")
```

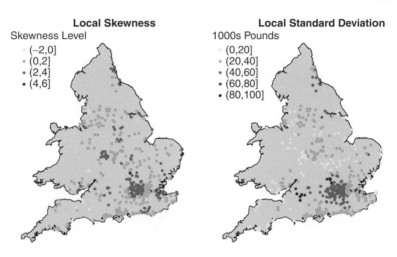

Figure 8.19 Geographically weighted skewness and standard deviation

Comparing figures side by side like this makes comparison easier – an idea strongly advocated by Tufte (1983), for example. Here, you can see the differences in spatial pattern between local skewness and standard deviation very clearly. The two patterns differ notably. One interesting trend in skewness is that there is a pattern towards the western side of London and the South-East for standard deviation to be greater – suggesting there are more houses that are relatively more variable. Further up the country it can be seen that variability is generally lower, although there is some more variability in the North-East.

Skewness seems to be largest in South Wales and the South-West of England, suggesting these places have a more notable 'upper tail' where there is a small number of *very* expensive houses. One possible explanation of this is that these places are popular choices for second 'holiday' homes, where there is a distinct housing submarket whose prices are driven up by relatively affluent buyers. Although these houses are perhaps less likely to be purchased with a mortgage arrangement, houses near to them will see similar rises in price. However, this is only a hypothesis, and would require further investigation. It demonstrates the value of exploratory work; we have noticed a pattern not easily identified by basic approaches, and a possible explanation, perhaps unearthing a process that might otherwise have gone undiscovered.

8.7.3 Exploring Non-Stationarity of Relationships

We can also map the geographically weighted correlation between the variables `PurPrice` and `FlrArea`. This allows the exploration of geographical variation in the strength of the association the between the two variables. The following code achieves this, producing Figure 8.20. A new R expression here is the `expression (rho)` term. R allows mathematical expressions to appear in graphics as well as text – the ρ in this case is the usual mathematical symbol for Pearson correlation.

```
# reset par(mfrow)
par(mfrow=c(1,1))
quick.map(localstats1$SDF,"Corr_PurPrice.FlrArea",
        expression(rho),"Geographically Weighted Pearson
        Correlation")
```

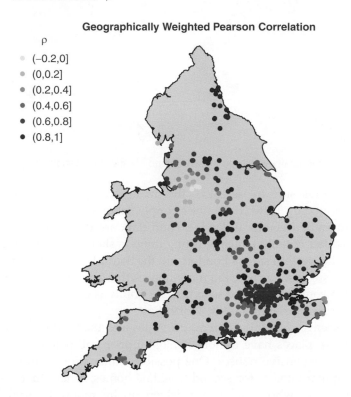

Geographically Weighted Pearson Correlation

ρ

- (−0.2,0]
- (0,0.2]
- (0.2,0.4]
- (0.4,0.6]
- (0.6,0.8]
- (0.8,1]

Figure 8.20   Geographically weighted Pearson correlation

Here the strongest linkage is in the North-East – and parts of East Anglia – suggesting in these cases that property size is very strongly linked to price. It is generally lower in the South-East – possibly other factors are more important here, such as whether the property has a garage, nearness to facilities and so on. Note that `gwss` also provides the Spearman correlation as described above. A pair of maps (Figure 8.21) is a useful way to compare the two kinds of correlation:

```
par(mfrow=c(1,2))
quick.map(localstats1$SDF,"Corr_PurPrice.FlrArea",
          expression(rho),
          "Geographically Weighted Pearson Correlation")
quick.map(localstats1$SDF,"Spearman_rho_PurPrice.FlrArea",
          expression(rho),
          "Geographically Weighted Spearman Correlation")
```

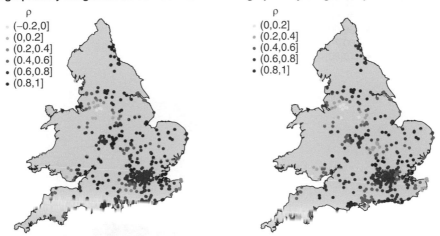

Geographically Weighted Pearson Correlation   **Geographically Weighted Spearman Correlation**

Figure 8.21   Comparison of geographically weighted correlation measures

This time, the 'small multiples' principle does a good job of demonstrating that the two kinds of local correlation show quite a similar story.

8.7.4 Robust, Quantile-Based Local Summary Statistics

As discussed earlier, there are quantile-based versions of the geographically weighted (GW) summary statistics, and `gwss` can supply these as well. In addition to the earlier summary statistics, a number of robust variants are provided:

Variable name	Statistic referred to
X_Median	GW median
X_IQR	GW interquartile range
X_QI	GW quantile imbalance

To obtain these in gwss, just add the option quantile=TRUE. Here, this is done and a map of geographically weighted medians (Figure 8.22) is produced:

```
# reset par(mfrow)
par(mfrow=c(1,1))
localstats2 <- gwss(houses.spdf,vars=c("PurPrice","FlrArea"),
                    bw=50000,quantile=TRUE)
quick.map(localstats2$SDF,"PurPrice_Median","1000\'s
        UK Pounds",
        "Geographically Weighted Median House Price")
```

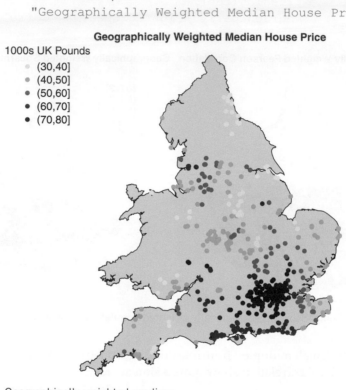

Figure 8.22 Geographically weighted medians

Finally, it is possible to inspect the other two robust geographically weighted summary statistics, the interquartile range and the quantile imbalance.

```
par(mfrow=c(1,2))
quick.map(localstats2$SDF,"PurPrice_IQR","1000\'s
        UK Pounds",
        "Geographically Weighted Interquartile Range")
quick.map(localstats2$SDF, "PurPrice_QI","1000\'s
        UK Pounds",
        "Geographically Weighted Quantile Imbalance")
```

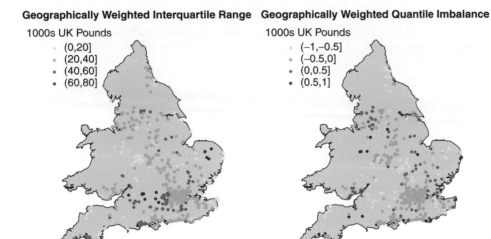

Figure 8.23 Geographically Weighted Interquartile Range and Quantile Imbalance

The interquartile ranges are quite similar to the standard deviations. Quantile imbalance is perhaps rather different – although extreme levels in the North-East might associate with the notably low median house prices compared to the means. However, recall from earlier discussions that the two measures are qualitatively quite different, and so it is less helpful to draw a direct comparision of quantile imbalance to skewness – the former focuses on the shape of the 'middle' 50% of the distribution, the latter on the contrast between high and low tails.

8.7.5 Geographically Weighted Regression

A final geographically weighted topic to be covered here is *geographically weighted regression* (GWR: Brunsdon *et al.*, 1996; Fotheringham *et al.*, 2002). As in the previous section, this is used to explore the relationships between several variables. The idea is to fit a regression model of the form:

$$z_i = a_0(u_i, v_i) + a_1(u_i, v_i)X_i + \varepsilon_i \qquad (8.12)$$

where z_i is a measured attribute at a location i, (u_i, v_i) are the coordinates of this location[3], X_i is a predictor variable associated with location i, a_0 and a_1 are functions of coordinates (u, v), and ε_i is a random normal variable with mean zero and variance σ^2. In the simple model, the ε_i are independent. This is essentially a regression model in which the coefficients are allowed to vary over space – further details and extension of the technique may be found in the references cited above. As with geographically weighted correlation, the idea is to explore the changes in relationship between

---

3 Typically if location i is a polygon rather than a point, (u_i, v_i) are the centroid coordinates.

two variables[4]. GWmodel incorporates a facility to compute GWR, using the function gwr.basic. Below, the GWR analysis is carried out for the model where z_i is the purchase price and X_i is the floor area:

```
gwr.res <- gwr.basic(PurPrice~FlrArea,
                     data=houses.spdf,bw=50000,
kernel='gaussian')
```

Here, the function takes a regression model specification PurPrice~FlrArea, a spatial points data frame with information relating to the variables and their location, and a bandwidth bw – as with other geographically weighted approaches, this is the radius of the kernel. The result (including quite a lot of related information) is stored in gwr.res, an object of class gwrm. A summary of the model can be obtained by printing the GWR object:

```
gwr.res
##    ***********************************************************************
##    *                       Package GWmodel                              *
##    ***********************************************************************
##    Program starts at: 2013-11-27 16:45:57
##    Call:
##    gwr.basic(formula = PurPrice ~ FlrArea, data = houses.spdf, bw = 50000)
##
##    Dependent (y) variable: PurPrice
##    Independent variables: FlrArea
##    Number of data points: 519
##    ***********************************************************************
##    *                    Results of Global Regression                    *
##    ***********************************************************************
##
##    Call:
##     lm(formula = formula, data = data)
##
##    Residuals:
##    Min      1Q Median     3Q       Max
## -80.22 -17.08  -3.49 12.13 189.42
##
##    Coefficients:
##               Estimate Std. Error t value Pr(>|t|)
##    (Intercept)    1.0695       3.6885    0.29     0.77
##    FlrArea                     0.6565 0.0342   19.20    <2e-16 ***
##
##    ---Significance stars
##    Signif. codes: 0 '***' 0.001 '**' 0.01 '*' 0.05 '.' 0.1 ' ' 1
##    Residual standard error: 29.6 on 517 degrees of freedom
##    Multiple R-squared: 0.416
##    Adjusted R-squared: 0.415
##    F-statistic: 369 on 1 and 517 DF, p-value: <2e-16
##    ***Extra Diagnostic information
##    Residual sum of squares: 454113
##    Sigma(hat): 29.64
##    AIC: 4995
##    AICc: 4995
```

---

4 Although it can be extended to consider several predictor variables

```
##  ****************************************************************************
##  *          Results of Geographically Weighted Regression               *
##  ****************************************************************************
##
##  ********************Model calibration information********************
##  Kernel function: gaussian
##  Fixed bandwidth: 50000
##  Regression points: the same locations as observations are used.
##  Distance metric: Euclidean distance metric is used.
##
##  ****************Summary of GWR coefficient estimates:******************
##              Min. 1st Qu. Median 3rd Qu.  Max.
##  X.Intercept. -42.700  -3.080  4.490   6.540 18.40
##  FlrArea        0.325   0.594  0.719   0.792  0.94
##  ************************Diagnostic information************************
##  Number of data points: 519
##  Effective number of parameters (2trace(S) - trace(S'S)): 28.69
##  Effective degrees of freedom (n-2trace(S) + trace(S'S)): 490.3
##  AICc (GWR book, Fotheringham, et al. 2002, p. 61, eq 2.33): 4840
##  AIC (GWR book, Fotheringham, et al. 2002,GWR p. 96, eq. 4.22): 4815
##  Residual sum of squares: 312583
##  R-square value: 0.5982
##  Adjusted R-square value: 0.5747
##
##  ****************************************************************************
##  Program stops at: 2013-11-27 16:46:06
```

One item within the gwr.res is called SDF and this is the spatial points data frame or spatial polygons data frame containing the estimates of $a_0(u, v)$ and $a_1(u, v)$ at the locations associated with the original data. These may be mapped in the same way as the local summary statistics earlier – the code below produces Figure 8.24.

```
# recut par (mfrow)
par(mfrow=c(1,1))
quick.map(gwr.res$SDF,"FlrArea",
          "1000's Uk Pounds per Square meter",
          "Geographically Weighted Regression Coefficient")
```

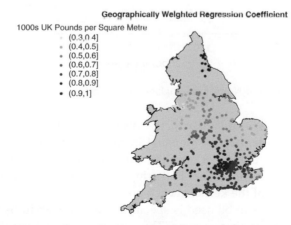

Figure 8.24   Geographically weighted regression coefficient

One interesting result here is the relatively high values of the coefficient in the North-East of England, despite the fact that the average price levels are actually quite low. One explanation of this is that there are two quite expensive houses in the North-East part of the dataset – which also have large floor areas; this can be seen in Figure 8.25, produced by the code below:

```
# Get coordinates
xy <- coordinates(gwr.res$SDF)
# Compute distance from a point in north east england
dne <- sqrt(rowSums(sweep(xy,2,c(452300,517200),"-")^2))
# Is each location less than 75km away?
in.ne <- dne < 75000
# Compare scatter plots for north east and rest of data
plot(houses.spdf$FlrArea,houses.spdf$PurPrice,type='n',
     xlab='Floor area (sq. m.)',
     ylab="Purchase Price (1000's pounds)")
points(houses.spdf$FlrArea[!in.ne],
       houses.spdf$PurPrice[!in.ne],col='grey85',pch=16)
points(houses.spdf$FlrArea[in.ne],
       houses.spdf$PurPrice[in.ne],col='black',pch=16)
```

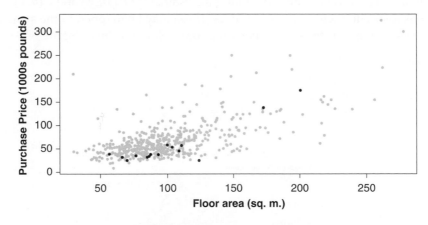

Figure 8.25 Comparison of North-East England against other areas

This illustrates the issue of *local outliers* – observations that are not untypical of the dataset as a whole, but are unusual in their region. To avoid the possible distortion of patterns due to local outliers, one approach is to use *adaptive band-width selection* – see, for example, Fotheringham et al. (2002). Here, rather than specifying the width of the kernel at each point $a_0(u, v)$ and $a_1(u, v)$ are estimated, the *number of data items* to be used is specified. The bandwidth is then chosen to include this number of observations. This will increase the bandwidth in areas where observations are sparser, and decrease in where they are denser. The option adaptive=TRUE instructs the gwr.basic function to use this approach. In this case, bw specifies the number of observations to include. Here the analysis is rerun using this approach – producing the map in Figure 8.26.

```
gwr.res.ad <- gwr.basic(PurPrice~FlrArea,
data=houses.spdf,adaptive=TRUE,bw=100), kernel='gaussian')
quick.map(gwr.res.ad$SDF,"FlrArea",
          "1000's Uk Pounds per Square meter",
          "Geographically Weighted Regression Coefficient")
```

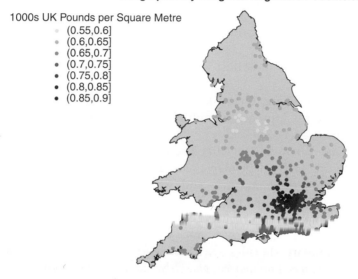

Figure 8.26 Geographically weighted regression coefficient using an adaptive bandwidth

The map produced above has similar geographical patterns outside of the North East, but the unusually high values of the coefficient in the North-East are no longer present.

The GWmodel package offers a number of other options – for example, an alternative approach to handling outliers in GWR as presented in Harris et al. (2010); and a number of diagnostics to identify collinearity. The latter is an issue in GWR (and indeed many other kinds of regression) when there are several predictor variables exhibiting correlation. GWmodel also offers other geographically weighted techniques, such as principal components analysis (Harris et al., 2011).

ANSWER TO SELF-TEST QUESTION

A fairly straightforward way to achieve this is to select the rows for which the significance is less than 0.05, and corresponding columns to give the names of the counties.

```
nc.sids.p@data[nc.lI[,5] < 0.05,c(11,18,19)]
```

```
##              NAME  BIR79 SID79
## 37029      Camden    350     2
## 37045   Cleveland   5526    21
## 37093        Hoke   1706     6
## 37095        Hyde    427     0
## 37155     Robeson   9087    26
## 37165    Scotland   2617    16
## 37177     Tyrrell    319     0
## 37187  Washington   1141     0
## 37189     Watauga   1775     1
```

REFERENCES

Anselin, L. (1995) Local indicators of spatial association – LISA. *Geographical Analysis*, 27: 93–115.

Benjamini, Y. and Hochberg, Y. (1995). Controlling the false discovery rate: A practical and powerful approach to multiple testing. *Journal of the Royal Statistical Society, Series B*, 57(1): 289–300.

Benjamini, Y. and Yekutieli, D. (2001) The control of the false discovery rate in multiple testing under dependency. *The Annals of Statistics*, 29(4): 1165–1188.

Brunsdon, C., Fotheringham, A.S. and Charlton, M. (1996) Geographically weighted regression: A method for exploring spatial nonstationarity. *Geographical Analysis*, 28: 281–289.

Brunsdon, C., Fotheringham, A.S. and Charlton, M. (2002) Geographically weighted summary statistics – a framework for localised exploratory data analysis. *Computers, Environment and Urban Systems*, 26(6): 501–524.

Ehrenberg, A. (1982) *A Primer in Data Reduction*. Chichester: John Wiley & Sons. Reprinted (2000) in the *Journal of Empirical Generalisations in Marketing Science*, 5: 1–391, and available from http://www.empgens.com.

Fotheringham, A.S., Brunsdon, C. and Charlton, M. (2002) *Geographically Weighted Regression: The Analysis of Spatially Varying Relationships*. Chichester: John Wiley & Sons.

Getis, A. and Ord, J. K. (1992) The analysis of spatial association by use of distance statistics. *Geographical Analysis*, 24(3): 189–206.

Harris, P., Brunsdon, C., and Charlton, M. (2011) Geographically weighted principal components analysis. *International Journal of Geographical Information Science*, 25(10): 1717–1736.

Harris, P., Fotheringham, A. and Juggins, S. (2010) Robust geographically weighed regression: A technique for quantifying spatial relationships between freshwater acidification critical loads and catchment attributes. *Annals of the Association of American Geographers*, 100(2): 286–306.

Holm, S. (1979) A simple sequentially rejective multiple test procedure. *Scandinavian Journal of Statistics*, 6: 65–70.

Ord, J.K. and Getis, A. (2010) Local spatial autocorrelation statistics: Distributional issues and an application. *Geographical Analysis*, 27(4): 286–306.

Permeger, T.V. (1998) What's wrong with Bonferroni adjustments. *British Medical Journal*, 316: (1236).

Šidàk, Z. (1967) Rectangular confidence region for the means of multivariate normal distributions. *Journal of the American Statistical Association*, 62: 626–633.

Tufte, E.R. (1983) *The Visual Display of Quantitative Information*. Cheshire, CT: Graphics Press.

Wilk, M. and Gnanadesikan, R. (1968) Probability plotting methods for the analysis of data. *Biometrika*, 55(1): 1–17.

9

R AND INTERNET DATA

9.1 INTRODUCTION

While the last few chapters have focused on spatial data analysis, and particularly on statistical approaches, this chapter considers another important aspect of working with spatial data, that of obtaining it from the internet. There are a number of ways that R can access internet data. Had this chapter been written some time ago, much emphasis would have been placed on *web scraping*, where output intended to create human-readable material (such as HTML files) is 'mined' using a computer program to extract relevant information. For example, the underlying HTML for web pages containing weather forecasts or share prices would be downloaded as they would for a web browser, but then the content would be scanned for patterns in their content that contained the information of interest – such as a formatted table with share prices or a table of forecasted maximum and minimum daily temperatures. Although this is still possible in some cases, the situation has perhaps bifurcated – some institutions have taken on board calls for open data, and provided *application program interfaces* (APIs) where direct requests may be made for data in machine-readable form, and others, perhaps initially unaware that data they published could be 'scraped' in this way and used in bulk, have adopted more complex practices in web site provision so that a basic 'scraping' approach is no longer possible.

For the situations in which an API is used, R provides generic tools for working with APIs, and also a number of packages intended to work directly with specific data providers, such as Google. In addition to this, web scraping can also be achieved, and most simply some data files may be directly accessed over the web. However, it is perhaps necessary to add a note of caution here. One issue with data from the internet is that data providers may occasionally change the format of API requests, or filenames, or of the dataset itself. Thus an approach that works at one point in time is not guaranteed to work indefinitely. In general, the problem is not irreparable – usually a reorganisation of the website has meant that some files are differently named, or the API has been modified, and existing code can be modified and become usable once more. However, for this reason it is important to have an understanding of the general principles involved in producing R code for accessing the data, rather than regarding code snippets as mystical incantations that can make certain items of data magically appear. The other consequence of this changeability leads the authors to issue a warning – what has just been said about changes in format means that although the examples given here work at the time of writing, we cannot guarantee that they will work without modification indefinitely.

It is worth noting that the exercises in this chapter involve accessing data over the internet in various ways. Service providers and operating systems often have differing rules regarding the circumstances and techniques used to access web-based information. For this reason, even when there have been no changes to websites, some of the exercises may fail to download information when working with some service providers. You may find you may need to use a different service provider (for example, working from home rather than from a public facility) or change some of the operating system settings (which we would only advise doing if you are fully aware of the consequences) to carry out the exercises successfully.

9.2 DIRECT ACCESS TO DATA

Let us begin with the situation in which data may be directly downloaded from the internet. R can deal with this in a number of ways. If the dataset on the internet is simply a text file, then the URL can sometimes be substituted for a filename with a number of commands. This works with read.csv and read.table, for example. A simple demonstration is provided here, via a Princeton University website, recording birth rates, an index of social setting and an index of family planning effort for a number of countries.[1] Here the data are read from the remote URL using read.table into a data frame called fpe:

```
fpe <-
read.table("http://data.princeton.edu/wws509/datasets/effort.dat")
head(fpe)
```

```
##              setting     effort     change
## Bolivia          46          0          1
## Brazil           74          0         10
## Chile            89         16         29
## Colombia         77         16         25
## CostaRica        84         21         29
## Cuba             89         15         40
```

It is then possible to analyse the data in the same way as any other data – here a scatterplot matrix of the variables is drawn (see Figure 9.1) to investigate relationships between the three variables. The panel=panel.smooth option causes a loess smooth (Cleveland, 1979) to be added to each scatter plot.

```
pairs(fpe,panel=panel.smooth)
```

---

1 See data.princeton.edu/R/readingData.html

Unfortunately, on Unix-based systems this approach works with URLs beginning with `http:` but not with the secured `https:` URLs. However, these URLs can be accessed using the `RCurl` package, discussed later in this chapter.

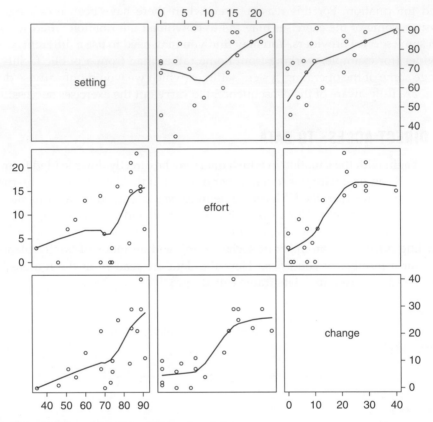

Figure 9.1   Scatter plot matrix of Princeton data

This approach can also be used to access code over the internet, via the `source` command. An example of this is found on the Bioconductor project[2] – on their website they describe themselves thus: 'Bioconductor is an open source, open development software project to provide tools for the analysis and comprehension of high-throughput genomic data. It is based primarily on the R programming language.' They provide a number of R packages, including a basic collection and a number of further optional packages. Although their aim is to develop code for a relatively specific area of application, some of these packages are of more general

2 `http://www.bioconductor.org`

use – for example, the `Rgraphviz` library for visualising graphs, as an alternative to the `iGraph` package. To install the base Bioconductor package collection (for R version 3.0.1 and later) enter

```
source("http://bioconductor.org/biocLite.R")
biocLite()
```

Then, to install `Rgraphviz`, enter:

```
source("http://bioconductor.org/biocLite.R")
biocLite("Rgraphviz")
```

Note that in both blocks of R, the command

```
source("http://bioconductor.org/biocLite.R")
```

is used. This runs some code located on the Bioconductor website to install the packages. Note also that this is not running a remote process. The remote code is read into R on the user's machine, and then executed on that machine. Although the intention here is to focus on running the remote code, rather than on the use of `Rgraphviz`, a brief example follows. This uses the `state.x77` data frame, supplied with the `datasets` package. This contains a number of variables recorded for each US state:

- Population estimate as of 1 July 1975 (`Population`)
- Income per capita, 1974 (`Income`)
- Illiteracy, 1970, as a percentage of population (`Illiteracy`)
- Life expectancy in years, 1969–1971 (`Life Exp`)
- Murder and non-negligent manslaughter rate per 100,000 population, 1976 (`Murder`)
- Percentage high-school graduates, 1970 (`HS Grad`)
- Mean number of days with minimum temperature below freezing, 1931–1960 in capital or large city (`Frost`)
- Land area in square miles (`Area`)

The correlations between each of these variables are computed, and the variable pairs whose absolute correlation exceeds 0.5 are noted. A graph is then created whose edges correspond to these pairs. Next, the graph is 'configured' – essentially locations for the nodes are specified, in a layout designed to limit the number of edge crossings. Finally, it is drawn.[3] The code below executes this procedure, and results in the graph seen in Figure 9.2:

```
# The following two packages are required:
require(Rgraphviz)
require(datasets)
# Load the state.x77 data
data(state)
# Which ones are 'connected' - i.e. abs correlation above
0.5
connected <- abs(cor(state.x77)) > 0.5
# Create the graph - node names are the column names
conn <- graphNEL(colnames(state.x77))
# Populate with edges - join variables that are TRUE in
'connected'
for (i in colnames(connected)) {
  for (j in colnames(connected)) {
    if (i < j) {
      if (connected[i,j]) {
        conn <- addEdge(i,j,conn,1)}}}}
# Create a layout for the graph
conn <- layoutGraph(conn)
# Specify some drawing parameters
attrs <- list(node=list(shape= "ellipse",
                        fixedsize=FALSE, fontsize=12))
# Plot the graph
plot(conn,attrs=attrs)
```

As can be seen, the population and area variables do not connect strongly with other variables (it is of note that these depend directly on the size of the state, while the others are state averages or per capita rates). Illiteracy is connected to the greatest number of other variables.

9.3 USING *RCURL*

The RCurl package[4] provides quite a lot of extra functionality for accessing data from the web. Essentially, it provides a set of tools to allow R to act as a web

---

3 As stated earlier, the aim here is not to provide a detailed tutorial on Rgraphviz, but the code block is commented, and further details are available at http://www.bioconductor.org/packages/2.12/bioc/vignettes/Rgraphviz/inst/doc/Rgraphviz.pdf

4 See http://www.omegahat.org/RCurl/ for full details.

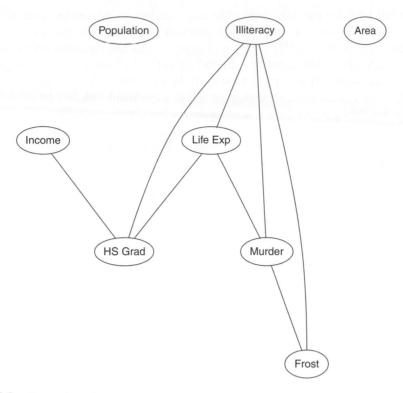

Figure 9.2 Illustration of `Rgraphviz`

client. This is done by providing a number of help functions. Perhaps the most basic is `getURL`: given a URL (including secure HTTPS and a number of other protocols, such as FTPS) this function returns the information located at the URL. In some cases this might be the content of an HTML file specifying a web page (which might possibly be used for web scraping), while in others it may be plain text (for example, the content of a CSV file). The latter situation will be considered here. The file `1871702.csv` is located on the UK government's server and contains the 2010 English Index of Multiple Deprivation (IMD) scores[5] in CSV format. This index combines measures of deprivation via a number of different dimensions (see Department for Communities and Local Government, 2012, for example), and the CSV file contains deprivation scores and ranks for each dimension, as well as an overall score[6] and rank for each Lower Super Output Area (LSOA) – in England there are 32,482 LSOAs in all. It also provides a look-up from LSOAs to larger areal units (such as Government Office Regions).

---

5 Contains public sector information licensed under the Open Government Licence v2.0.
6 Higher scores imply a greater degree of deprivation.

The full URL for this file appears in the code below. As can be seen, this URL uses the HTTPS protocol. The `getURL` function is used to read the contents of the file into `temp`. The `getURL` function always returns the information of the URL into a single character variable – including control characters such as carriage returns. The information is not particularly helpful in this form. The content is in fact a CSV file, and a command such as `read.csv` would ideally be used to read this content into a data frame. Fortunately R offers this possibility, via the `text-Connection` function. Given a character argument (such as that returned by `getURL`) this function creates a *connection* – a kind of pseudofile that can be read by a function usually requiring a filename as input. The content of the pseudofile is just the character content of the argument to `textConnection`. Thus, by storing the information obtained from `getURL` in a temporary variable, and then using this variable as input to `textConnection` and finally inputting this to `read.csv`, the file may be read into a data frame. This is set out below for Apple Mac users (see the notes following for MS Windows users):

```
library(RCurl)  # Load RCurl
# Get the content of the URL and store it into 'temp'
stem <-
'https://www.gov.uk/government/uploads/system/uploads'
file1 <- '/attachment_data/file/15240/1871702.csv'
temp <- getURL(paste0(stem,file1))
# Use textConnection to read the content of temp
# as though it were a CSV file
imd <- read.csv(textConnection(temp))
# Check - this gives the first 10 column names of the
data frame
head(colnames(imd),n=10)

##   [1]  "LSOA.CODE"
##   [2]  "PRE.2009.LA.CODE"
##   [3]  "PRE.2009.LA.NAME"
##   [4]  "POST.2009.LA.CODE"
##   [5]  "POST.2009.LA.NAME"
##   [6]  "GOR.CODE"
##   [7]  "GOR.NAME"
##   [8]  "IMD.SCORE"
##   [9]  "RANK.OF.IMD.SCORE..where.1.is.most.deprived."
##   [10] "INCOME.SCORE"
```

MS Windows users should ignore the line:

```
temp <- getURL(paste0(stem,file1))
```

and replace

```
imd <- read.csv(textConnection(temp))
```

with

```
imd <- read.csv(paste0(stem,file1))
```

If a number of CSV files are going to be read in this way (i.e. via a URL using the HTTPS protocol) it may be helpful to define a function read.csv.https to do this in a single command on a Mac:

```
read.csv.https <- function(url) {
    temp <- getURL(url)
    return(read.csv(textConnection(temp)))
}
```

and in MS Windows:

```
read.csv.https <- function(url) return(read.csv(url))
```

This function is then used in the following code block to create a boxplot of the IMD for each GOR in England. The result is reproduced in Figure 9.3.

```
# Download the csv data and put it into 'imd2'
imd2 <- read.csv.https(paste0(stem,file1))
# Modify the margins around the plot, to fit the GOR
# names into the left-hand margin
par(mar=c(5,12,4,2) + 0.1)
# Create the boxplot. The 'las' parameter specifies y-axis
# labelling is horizontal, x-axis is vertical
boxplot(IMD.SCORE~GOR.NAME,data=imd,horizontal=TRUE,las=2)
```

The boxplots show patterns varying across England – the lowest median levels of the IMD are in the East of England and South-East GORs, although London has a higher level. The North-East has the highest median level. However, the East of England actually has the highest IMD for an individual LSOA – and it can also be seen that some GORs have a more prominent upper tail than others – suggesting that some parts of England are more prone to small 'pockets of deprivation' than others. The variation in distribution shape across the UK also suggests that geographically weighted summary statistics may be a useful exploratory tool here.

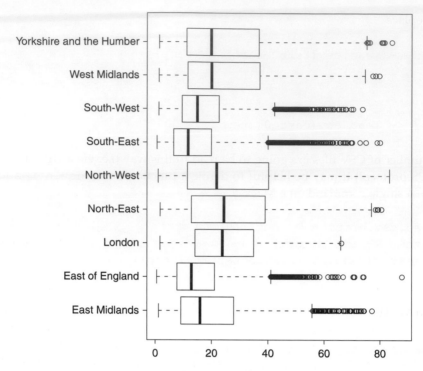

Figure 9.3 Boxplot of IMDs by Government Office Regions

9.4 WORKING WITH APIs

As well as providing 'raw' text files, many websites provide 'bespoke' data in response to requests – for example, all of the detached houses for sale in a given locality, or all of the crimes occurring in a given rectangular region. Obtaining data often takes the form of a client request, followed by a server response. The requests specify the information to be returned – for example, a location which is the centre of an area for crimes to be returned. It is often possible to specify these requests as part of a URL. The protocol for these specifications is essentially the API. For example, the `police.uk` website allows requests of the form:

```
http://data.police.uk/api/crimes-street/all-crime?lat=<latitude>
    &lng=<longitude>&date=<date>
```

where the items in angle brackets are replaced by actual values – such as

```
http://data.police.uk/api/crimes-street/all-crime?lat=53.401422
    &lng=-2.965075&date=2013-04
```

Note the lines are not broken in practice – this was done here just to fit the URLs on the page. These return all crimes in a one-mile radius of the specified latitude and longitude, for the month specified by <date>. It can therefore be seen that the requests consist of a number of named arguments (here, lat, lng and date).

It is quite possible to construct requests as above, and simply use getURL to retrieve the results. However, it is also possible to use getForm, which accepts the named parameters in the same format as named parameters in R. For example:

```
crimes.buf <- getForm(
    'http://data.police.uk/api/crimes-street/all-crime',
    lat=53.401422,
    lng=-2.965075,
    date="2013-04")
```

Although functionally identical, this format is easier to read – a useful characteristic when revisiting old code. Note, however, that as with getURL, the information returned is not quite ready to be used. As before, it is returned as a single character string, although this time the data is in *JavaScript Object Notation* (JSON) format, rather than CSV. JSON is a more sophisticated format, allowing lists with named elements, arrays and other forms of data to be represented. In particular, it allows lists within lists, and so on, to be represented. The crime data here is returned in this format. The data item that the JSON format character string represents consists of a list of items, one for each crime. Each item is itself a list, which contains at least the following items:

- Crime category (category)

- Unique crime identifier (persistent_ id)

- Month of the crime (month)

- A list item (location) containing the approximate crime latitude (latitude), approximate crime longitude (longitude), along with street details (street), including an ID number for the street (id) and a street name (name), specifiying a degree of uncertainty (e.g. 'On or near Florizel Street')

- A location type (location_type), either 'Force' or 'BTP' (British Transport Police)

In fact some further items are present, but we will focus on the ones listed, as they supply location, date and crime type. To convert the variable crimes.buf from a single character into a usable R object, the function fromJSON in the package rjson will be used:

```
require(rjson)
crimes <- fromJSON(crimes.buf)
```

The variable `crimes` is now an R list object, whose items meet the description above. To check this, enter:

```
crimes[[1]]

## $category
## [1] "anti-social-behaviour"
##
## $location_type
## [1] "Force"
##
## $location
## $location$latitude
## [1] "53.408246"
##
## $location$street
## $location$street$id
## [1] 912187
##
## $location$street$name
## [1] "On or near Adderley Street"
##
##
## $location$longitude
## [1] "-2.949301"
##
##
## $context
## [1] " "
##
## $outcome_status
## NULL
##
## $persistent_id
## [1] "865f4241f44bea75b34ffc7f02924d5ab9cfad6db182
4f4fdd9305f68b558641"
##
## $id
## [1] 23097276
##
## $location_subtype
## [1] " "
##
## $month
## [1] "2013-04"
```

This is the first item describing a crime, in a list of all crimes within a one-mile radius of the location 53.401422°N, 2.965075°W, in April 2013. This is a helpful object format for storing complex information – for example, the street name and ID are in a list within a list within a list. However, most data analysis in R uses the more familiar vector, matrix and data frame formats. The next step is to extract the relevant information from crimes. This is a two-stage process:

1. Create a function to extract the information needed from an individual list item
2. Use sapply to apply the function to each item in the list, and recombine the results into an array

The method is illustrated below – here the function getLonLat extracts longitude and latitude

```
getLonLat <- function(x) as.numeric(c(x$location$longitude,
           x$location$latitude))
crimes.loc <- t(sapply(crimes,getLonLat))
head(crimes.loc)

##          [,1]   [,2]
## [1,] -2.949 53.41
## [2,] -2.949 53.41
## [3,] -2.949 53.41
## [4,] -2.949 53.41
## [5,] -2.949 53.41
## [6,] -2.949 53.41
```

The as.numeric function is used, since the latitude and longitude are stored as characters. Note that the sapply function returns the listwise results as one *column* per item, whereas data frames and matrices are usually formatted as one row per item. Thus the t function is applied, which transposes rows and columns.

Next, some of the attribute data for each of the crimes is extracted. This is done in the same way:

```
getAttr <- function(x) c(
  x$category,
  x$location$street$name,
  x$location_type)
crimes.attr <- as.data.frame(t(sapply(crimes,getAttr)))
colnames(crimes.attr) <- c("category", "street",
"location_type")
head(crimes.attr)
```

```
##                  category                       street location_type
## 1 anti-social-behaviour On or near Adderley Street          Force
## 2 anti-social-behaviour On or near Adderley Street          Force
## 3 anti-social-behaviour On or near Adderley Street          Force
## 4 anti-social-behaviour On or near Adderley Street          Force
## 5 anti-social-behaviour On or near Adderley Street          Force
## 6 anti-social-behaviour On or near Adderley Street          Force
```

Here, the matrix created is converted to a data frame (with as.data.frame). Inspecting the top of the data frame created, it may be seen that the crimes are located in Liverpool, UK, and that the BTP crimes are generally associated with railway stations (such as Liverpool Central). Although the crimes have a spatial identifier, in this case they are not associated with streets. Finally, the location and attribute information can be combined to provide a spatial points data frame:

```
library(GISTools)
crimes.pts <- SpatialPointsDataFrame(crimes.loc,crimes.attr)
# Specify the projection - in this case just geographical
coordinates
proj4string(crimes.pts) <- CRS("+proj=longlat")
# Note that 'head' doesn't work on SpatialPointsDataFrames
crimes.pts[1:6,]
```

```
##         coordinates              category                  street
## 1 (-2.949, 53.41) anti-social-behaviour On or near Adderley Street
## 2 (-2.949, 53.41) anti-social-behaviour On or near Adderley Street
## 3 (-2.949, 53.41) anti-social-behaviour On or near Adderley Street
## 4 (-2.949, 53.41) anti-social-behaviour On or near Adderley Street
## 5 (-2.949, 53.41) anti-social-behaviour On or near Adderley Street
## 6 (-2.949, 53.41) anti-social-behaviour On or near Adderley Street
##   location_type
## 1         Force
## 2         Force
## 3         Force
## 4         Force
## 5         Force
## 6         Force
```

It is also possible to create further spatial points data frames by taking subsets of the data. This creates a set with incidents of anti-social behaviour only:

```
asb.pts <- crimes.pts[crimes.pts$category==
"anti-social-behaviour",]
```

This creates a set with criminal damage and arson cases:

```
cda.pts <- crimes.pts[crimes.pts$category==
"criminal-damage-arson",]
```

These data will be revisited, but for now a plot contrasting the locations of anti-social behaviour against criminal damage and arson crimes can be created (Figure 9.4):

```
plot(asb.pts,pch=16,col= 'grey70')
plot(cda.pts,pch=16,col= 'black',add=TRUE)
legend('bottomright',c("Antisocial behaviour",
"Criminal damage"),
   col=c("grey70", "black"),pch=16)
```

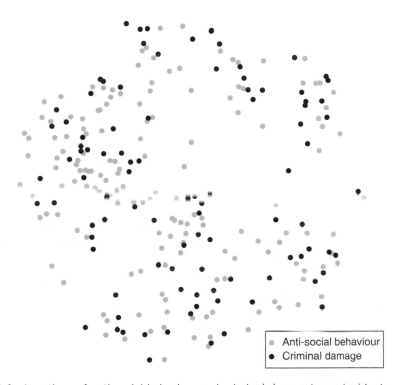

Figure 9.4 Locations of anti-social behaviour and criminal damage/arson incidents

One thing to note here is that although the locations are stored as latitude and longitude, so that directly plotting coordinates as x and y locations would give a distorted map, the plot method recognises this (from the proj4string) and corrects for it. As can be seen, both sets of points lie within a circle; however, without this correction they would appear to lie within an ellipse.

9.4.1 Creating a Statistical 'Mashup'

In this section, another API will be accessed, and the information obtained from it will be used in conjunction with the police.uk API. The new API is provided by Nestoria[7] and supplies lists of housing properties that are currently for sale. The API can be accessed via getForm in much the same way as the police.uk site[8]. Among other things, this supplies the asking price, latitude and longitude of properties. In the example below, a sample of 50 three-bedroom terraced houses is retrieved, and decoded from JSON form into an R object:

```
terr3bed.buf <- getForm("http://api.nestoria.co.uk/api",
   action= 'search_listings',
   place_name= 'liverpool',
   encoding= 'json',
   listing_type= 'buy',
   number_of_results=50,
   bedroom_min=3,bedroom_max=3,
   keywords= 'terrace')

terr3bed <- fromJSON(terr3bed.buf)
```

The warning appears because the keyword encoding is also used by the get-Form function directly, as well as a keyword in the Nestoria API. However, in this case, it is interpreted as a Nestoria keyword, which is required in the example, therefore the warning may be ignored.

The results are now stored as a list in terr3bed$response$listings. Inside each item in the list, a number of other items are stored. Among those of interest here are price, longitude and latitude – (further details of the keywords in the API and the information returned can be found at http://www.nestoria.co.uk/help/api). The following code extracts these and stores them in a data frame:

```
getHouseAttr <- function(x) {
   as.numeric(c(x$price/1000,x$longitude,x$latitude))
}

terr3bed.attr <- as.data.frame(t(sapply(
terr3bed$response$listings,getHouseAttr)))
```

---

7 http.//nestoria.co.uk

8 When using this API, follow the guidelines at http://www.nestoria.co.uk/help/api

```
colnames(terr3bed.attr) <- c("price", "longitude",
"latitude")
head(terr3bed.attr)
```

```
##        price   longitude    latitude
## 1   150.00      -2.926       53.42
## 2    69.95      -2.840       53.42
## 3    74.95      -3.034       53.38
## 4    56.00      -2.930       53.42
## 5    67.50      -2.951       53.43
## 6    79.00      -2.948       53.43
```

Note that prices are divided by 1000 – this is just to return simpler numbers for formatting. Next, these data are combined with police.uk data. Essentially, the aim here is to provide a further data item to terr3bed.attr – a count of the number of household burglaries occurring within a one-mile radius of each house during April 2013. This gives a measure of the frequency of burglaries that occur close to each house. This rate will then be compared to the price of each house. By restricting the study to three-bedroom terraced houses, it is hoped that much of the price variation attributed to the characteristics of the house itself will be controlled.

The code to create this extra variable is shown below:

```
# Create an extra column to contain burglary rates
terr3bed.attr <- transform(terr3bed.attr,burgs=0)

# For each house in the data frame
for (i in 1:50) {
  # Firstly obtain crimes in a 1-mile radius of the
  houses
  # latitude and longitude and decode it from JSON form
  crimes.near <- getForm(
  "http://data.police.uk/api/crimes-street/all-crime",
  lat=terr3bed.attr$latitude[i],
  lng=terr3bed.attr$longitude[i],
  date= "2013-04")
  crimes.near <- fromJSON(crimes.near)
  crimes.near <- as.data.frame(t(sapply(
  crimes.near,getAttr)))
  # Then from the 'category' column count the number of
  burglaries
  # and assign it to the burgs column
  terr3bed.attr$burgs[i] <- sum(crimes.near[,1] == 'burglary')
```

```
    # Pause before running next API request - to avoid
    overloading
    # the server
    Sys.sleep(0.7)
    # Note this stage may cause the code to take a minute
    or two to run
  }
```

Essentially this code makes a call to the `police.uk` API for each entry in the house price data frame. Once it has run, the relationship between price and burglary rate may be plotted as a scatter plot. As one or two house prices are very high, a log scale is used for the *y*-axis (the house price axis). The following code produces Figure 9.5:

```
plot(price~burgs,data=terr3bed.attr,log= 'y',
     xlab= 'Burglaries in a 1-mile radius',
     ylab= 'House Price (1000s pounds)')
```

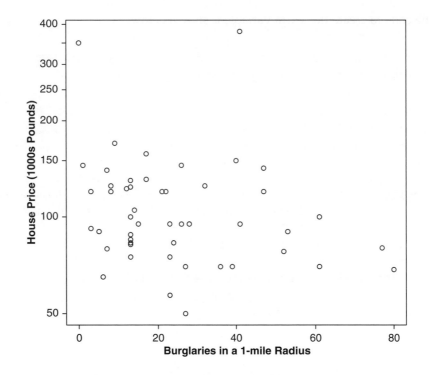

Figure 9.5   Scatter plot of burglary rate against house price

The scatter plot suggests some evidence for an inverse relationship between price and burglary rates. Finally, a regression model may be fitted – again, the y value is logged:

```
summary(lm(log(price)~burgs,data=terr3bed.attr))
```

```
##
## Call:
## lm(formula = log(price) ~ burgs, data = terr3bed.attr)
##
## Residuals:
##     Min      1Q  Median      3Q     Max
## -0.714  -0.231  -0.051   0.172   1.373
##
## Coefficients:
##             Estimate Std. Error t value Pr(>|t|)
## (Intercept)  4.73979    0.08671   54.66   <2e-16 ***
## burgs       -0.00421    0.00279   -1.51    0.14
## ---
## Signif. codes: 0 '***' 0.001 '**' 0.01 '*' 0.05 '.' 0.1
' ' 1
##
## Residual standard error: 0.376 on 48 degrees of freedom
## Multiple R-squared: 0.0451,Adjusted R-squared: 0.0252
## F-statistic: 2.27 on 1 and 48 DF, p-value: 0.139
```

This indicates that there is a significant negative effect – as the burglary rate increases, the house price decreases.

One final issue to be aware of with the Nestoria API is that it operates in real time – so that a request returns a list of houses that are currently on the market. This implies that running the code above at a future point may well not return the same results as listed here, since different data will be returned. It is suggested also that runs of the analysis in the future should use a more recent month for recorded crimes than April 2013. This month is being used at the time of writing since it is the most current.

9.5 USING SPECIFIC PACKAGES

Although it is possible to access many APIs using the RCurl package as a toolkit, there are a number of R packages that are designed to access specific APIs, such as Google Maps or Twitter. The main advantage of these is that they contain a number of predefined functions to unpack the data, or perhaps allow the user to merge other kinds of data. One example of this is the RgoogleMaps package. This allows the downloading of Google Maps tiles as backdrops for maps. The tiles are stored as raster images, and are based on a pixel-oriented coordinate system that runs from –320 to 320 in both the *x* and *y* directions. The package provides tools for both the downloading of the map tiles, and conversion of other coordinate systems (mainly latitude and longitude) to this system, to allow plotting.

The example here demonstrates the use of the `RgoogleMaps` package in conjunction with the crime data download earlier, and used in the code to generate Figure 9.4, in particular `asb.pts`. If this object is not currently defined in your R session, it is advisable to rerun the code in Section 9.4.

The `GetMap` function in `RgoogleMaps` finds a Google Maps tile containing a supplied latitude and longitude, at a given 'zoom level' – here the latitude and longitude are the same ones used as the centre of the search circle used in the Liverpool example above. A zoom level of 14 (high is more 'zoomed in') has been found experimentally to contain the extracted incidents, and is chosen here.

```
require(RgoogleMaps)
LivMap <- GetMap(c(53.401422,-2.965075),zoom=14)
```

Note that this obtains a tile which has 640 × 640 pixels, is stored in the object `LivMap` and accessed via `LivMap$myTile`. The R function `rasterImage` allows this to be added to a plot. This map, now obtained, will be used as the backdrop to the crime data. A convenient way to work with this is to create a function `backdrop` that draws an empty plot (with limits –320 to 320 in each dimension) and then add the bitmap to this. Subsequent use of `points`, `polygons` and so on can then add to this backdrop. The function is defined below:

```
backdrop <- function(gmt) {
  # Set x and y plot limits
  limx <- c(-320,320)
  limy <- c(-320,320)
  # Make the map fill the entire window
  par(mar=c(0,0,0,0))
  # Create the empty plot
  plot(limx,limy,type= 'n',asp=1,
       xlab= '',ylab= '',xaxt= 'n',yaxt= 'n',bty= 'n')
  # Draw a box around it
  box()
  # Fill it with the raster map
  rasterImage(gmt$myTile,-320,-320,320,320)
  }
```

Having defined the function, a backdrop map may be created (see Figure 9.6):

```
backdrop(LivMap)
```

Figure 8.6 Google Maps backdrop for Liverpool

The function LatLon2XY.centered takes a given tile and a set of latitudes and longitudes, and returns a set of transformed coordinates corresponding to the pixel locations in the tile. Note that the coordinate system is centred on the origin, so that pixel locations are labelled in the range −320 to 320 in the x and y directions. This function takes three arguments – the downloaded Google Maps object, a vector of latitudes and a vector of longitudes. Here these are extracted from asb.pts:

```
asb.XY <- LatLon2XY.centered(LivMap,
                            coordinates(asb.pts)[,2],
                            coordinates(asb.pts)[,1])
```

The coordinates function extracts the longitude and latitude from asb.pts. The order they are stored in is longitude, latitude, but LatLon2XY.centered requires them in reverse order – thus column 2 is passed as the first coordinate argument, followed by column 1. In each of the two transformed objects the items newX and newY contain the coordinates in the Google Maps tile system.

Essentially this is a map projection, but one that is localised to the particular tile request. The centre of the image has coordinates (0, 0), and the values generally refer to pixel locations in the raster backdrop image. It is now possible to plot the crimes on the backdrop. This plots the anti-social behaviour incidents on the backdrop, yielding Figure 9.7:

```
backdrop(LivMap)
points(asb.XY$newX,asb.XY$newY,
       pch=16,col= 'darkred',cex=1.5)
points(asb.XY$newX,asb.XY$newY,
       pch=16,col= 'white',cex=0.75)
```

Figure 9.7 Locations of anti-social behaviour incidents

Here two dots are drawn for each location – this gives the two-colour dot effect observed in the figure and makes the locations stand out on the map. However, it is important to recall that the crime locations given here are only approximate. Careful inspection of Figure 9.7 shows that many of these points occur in the middle of a street. This is not because the events actually occur in these locations. In fact, locations are specified as being 'on or near Brownlow Hill' or similar, and the points supplied are just label points for these descriptions. Thus, the maps produced are useful for identifying broader trends (for example, identifying parts of the city where events are more prevalent), but are not good for more geographically precise studies (for example, investigating whether street corners are more likely sites for anti-social behaviour than other parts of the street).

Given this imprecision in location, a more 'visually honest' approach is to draw much larger dots around the points, so that less spatial precision is implied. The points are also drawn with relatively high transparency, and so the effect of having a number of points close to each other may be seen, as in Figure 9.8, created by the code here:

```
backdrop(LivMap)
points(asb.XY$newX,asb.XY$newY,
       pch=16,col=rgb(0.7,0,0,0.15),cex=3)
```

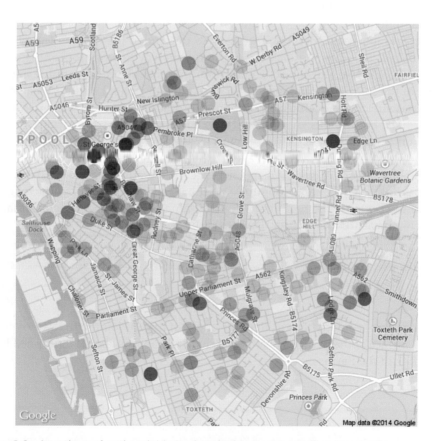

Figure 9.8 Locations of anti-social behaviour incidents representing imprecision

An alternative might be to use kernel density estimation, as discussed in Chapter 6. Looking at this map, it can be seen that quite a large 'hot spot' occurs just south of Dale Street – this is the main shopping precinct in the city, and also contains a number of bars and clubs. Another appears at the western side of London Road.

A further fact that should be considered here is that of data extent. Due to the nature of the `police.uk` API data provision, this dataset consists of points in a one-mile radius around the query point, and therefore in the maps created here, there are no crimes plotted outside this zone. However, it is important to realise that the non-appearance of crimes is due to an artefact of the data provision, not to the absence of crime. For this reason, it is perhaps helpful to 'grey out' parts of the map for which data are not provided. The greyed-out areas of the map can still provide context, but the visual implication is that they are not part of the study area. A way of providing a greyed-out effect is to draw a polygon on the map whose colour is a transparent grey. The shape of the polygon is a rectangle with the same edges as the map tile, but with a circular hole coinciding with the one-mile radius sample area. The hole is therefore shares its centre with the rectangle.

To create this rectangle, it is necessary to determine the radius of the hole in Google Maps tile units. A quick but approximate way to work this out is to note that the Google Maps tile object contains information about the latitude and longitude of the south-west and north-east corners of the map. Latitudes of a point P are angles subtended between a point on the equator and P on a *great circle* passing through both points. A great circle is a circle that has the largest possible radius on a given sphere. A simplifying assumption here is that the Earth is a perfect sphere – if this is the case, and the latitudes of the northern and southern limits of the tile are ϕ_1 and ϕ_2 respectively, then the angle subtended between a pair of points with the same longitude on the upper and lower boundaries of the tile and the centre of the Earth is $\phi_1-\phi_2$. Assuming (as in normal practice) that the angles are measured in degrees, then, in radians, this angle is

$$\frac{\pi}{180}(\phi_1-\phi_2)$$

(9.1)

and then basic geometry tells us that the length of the line joining the pair of points (on the surface of the Earth) is just this angle in radians (as above) multiplied by R, the radius of the Earth:

$$\frac{R\pi}{180}(\phi_1-\phi_2)$$

(9.2)

The NASA Earth Fact Sheet[9] shows that the mean radius of the Earth is 6371.0 km – or 3959 miles. Note that this is an approximation – in reality the radius of the Earth is not constant, as it is not a perfect sphere, so the volumetric mean radius (i.e. the radius giving the correct volume of the Earth if it *were* a sphere) is used here. Since the search radius is 1 mile, the distance from the south to the north of the tile is computed as below:

```
# Compute distance along side of map tile
# components BBOX$ur and BBOX$ll give lat/long of upper
right and
# lower left of the map tile
dist.ns <- (3959 * pi / 180) * (LivMap$BBOX$ur[,1] -
LivMap$BBOX$ll[,1])
dist.ns

## [1] 2.263
```

In the Google coordinate system, this distance is 640 units – and so the conversion factor is 640/2.263 = 282.8126. Thus, a circle of radius 282.8126 in Google units represents a circle of radius 1 mile. This can be verified visually – as below:

```
# Set conversion factor between pixels and miles
cf <- 282.8126
theta <- seq(0,pi*2,l=100) # Angles for points on a
circle
# (sin,cos) Circle is of radius 1 so multiply by cf
# to get 1 mile in pixel units
circle <- cbind(sin(theta),cos(theta)) * cf
backdrop(LivMap) # So draw it on the backdrop map...
# Draw the circle - note that (0,0) in pixel coords
# is the centre of the map.
polygon(circle,col=rgb(0.5,0,1,0.1))
# Plot the crimes as well, to compare with the 1 mile
radius circle
points(asb.XY$newX,asb.XY$newY,pch=16,col= 'blue')
```

As can be seen in Figure 9.9, this approach has been quite effective – the furthest points lies more or less exactly on the boundary of the one-mile-radius circle drawn on the map. However, the success of the approximation is mainly due to the fact that the curvature of the Earth's surface in an area of around 5 square miles as used here is negligible!

---

9 http://nssdc.gsfc.nasa.gov/planetary/factsheet/earthfact.html

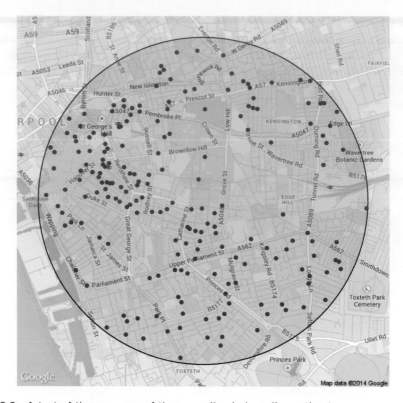

Figure 9.9 A test of the accuracy of the one-mile circle radius estimate

Finally, this information may be used to create the greyed-out map. Note that the polygon used to create the hole is essentially a rectangle with a zero-length slit cut into it, to meet the boundary of the hole. Running the code below results in the map in Figure 9.10.

```
hole.bg <- rbind(circle,
            1.02*cbind(c(0,-320,-320,320,320,0),
                      c(320,320,-320,-320,320,320)))
# The above creates a polygon shape equivalent to a
# rectangular tile with a circular hole.
backdrop(LivMap) # So draw the backdrop map...
points(asb.XY$newX,asb.XY$newY,pch=16,
      col=rgb(1,0,0,0.1),cex=3)    # Plot the crimes
  # next draw the tile-with-a-hole -
polygon(hole.bg,col=rgb(0,0,0,0.2),border=NA)
```

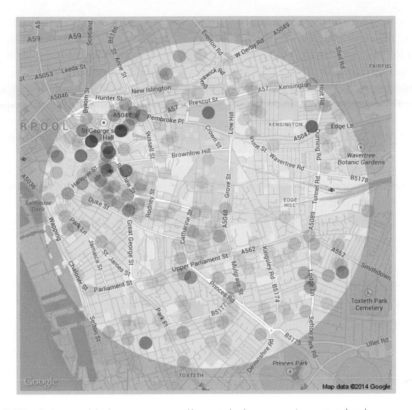

Figure 9.10 Anti-social behaviour map with non-study area region greyed out

Self-Test Question. In the above code, the circle radius is slightly larger than 320 (actually 1.02 times 320) – why do you think this is?

9.6 WEB SCRAPING

The final aspect of web-based information gathering to be covered here is *web scraping*. As mentioned earlier, this is perhaps the oldest approach to obtaining information from the web, and involves directly reading information from HTML code used to create human-readable content. This process is the successor to early techniques to extract information from Teletext pages through USB TV tuners for computers.[10] The arrival of APIs means that this technique has been less frequently used in recent years, but it is still needed occasionally. The method used for web scraping in R typically involves techniques for text pattern searching and pattern

---

10 See http://nxtvepg.sourceforge.net/man-ttx_grab.html, for example.

extraction, which is mostly achieved through the use of *regular expressions* – see Aho (1990), for example. Regular expressions are a way of specifying patterns to search for in character data. The very simplest expression is just a direct string – for example, the pattern `'chris'` simply specifies the five letters c, h, r, i and s appearing in sequence in a string. Thus, the string `'chris brunsdon'` would match this expression, since it has these five letters appearing in sequence. However, the string `'lex comber'` would not prove a match. Also, it should be noted that `'Chris Brunsdon'` does not match, because regular expressions discriminate between upper- and lower-case characters.

If one wanted to find strings that contain either `'Chris'` or `'chris'`, one possible regular expression might be `'[Cc]hris'` – a sequence of characters inside square brackets will match a stream with *any* of these characters where the square-bracketed list occurs. Any number of characters may lie within the square brackets. Also, sequences may be specified: for example, `'[0-9]'` matches any single numeric digit. Also, some postfix modifiers may be used: a character or pattern followed by `'+'` means that the character or pattern may be repeated one or more times – thus `' [0-9]+ '` matches a whole number preceded and succeeded by a space (note that spaces are also matched). A number of other modifiers and pattern specifiers exist. Some notable ones are listed here:

- `'*'` A pattern preceding this symbol may be repeated zero or more times – e.g. `'Chris[0-9]*'` matches `'Chris'`, `'Chris1'`, `'Chris2013'` and so on, since the pattern preceding the `'*'` is `'[0-9]'`.

- `'?'`: A pattern preceding this symbol may be repeated zero or one times – e.g. `'-?[0-9]+'` matches a positive or negative whole number – since the `'?'` is preceded by `'-'`.

- `'.'`: This pattern matches any character – e.g. `'#.*'` would match a Twitter hashtag, since this is a hash character followed by any combination of characters.

- `'^'`: This pattern matches the beginning of a line – e.g. `'^[0-9]'` matches a line starting with a numeric character.

- `'$'`: This pattern matches the end of the line – e.g. `'!$'` matches a line ending with an exclamation mark.

- `'\'`: If this symbol is placed in front of one of the special symbols it implies the special symbol should be matched literally rather than take on its special meaning – e.g. `'\.doc'` matches `'.doc'` – the 'dot' is taken literally rather than matching any character.

The above list is a very brief overview of a fairly involved topic. A comprehensive treatment is given in Friedl (2002).

These patterns may be used in R via a number of related functions. The function grepl takes two arguments, the first a pattern and the second an array of one or more character variables. It returns TRUE for each character value that matches the pattern, and FALSE for each one that does not:

```
grepl('Chris[0-9]*',c('Chris', 'Lex', 'Chris1999', 'Chris
Brunsdon'))

## [1] TRUE FALSE   TRUE TRUE
```

Also, the grep function returns the indices of the items in the list that match:

```
grep('Chris[0-9]*',c('Chris', 'Lex', 'Chris1999', 'Chris
Brunsdon'))

## [1] 1 3 4
```

Finally, grep with the value=TRUE option returns the actual matching character strings.

```
grep('Chris[0-9]*',c('Chris', 'Lex', 'Chris1999',
'Chris Brunsdon'), value=TRUE)

## [1] "Chris"       "Chris1999"       "Chris Brunsdon"
```

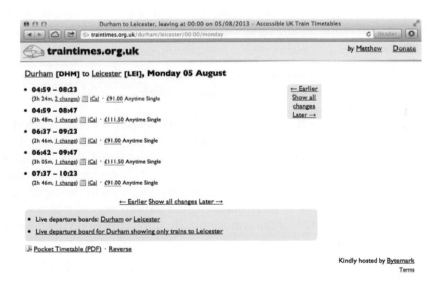

Figure 9.11 A typical accessible UK train timetables web view

These functions are the key tools in R for finding the lines in the HTML code that contain the information of interest when web scraping. This is best illustrated with a practical example.

9.6.1 Scraping Train Times

The 'Accessible UK Train Timetables website'[11] provides a simple interface to UK train timetable information. This is an unofficial site, but acknowledges National Rail Enquiries for allowing the site to use information from the official site.[12] The main advantage of the unofficial site here is that it provides a very simple query system. For example, `http://traintimes.org.uk/durham/leicester/00:00/monday` returns a web page listing train times for journeys from Durham to Leicester after midnight on the Monday following the date of the request.

Suppose it is wished to extract the departure and arrival times from this web page. The HTML content of the web page can be read into a character array (one element of the array being one line of the HTML file) using `readLines`. Note that as this a simple HTTP resource, `Rcurl` is not needed here:

```
web.buf <- readLines(
    "http://traintimes.org.uk/durham/leicester/00:00/monday")
```

If you are curious you might type in `web.buf` to see what the HTML looks like. Next, `grep` can be used to select the lines in the HTML corresponding to the train departure and arrival times. These all take the form dd:dd – dd:dd, where each dd is a two-digit number (for example, 04:59 – 08:23), and an appropriate regular expression is '[0-2][0-9]:[0-5][0-9].*[0-2][0-9]:[0-5][0-9]' – this accounts for the fact that the first digit of the hour must be 0, 1 or 2, and the first digit of the minute cannot exceed 5.

```
times <- grep(
            "[0-2][0-9]:[0-5][0-9].*[0-2][0-9]:[0-5]
            [0-9]",web.buf,value=TRUE)
```

Again, typing in `times` will verify that the lines of interest have been selected. The previous stages have selected the lines actually containing the information of interest. The next stage is to extract the specific information required. Each line has two times, with the pattern '[0-2][0-9]:[0-5][0-9]'. A companion function to `grep` is `gregexpr` – this returns a list giving the locations in the input strings where the part of the string actually matching the pattern begins. It also supplies information about the length of the pattern match. If the pattern occurs more than once, a vector of locations is given:

11 http://traintimes.org.uk
12 http://www.nationalrail.co.uk

```
locs <- gregexpr("[0-2][0-9]:[0-5][0-9]",times)
# Show the match information for times[1]
locs[[1]]

## [1] 46 60
## attr(,"match.length")
## [1] 5 5
## attr(,"useBytes")
## [1] TRUE
```

Thus, for the strings selected in `times` there are two matches, one for the departure time and one for the arrival. If x is the location of the time within the string, then characters x and $x + 1$ supply the hours, and characters $x + 3$ and $x + 4$ supply the minutes. In the final section of code these pieces of information are extracted and converted into numerical values. Finally, a new column is added to the data frame which is the duration of the journey in decimal hours:

```
timedata <- matrix(0,length(locs),4)
ptr <- 1
for (loc in locs) {
timedata[ptr,1] <- as.numeric(substr(times[ptr],loc[1],
loc[1]+1))
timedata[ptr,2] <- as.numeric(substr(times[ptr],loc[1]+3,
loc[1]+4))
timedata[ptr,3] <- as.numeric(substr(times[ptr],loc[2],
loc[2]+1))
timedata[ptr,4] <- as.numeric(substr(times[ptr],loc[2]+3,
loc[2]+4))
ptr <- ptr + 1
}
colnames(timedata) <- c('h1', 'm1', 'h2', 'm2')
timedata <- transform(timedata,duration = h2 + h2/60 - h1 -
m1/60)
timedata
```

```
##          h1     m1     h2     m2     duration
## 1        12     48     15     22        2.450
## 2        13     48     16     23        2.467
## 3        14     48     17     23        2.483
## 4        15     16     18     24        3.033
## 5        16     48     19     24        2.517
```

Although this is a fairly basic example, it provides an indication of the approach used to extract information from 'raw' HTML data. However, it is important to realise that if the design of the web page is changed, it may be necessary to revisit any web-scraping code, since the patterns specifying the data of interest may need to be altered. This would be the case if the website in the example altered the format for displaying times from hh:mm to hhmm (to display 0823 instead of 08:23).

ANSWER TO SELF-TEST QUESTION

The hole is intentionally slightly larger than the map tile as when the size match is exact, parts of the boundary pixels of the map tiles are not blanked out.

REFERENCES

Aho, A. (1990) Algorithms for finding patterns in strings. In J. van Leeuwen (ed.), *Handbook of Theoretical Computer Science, Volume A: Algorithms and Complexity*, pp. 255–300. Cambridge, MA: MIT Press.

Cleveland, W.S. (1979) Robust locally weighted regression and smoothing scatterplots. *Journal of the American Statistical Association*, 74: 829–836.

Department for Communities and Local Government (2012) Tracking economic and child income deprivation at neighbourhood level in England, 1999–2009. Neighbourhoods Statistical Release. London: DCLG. https://www.gov.uk/government/uploads/system/uploads/attachment_data/file/36446/Tracking_Neighbourhoods_Stats_Release.pdf

Friedl, J. (2002) *Mastering Regular Expressions*. Sebastopol, CA: O'Reilly.

EPILOGUE

THE FUTURE OF R AS A TOOL FOR GEOCOMPUTATION

Considering the future of R is not an easy task – it is an already complex language, with what some may argue is an even more complex collection of libraries, covering a wide range of techniques and application areas, many of which extend beyond the original purpose of R as a programming language and interactive environment for statistical data analysis. The existence of this book – much of which is about using R as a tool for manipulating geographical information, and the production of maps – is evidence of this. If the authors had considered the future of R at the point of its first public release in 1995, we admit it would be highly unlikely that we could have predicted the current situation.

For this reason, perhaps the best we can offer is to outline aspects of a future pathway for R *as we would like to see it*. A number of aspects will be considered:

- Extensions of R as a language
- Improvements 'under the bonnet'
- Coexistence with other software

EXTENSION OF R AS A LANGUAGE

In this section, we will consider extensions to the existing R syntax. These are not fully fledged *extensions* in the sense that they can be written using existing R code, but can be considered as extensions in that they introduce new idioms to R – and provide novel ways to express the solutions to certain data analysis problems. An example of a package providing such extensions is Hadley Wickham's `plyr` package. Using this package – as illustrated in Chapter 7 – one can, for example, use the `colwise` function to transform a function operating on a one-dimensional list (such as median) to one that summarises each column is a data frame:

```
library(plyr)
# Create a data frame with three columns (x, y and z)
```

```
test.set <- data.frame(x = rnorm(100, 1, 1),
                       y = rnorm(100, 2, 1),
                       z = rnorm(100, 3, 1))
median.by.col <- colwise(median)
median.by.col(test.set)


##          x       y       z
## 1   0.8295   1.804   3.057
```

The method can also be used for user-defined functions. Here a harmonic mean, given by

$$\tilde{x} = \frac{n}{\dfrac{1}{x_1} + \dfrac{1}{x_2} + \ldots + \dfrac{1}{x_n}} \tag{10.1}$$

is defined in R and a columnwise version is created

```
h.mean <- function(x) 1/mean(1/x)
h.mean.by.col <- colwise(h.mean)
h.mean.by.col(test.set)


##          x       y       z
## 1   0.5911   1.709   2.639
```

Although this code could have existed in very early versions of R, the provision of `plyr` has made it much more commonplace. The key idea here is that of a 'function modifier' – a function that takes another function as its argument, and returns a modified function. Certain function modifiers are commonly used – for example, creating row- or columnwise versions of data summary functions in this way is perhaps a more intuitive approach than the use of functions such as `apply` and `sweep`. This approach leads to a clear and compact method of defining certain functions that could be regarded as a programming tool in its own right – and indeed as an extension of the R language, in the sense that the code in `plyr` provides new tools for coding in general, rather than implementing some specific statistical method. Other such extensions are also appearing – for example, the `iterators` and `foreach` packages provide new approaches to dealing with loops in R that are intuitive, powerful and well suited to parallel and cloud-based computing.

IMPROVEMENTS 'UNDER THE BONNET'

The previous section considered ways in which R is changing that relate directly to the user-facing part of R – adding to the R language will change the way coders interact with R as a tool. However, another aspect of R that undergoes change is its internal design. The most obvious kind of 'invisible' change is when internal algorithms or memory management are made more efficient. The only difference in user experience is that issuing the same commands leads to a faster result or more effective memory usage by the R process. An example of this is the recent release of R 3.0.0, where a previous limit on the maximum number of elements in a vector (of 2^{31}) was removed, due to changes in internal memory management.

An example of a 'near-invisible' change is the implementation of a sparse matrix package `SparseM` that provides efficient algorithms for matrix algebra when many of the elements of the matrices being processed are zero. In R, the operations appear to be the same as for standard matrices, but results are achieved more rapidly.

The trend to process increasingly large datasets suggests that technical improvements to the architecture of R will continue, to ensure efficient running of algorithms developed in R. There is, however, one hurdle in the internal architecture that is more difficult to overcome. R generally works on a model of 'pass by value'. That is, if a function `f(x)` is passed an argument x, a new copy of x is made and stored in memory, and `f` operates on this copy. In many ways this is a good approach – it stops `f` from interfering with the value of x in the command line environment:

```
x <- 5
f <- function(x) {
   x <- x + 1
   print(x^x)
}
f(x)

## [1] 36

x

## [1] 5
```

In the above code, the value of x was changed inside the function, but because the function manipulates the copy of x and not x itself, the value of x on the command line remains unaltered. The benefit is that this stops functions from having unseen side effects. However, the cost is that if x were a very large array (say, a gigabyte), then when the function was called, an extra gigabyte of storage would be needed. This leads to memory-hungry applications, and also slows code down, as a gigabyte's worth of data must be copied each time `f` is called. Other languages deal with this by simply copying the memory location of x to the function when it is called – this approach is called 'pass by reference'. This is faster (as only the memory address, not the whole of x, needs to be transferred), and needs less memory, as the data content is not duplicated. However, the drawback is that it *is* now possible to overwrite parts of the original x from inside the function – so that new software is harder to debug.

One R enhancement to deal with this can be thought of as both an extension to the language and a change in internal architecture – the *reference class*. This is a new kind of R class whose objects are passed to methods using the 'pass by reference' approach. As larger datasets become available, increased use of reference classes is a likely consequence.

COEXISTENCE WITH OTHER SOFTWARE

A final area where R is currently extending, and we feel will continue to extend, is its ability to work with other software. This can occur in a number of ways. For example, some may feel that the extension of R to handle 'pass by reference' techniques leads to a complication in the overall view of R, and is perhaps drifting away from its original purpose as an interactive data analysis tool. In terms of big data, one path forward might be to manipulate and summarise a very large dataset using some other software best suited to that task and pass the preprocessed data on to R. The Rcpp package facilitates such an approach; it provides a framework for creating functions in C++ (a compiled language that does allow passing by reference and is well suited to the preprocessing tasks outlined above) and creating an interface to R, so that the C++ functions can be called directly from R. This approach allows a division of labour between the two languages that can be achieved in an intuitive way.

A further example is RStudio. This is an integrated development environment for R that runs on Windows, Mac, or Linux computers with a number of user-friendly features. It provides a graphical front-end for R and includes a console, a scripting window, a graphics window, and an R workspace window. Some of its key features are a colour coded text editor (also present on the Mac R package), an integrated help and graphics and an interactive debugger. It also has tools that aid the development of packages. It can be downloaded from http://www.rstudio.com/ide/download/desktop; once installed, it has the same functionality as R, uses exactly the same code and draws from the packages installed in normal R libraries. It provides a standard interface to R (i.e. the Windows, Linux and Mac versions are the same), and many users find this environment easier to develop their code, especially users who are new to R.

Another example of R's coexistence with other software includes both the Sweave and knitr packages. These allow R to be embedded in LaTeX, a tool for creating documents. The code is executed, and the output automatically included in the final document. When Sweave and knitr files are compiled in RStudio (or R) all the outputs of the data analysis, such as the code itself, any maps, tables or graphs, are created on the fly and inserted into the final document. Sweave comes with the standard R installation and is described in full at `http://www.stat.uni-muenchen.de/~leisch/Sweave/`. The `knitr` package is described at `http://yihui.name/knitr/` and has to be installed. They both compile .Rnw scripts and generate L^A^T~E~X files that can be directly converted to PDF files in RStudio. In fact, this book, including all the code snippets, examples, exercises and figures, was created and compiled in `knitr`. Embedding the code in the document in this way has a number of advantages. First, it supports dynamic data analysis, allowing analyses to be updated automatically if the data or the analysis change. Second, it provides a transparent and reproducible research environment: rather than inserting a graph or table from Excel for example, the `Sweave` document contains the R code necessary to generate each figure or table, allowing for reproducible research. At the time of writing, reproducibility in research is seen as an important issue, and so tools of this kind are also likely to become important.

As a final example, the `shiny` framework and package provide a tool for creating interactive web pages using R.[1] To do this, shiny defines *reactive expressions* – chunks of R code that are linked to the values of sliders, buttons and other widgets, so that they are re-evaluated whenever the user interacts; these in turn are connected to output widgets such as graph panels, so that graphical and textual outputs and so on may be interactively linked. It has two components: a user interface definition (defining buttons, sliders and so on) and a 'server' definition that specifies the actions associated with these components of the interface. In terms of spatial data analysis, `shiny` offers the opportunity to generate interactive web mapping using R, without any knowledge of HTML, style sheets or JavaScript. However it is sufficiently flexible that it may be augmented with HTML to modify the default styles of the interface or functionality.

FINALLY...

If you have worked through the book, you are now proficient in the use of R for the analysis and visualisation of spatial data. The utilities described in this chapter will allow you to extend and develop your R-based projects and applications. Perhaps one of the best ways to further your understanding of R is to explore possibilities such as these. We hope that you will enjoy doing this as much as we have enjoyed exploring them in order to produce this book.

CB, AC

---

1 `http://shiny.rstudio.com`

INDEX

Page numbers in *italic* indicate figures.